The Challenge of
Carl Schmitt

PHRONESIS

A series from Verso edited by
Ernesto Laclau and Chantal Mouffe

There is today wide agreement that the left-wing
project is in crisis. New antagonisms have emerged
– not only in advanced capitalist societies but also
in the Eastern bloc and in the Third World – that
require the reformulation of the socialist ideal in
terms of an extension and deepening of democracy.
However, serious disagreements exist as to the
theoretical strategy needed to carry out such a task.
There are those for whom the current critique of
rationalism and universalism puts into jeopardy the
very basis of the democratic project. Others argue
that the critique of essentialism – a point of
convergence of the most important trends in contemporary theory: post-structuralism, philosophy
of language after the later Wittgenstein, post-
Heideggerian hermeneutics – is the necessary condition for understanding the widening of the field
of social struggles characteristic of the present stage
of democratic politics. *Phronesis* clearly locates itself
among the latter. Our objective is to establish a
dialogue between these theoretical developments
and left-wing politics. We believe that an anti-
essentialist theoretical stand is the sine qua non of
a new vision for the Left conceived in terms of a
radical and plural democracy.

The Challenge of
Carl Schmitt

◆

Edited by
CHANTAL MOUFFE

VERSO
London • New York

First published by Verso 1999
© in the collection Verso 1999
© in individual contributions the contributors 1999

Verso
UK: 6 Meard Street, London W1V 3HR
USA: 180 Varick Street, New York, NY 10014–4606

Verso is the imprint of New Left Books

ISBN 978-1-859-84244-7

British Library Cataloguing in Publication Data
A catalogue record for this book is available from the British Library

Library of Congress Cataloging-in-Publication Data
A catalog record for this book is available from the Library of Congress

Typeset by SetSystems Ltd, Saffron Walden, Essex
Printed by Biddles Ltd, Guildford and King's Lynn

Contents

Acknowledgements

Three of the essays in this volume have been previously published in English: Paul Hirst, 'Carl Schmitt's Decisionism', in *Telos* 72, Summer 1987; Ulrich K. Preuss, 'Political Order and Democracy: Carl Schmitt and His Influence', in *Poznam Studies in the Philosophy of the Sciences and the Humanities* 33, 1993; Chantal Mouffe, 'Carl Schmitt and the Paradox of Liberal Democracy', in *The Canadian Journal of Law and Jurisprudence* X, 1, 1997.

I am grateful to the authors and publishers for their permission to reprint these essays, and to George Schwab for authorizing publication of the first English translation of Schmitt's 'Ethic of State and Pluralistic State'.

Special thanks to Daniel Hahn for his editorial assistance and his important collaboration on translations.

Chantal Mouffe

Introduction: Schmitt's Challenge

Why should we read Carl Schmitt today? Does his friend–enemy conception of politics retain some pertinence in our 'post-political' age? Do liberal democrats have something to learn from his critique of liberalism? Is his theory of sovereignty still relevant in a globalized world? These are some of the issues that an international group of theorists – all identified with the Left, from a variety of disciplines – address in this volume.

To be sure, these authors do not all evaluate Schmitt's achievements in the same way, and some are more critical than others; but they all agree that he needs to be taken seriously. In spite of his moral flaws, he is an important political thinker whose work it would be a great mistake to dismiss merely because of his support for Hitler in 1933. No doubt Schmitt is an adversary, but an adversary of remarkable intellectual quality, and one from commerce with whom we could benefit. Ignoring his views would deprive us of many insights that can be used to rethink liberal democracy with a view to strengthening its institutions.

That Schmitt is one of the great political and legal theorists of this century is now widely recognized. Witness the recent boom in translations of his work, and the increasing number of studies dedicated to his thought. His amazing erudition and the breadth of his reflections – which always fascinated those who encountered him – help to explain his impact on so many different fields. Several chapters in this volume examine his production in a variety of domains, and they all testify to the wide range of his interests and the depth of his knowledge of culture. From political theory – the subject of many discussions – to geopolitics (explored by Jean-François Kervégan) and juridical science (examined by Agostino Carrino) Schmitt's contribution to the understanding of our modern political condition cannot be denied. His questions, disquieting as they are, still haunt our supposedly pacified world.

One of the aims of this reader is to acknowledge Schmitt's importance as a theorist and his place at the centre of this century's intellectual life.

By scrutinizing the multiple links that can be established with – among others – authors like Karl Marx (Jorge Dotti), Max Weber (Catherine Colliot-Thélène), Hermann Heller (David Dyzenhaus) and Max Adler (Grigoris Ananiadis), a number of the chapters testify to the diversity of his interests and to his being a crucial point of reference in many debates. Moreover, the influence of his constitutional approach has been widespread – not least, as Ulrich Preuss shows, in postwar Germany, despite the fact that he was banned from academic life there after 1945.

It is clear that those who strongly object to his growing recognition on spurious grounds of academic quality are prompted by other motives. To be sure, Schmitt says things that are very unpleasant to liberal ears; but as Preuss suggests, the aversion they incite probably comes from the truth that lies within them. However, it is not by shying away from uncomfortable insights – because they disturb our dogmatic certainties – that we will be able to come to terms with the tasks facing democracy today. Only by lucidly confronting the blind spot of liberalism will we begin to grasp the terms of our current predicament.

Hence the central objective of this collection: to argue that at this juncture, Schmitt's thought serves as a warning against the dangers of complacency that a triumphant liberalism entails. Indeed, his conception of the political brings the crucial deficiencies of the dominant liberal approach to the fore. It should shatter the illusions of all those who believe that the blurring of frontiers between Left and Right, and the steady moralization of political discourse, constitute progress in the enlightened march of humanity towards a new world order and a cosmopolitan democracy.

Indeed, humanitarian rhetoric has today displaced political stakes and, with the collapse of communism, Western liberals imagine that antagonisms have been eradicated. Having reached the stage of 'reflexive modernity', ethics can now replace politics. We are told that with the development of 'post-conventional identities', the archaic forms of friend-and-enemy politics are on the wane. The conditions are claimed to be ripe for 'deliberative' or 'dialogic' forms of democracy to be implemented internationally. Alas, Schmitt's insistence on the ineradicable dimension of conflictuality inherent in 'the political', and on the political 'exterior' of law, reveal all this to be wishful thinking. Besides, as Paul Hirst argues, Schmitt's 'decisionism' challenges the liberal-democratic theory of sovereignty in a way that shows most formal constitutional doctrines to be junk. No wonder he awakens such passionate animosity among liberals!

When we take a look at the current state of democratic politics through a Schmittian lens, we realize how much the process of neutralization and depoliticization, already noticed by Schmitt, has progressed.

Does not one of the most fashionable discourses nowadays proclaim the 'end of politics'? According to this perspective, the cycle of confrontational politics dominant in the West since the French Revolution has come to an end. The Left–Right distinction is now irrelevant, since it was anchored in a social bipolarity that has ceased to exist. Now the majority of the people in advanced industrial societies belong to the middle classes. The disappearance of class identities and the end of the bipolar system of confrontation have rendered conventional politics obsolete. Consensus finally reigns with respect to the basic institutions of society, and the lack of any legitimate alternative means that this consensus will not be challenged. Liberal-democratic capitalism has imposed itself as the only rational solution to the problem of organizing modern societies; its legitimacy could be put into question only by 'unreasonable' elements. The only way forward is a 'third way' beyond Right and Left, where a consensual politics at the centre will replace outdated confrontations.

Such a model presupposes that the political – in Schmitt's sense of friend–enemy relations – has been eradicated, and that an inclusive consensus among 'the people' is now possible. This type of consensual politics chimes with what liberal-democratic political theory is proposing under the name of 'deliberative democracy'. Rejecting the 'aggregative' model of democracy as negotiation of interests – which, with the development of mass democracy, had become the standard consensus – contemporary liberals advocate a different view of the nature of the liberal-democratic consensus. They affirm that a simple *modus vivendi* is not enough, and that a democratic society requires a stronger form of consensus, a moral one, based on impartiality and resulting from rational deliberation. Here again, what is erased is the antagonistic dimension which precludes any form of rational resolution through deliberation. To deny antagonisms in theory, however, does not make them disappear. They continue to manifest themselves, but with the proviso that now they can be perceived only as eruptions of the 'irrational' by those liberals who have denied their existence. Hence their impotence in dealing with the manifold forms of emergence of the political in its Schmittian sense. This is why, as Slavoj Žižek contends, reference to Schmitt is vital if we are to detect the deadlocks of 'post-political' liberal tolerance. Grasping the nature of what he calls Schmittian 'ultra-politics' can help us counteract the re-emergence of a similar type of politics in the various contemporary forms of fundamentalism. There is another field in which a discussion of Schmitt's theses is to be welcomed, which concerns the role of the state. According to David Dyzenhaus, Schmitt's reflections on the ethics of the state – most forcefully presented in his important essay 'Ethic of State and Pluralistic State', available in English for the first time in this volume – could contribute to the much-needed debate about how to rescue the state from its present situation of general discredit.

The different contributors agree that the problems highlighted by Schmitt need careful consideration, and that his central assertion – the necessity of seeing conflict as the crucial category of politics – cannot be ignored. Nevertheless, they consider that in general his solutions cannot be accepted, and that liberalism should not be rejected *in toto*. Certainly, liberalism needs to be taken to task in so far as, in its rationalist and individualistic formulation, it is unable to acknowledge the ineradicability of antagonism and the impossibility of a final reconciliation through reason; moreover, its incapacity to grasp the collective dimension of social life as constitutive, and the fact that political subjects are always collective subjects, have very damaging consequences for democratic politics. But those problems, once identified, can be tackled. What is called for is the elaboration of a truly 'political liberalism'. Contrary to the Rawlsian version of political liberalism, this would be a liberalism that comes to terms with 'the political' in its dimension of conflict/ antagonism, and acknowledges that the social is always instituted polit- ically through hegemonic configurations. To recognize the constitutive role of power relations implies abandoning the misconceived ideal of a reconciled democratic society. Democratic consensus can be envisaged only as a *conflictual consensus*. Democratic debate is not a deliberation aimed at reaching *the one* rational solution to be accepted by all, but a confrontation among adversaries. Indeed, the category of the adversary is crucial to redefining liberal democracy in a way that does not negate the political in its antagonistic dimension. The adversary is in a certain sense an enemy, but a legitimate enemy with whom there exists a common ground. Adversaries fight against each other, but they do not put into question the legitimacy of their respective positions. They share a common allegiance to the ethico-political principles of liberal democ- racy. However, they disagree about their meanings and their forms of implementation, and such a disagreement is not one that could be resolved through rational argument. Hence the antagonistic element in the relationship. Conceived in such a way, liberal-democratic politics can be seen as a consistent and never fully achieved enterprise to diffuse the antagonistic potential present in human relations. By creating the con- ditions for possible conflicts to take the form of confrontations among adversaries (agonism), it attempts to avoid a frontal struggle between enemies (antagonism).

It is important to emphasize that the political conception of the adver- sary that I am delineating here is missing not only from current liberal thought but also from Schmitt himself. Indeed, the main limitation of Schmitt's friend–enemy distinction is that while he asserts the conflictual nature of the political, he does not permit a differential treatment of this conflictuality. It can manifest itself only in the mode of antagonism, where the two sides are in complete opposition and no common symbolic ground exists between them. According to Schmitt, there is no possibility of pluralism – that is, legitimate dissent among friends – and conflictuality is relegated to the exterior of the democratic unity.

In the case of liberalism, the position of the adversary is excluded in a different way. This might seem surprising at first sight. Should not such a view make room for conflict and opposition, since the specificity of modern pluralist democracy consists in breaking with the symbolic representation of society as an organic body, and in legitimizing conflict? However, such a conflict is either reduced to a conflict of interests, to be managed through negotiation – as in the model of interest-group pluralism – or visualized as resolvable through rational deliberation thanks to the adoption of an impartial standpoint, as in the deliberative model. In both cases, what is foreclosed is the properly antagonistic dimension, the dimension that would preclude the possibility of a rational solution. For liberalism, the opponent is not an adversary in the political sense of the term. Rather, as Schmitt points out, it is either a competitor or a debating partner. This is why he declared that liberalism could only oscillate between ethics and economics, and was bound to miss the specificity of the political. The problem with his own conception, however, is that it finally leads to another form of negation of the political, this time by confining it outside democratic association.

What is at stake in answering Schmitt's challenge, therefore, is devising ways in which *antagonism* can be transformed into *agonism*. The tension between the democratic logic of popular sovereignty and the liberal logic of individual rights needs to be acknowledged so that it can be negotiated in a way that does not destroy the basis of political association. How can one envisage a democratic form of commonality which makes room for *conflictual* pluralism? This is clearly one of the key tasks confronting liberal-democratic societies today, given the increasing fragmentation of identities and the multiplication of new forms of conflictuality.

A last word in order to avoid possible misunderstandings: I hope that by now it is evident that what is being advocated in this volume is not some kind of 'left-wing Schmittism' that would agree with Schmitt that liberalism and democracy are in contradiction, and conclude that liberalism is therefore to be discarded. There are indeed people who take such a position, but it is very far from the position defended here. All the contributors are 'left liberals' of some sort, and they do not want to relinquish the great contribution made by the liberal tradition to the modern conception of democracy. But they also believe that this tradition needs to be redefined. Their interest in Schmitt comes from their conviction that through a discussion of his work we can get a better grasp of the deficiencies of the dominant liberal framework. Such an awareness is the precondition for the search for possible remedies. The strategy is definitively not to read Schmitt to attack liberal democracy, but to ask how it could be improved. To think both *with* and *against* Schmitt – this is the thrust of our common endeavour.

1

Carl Schmitt's Decisionism

Paul Hirst

Since 1945 Western nations have witnessed a dramatic reduction in the variety of positions in political theory and jurisprudence. Political argument has been virtually reduced to contests within liberal-democratic theory. Even radicals now take representative democracy as their unquestioned point of departure. There are, of course, some benefits following from this restriction of political debate. Fascist, Nazi and Stalinist political ideologies are now beyond the pale. But the hegemony of liberal-democratic political argument tends to obscure the fact that we are thinking in terms which were already obsolete at the end of the nineteenth century.

Nazism and Stalinism frightened Western politicians into a strict adherence to liberal democracy. Political discussion remains excessively rigid, even though the liberal-democratic view of politics is grossly at odds with our political condition. Conservative theorists like Hayek try to re-create idealized political conditions of the mid nineteenth century. In so doing, they lend themselves to some of the most unsavoury interests of the late twentieth century – those determined to exploit the present undemocratic political condition. Social-democratic theorists also avoid the central question of how to ensure public accountability of big government. Many radicals see liberal democracy as a means to reform, rather than as what needs to be reformed. They attempt to extend governmental action, without devising new means of controlling governmental agencies. New Right thinkers have reinforced the situation by pitting classical liberalism against democracy, individual rights against an interventionist state. There are no challenges to representative democracy, only attempts to restrict its functions. The democratic state continues to be seen as a sovereign public power able to assure public peace.

The terms of debate have not always been so restricted. In the first three decades of this century, liberal-democratic political theory and the notion of popular sovereignty through representative government were widely challenged by many groups. Much of this challenge, of course, was demagogic rhetoric presented on behalf of absurd doctrines of social reorganization. The anti-liberal criticism of Sorel, Maurras or Mussolini may be occasionally intriguing, but their alternatives are poisonous and, fortunately, no longer have a place in contemporary political discussion. The same can be said of much of the ultra-leftist and communist political theory of this period.

Other arguments are dismissed only at a cost. The one I will consider here – Carl Schmitt's 'decisionism' – challenges the liberal-democratic theory of sovereignty in a way that throws considerable light on contemporary political conditions. His political theory before the Nazi seizure of power shared some assumptions with fascist political doctrine and he did attempt to become the 'crown jurist' of the new Nazi state. Nevertheless, Schmitt's work asks hard questions and points to aspects of political life too uncomfortable to ignore. Because his thinking about concrete political situations is not governed by any dogmatic political alternative, it exhibits a peculiar objectivity.

Schmitt's situational judgement stems from his view of politics or, more correctly, from his view of the political as 'friend–enemy' relations, which explains how he could change suddenly from contempt for Hitler to endorsing Nazism. If it is nihilistic to lack substantial ethical standards beyond politics, then Schmitt is a nihilist. In this, however, he is in the company of many modern political thinkers. What led him to collaborate with the Nazis from March 1933 to December 1936 was not, however, ethical nihilism, but above all concern with order. Along with many German conservatives, Schmitt saw the choice as either Hitler or chaos. As it turned out, he saved his life but lost his reputation. He lived in disrepute in the later years of the Third Reich, and died in ignominy in the Federal Republic. But political thought should not be evaluated on the basis of authors' personal political judgements. Thus the value of Schmitt's work is not diminished by the choices he made.

Schmitt's main targets are the liberal-constitutional theory of the state and the parliamentarist conception of politics. In the former, the state is subordinated to law; it becomes the executor of purposes determined by a representative legislative assembly. In the latter, politics is dominated by 'discussion', by the free deliberation of representatives in the assembly. Schmitt considers nineteenth-century liberal democracy anti-political and rendered impotent by a rule-bound legalism, a rationalistic concept of political debate, and the desire that individual citizens enjoy a legally guaranteed 'private' sphere protected from the state. The political is none of these things. Its essence is struggle.

In *The Concept of the Political* Schmitt argues that the *differentia specifica* of the political, which separates it from other spheres of life, such as religion or economics, is friend–enemy relations. The political comes into being when groups are placed in a relation of enmity, where each comes to perceive the other as an irreconcilable adversary to be fought and, if possible, defeated. Such relations exhibit an existential logic which overrides the motives which may have brought groups to this point. Each group now faces an opponent, and must take account of that fact: 'Every religious, moral, economic, ethical, or other antithesis transforms itself into a political one if it is sufficiently strong to group human beings effectively according to friends and enemy.'[1] The political consists not in war or armed conflict as such, but precisely in the relation of enmity: not competition but confrontation. It is bound by no law: it is prior to law.

For Schmitt: 'The concept of the state presupposes the concept of the political.'[2] States arise as a means of continuing, organizing and channelling political struggle. It is political struggle which gives rise to political order. Any entity involved in friend–enemy relations is by definition political, whatever its origin or the origin of the differences leading to enmity: 'A religious community which wages wars against members of other religious communities or engages in other wars is already more than a religious community; it is a political entity.'[3] The political condition arises from the struggle of groups; internal order is imposed to pursue external conflict. To view the state as the settled and orderly administration of a territory, concerned with the organization of its affairs according to law, is to see only the stabilized results of conflict. It is also to ignore the fact that the state stands in a relation of enmity to other states, that it holds its territory by means of armed force and that, on this basis of a monopoly of force, it can make claims to be the lawful government of that territory. The peaceful, legalistic, liberal bourgeoisie is sitting on a volcano and ignoring the fact. Their world depends on a relative stabilization of conflict within the state, and on the state's ability to keep at bay other potentially hostile states.

For Hobbes, the political state arises from a contract to submit to a sovereign who will put an end to the war of all against all which must otherwise prevail in a state of nature – an exchange of obedience for protection. Schmitt starts where Hobbes leaves off – with the natural condition between organized and competing groups or states. No amount of discussion, compromise or exhortation can settle issues between enemies. There can be no genuine agreement, because in the end there is nothing to agree about. Dominated as it is by the friend-or-enemy alternative, the political requires not discussion but decision. No amount of reflection can change an issue which is so existentially primitive that it precludes it. Speeches and motions in assemblies should not be contraposed to blood and iron but with the moral force of the

decision, because vacillating parliamentarians can also cause considerable bloodshed.

In Schmitt's view, parliamentarism and liberalism existed in a particular historical epoch between the 'absolute' state of the seventeenth
century and the 'total state' of the twentieth century. Parliamentary
discussion and a liberal 'private sphere' presupposed the depoliticization
of a large area of social, economic and cultural life. The state provided a
legally codified order within which social customs, economic competition, religious beliefs, and so on, could be pursued without becoming
'political'. 'Politics' as such ceases to be exclusively a matter of the state
when 'state and society penetrate each other'.[4] The modern 'total state'
breaks down the depoliticization on which such a narrow view of politics
could rest:

> Heretofore ostensibly neutral domains – religion, culture, education, the
> economy – then cease to be neutral. . . . Against such neutralizations and
> depoliticizations of important domains appears the total state, which poten-
> tially embraces every domain. This results in the identity of state and society.
> In such a state . . . everything is at least potentially political, and in referring
> to the state it is no longer possible to assert for it a specifically political
> characteristic.[5]

Democracy and liberalism are fundamentally antagonistic. Democracy
does away with the depoliticizations characteristic of rule by a narrow
bourgeois stratum insulated from popular demands. Mass politics means
a broadening of the agenda to include the affairs of all society – everything is potentially political. Mass politics also threatens existing forms
of legal order. The politicization of all domains increases pressure on the
state by multiplying the competing interests demanding action; at the
same time, the function of the liberal legal framework – the regulating of
the 'private sphere' – becomes inadequate. Once all social affairs become
political, the existing constitutional framework threatens the social order:
politics becomes a contest of organized parties seeking to prevail rather
than to achieve reconciliation. The result is a state bound by law to allow
every party an 'equal chance' for power: a weak state threatened with
dissolution.

Schmitt may be an authoritarian conservative. But his diagnosis of the
defects of parliamentarism and liberalism is an objective analysis rather
than a mere restatement of value preferences. His concept of 'sovereignty' is challenging because it forces us to think very carefully about
the conjuring trick which is 'law'. Liberalism tries to make the state
subject to law. Laws are lawful if properly enacted according to set
procedures; hence the 'rule of law'. In much liberal-democratic constitutional doctrine the legislature is held to be 'sovereign': it derives its law-

making power from the will of the people expressed through their representatives. Liberalism relies on a constituting political moment in order that the 'sovereignty' implied in democratic legislatures be unable to modify at will not only specific laws but also law-making processes. It is therefore threatened by a condition of politics which converts the 'rule of law' into a merely formal doctrine. If the 'rule of law' is simply the people's will expressed through their representatives, then it has no determinate content and the state is no longer substantively bound by law in its actions.

Classical liberalism implies a highly conservative version of the rule of law and a sovereignty limited by a constitutive political act beyond the reach of normal politics. Democracy threatens the parliamentary-constitutional regime with a boundless sovereign power claimed in the name of the 'people'. This reveals that all legal orders have an 'outside'; they rest on a political condition which is prior to and not bound by law. A constitution can survive only if the constituting political act is upheld by some political power. The 'people' exist only in the claims of that tiny minority (their 'representatives') which functions as a 'majority' in the legislative assembly. 'Sovereignty' is thus not a matter of formal constitutional doctrine or essentially hypocritical references to the 'people'; it is a matter of determining which particular agency has the capacity – outside of law – to impose an order which, because it is political, can become legal.

Schmitt's analysis cuts through three hundred years of political theory and public law doctrine to define sovereignty in a way that renders irrelevant the endless debates about principles of political obligation or the formal constitutional powers of different bodies:

> From a practical or theoretical perspective, it really does not matter whether an abstract scheme advanced to define sovereignty (namely, that sovereignty is the highest power, not a derived power) is acceptable. About an abstract concept there will be no argument. . . . What is argued about is the concrete application, and that means who decides in a situation of conflict what constitutes the public interest or interest of the state, public safety and order, *le salut public*, and so on. The exception, which is not codified in the existing legal order, can at best be characterized as a case of extreme peril, a danger to the existence of the state, or the like. But it cannot be circumscribed factually and made to conform to a preformed law.

Brutally put: 'Sovereign is he who decides on the exception.'[7] The sovereign is a definite agency capable of making a decision, not a legitimating category (the 'people') or a purely formal definition (plenitude of power, etc.). Sovereignty is *outside* the law, since the actions of the sovereign in the state of exception cannot be bound by laws. To claim that this is anti-legal is to ignore the fact that all laws have an outside, that they exist because of a substantiated claim on the part of some agency to be the dominant source of binding rules within a territory. The sovereign determines the possibility of the 'rule of law' by deciding on the exception: 'For a legal order to make sense, a normal situation must exist, and he is sovereign who definitely decides whether this normal situation actually exists.'[8]

Schmitt's concept of the exception is neither nihilistic nor anarchistic; it is concerned with the preservation of the state and the defence of legitimately constituted government and the stable institutions of society. He argues that 'the exception is different from anarchy and chaos'.[9] It is an attempt to restore order in a political sense. While the state of exception can know no norms, the actions of the sovereign within the state must be governed by what is prudent to restore order. Barbaric excess and pure arbitrary power are not Schmitt's object. Power is limited by a prudent concern for the social order; in the exception, 'order in the juristic sense still prevails, even if it is not of the ordinary kind'.[10] Schmitt may be a relativist with regard to ultimate values in politics. But he is certainly a conservative concerned with defending a political framework in which the 'concrete orders' of society can be preserved, which distinguishes his thinking from both fascism and Nazism in their subordination of all social institutions to such idealized entities as the Leader and the People. For Schmitt, the exception is never the rule, as it is with fascism and Nazism. If he persists in demonstrating how law depends on politics, the norm on the exception, stability on struggle, he points up the contrary illusions of fascism and Nazism. In fact, Schmitt's work can be used as a critique of both. The ruthless logic in his analysis of the political, the nature of sovereignty, and the exception demonstrates the irrationality of fascism and Nazism. The exception cannot be made the rule in the 'total state' without reducing society to such a disorder through the political actions of the mass party that the very survival of the state is threatened. The Nazi state sought war as the highest goal in politics, but conducted its affairs in such a chaotic way that its war-making capacity was undermined and its war aims became fatally overextended. Schmitt's friend–enemy thesis is concerned with avoiding the danger that the logic of the political will reach its conclusion in unlimited war.

Schmitt modernizes the absolutist doctrines of Bodin and Hobbes. His jurisprudence restores – in the exception rather than the norm – the sovereign as uncommanded commander. For Hobbes, laws are orders given by those with authority – *autoritas non veritas facit legem*. Confronted with complex systems of procedural limitation in public law and with the formalization of law into a system, laws became far more complex than orders. Modern legal positivism could point to a normal liberal-parliamentary legal order which did and still does appear to contradict Hobbes. Even in the somewhat modernized form of John Austin, the Hobbesian view of sovereignty is rejected on all sides. Schmitt shared neither the simplistic view of Hobbes that this implies, nor the indifference of modern legal positivism to the political foundation of law. He founded his jurisprudence neither on the normal workings of the legal order nor on the formal niceties of constitutional doctrine, but on a condition quite alien to them. 'Normalcy' rests not on legal or constitutional conditions but on a certain balance of political forces, a certain capacity of the state to impose order by force should the need arise. This is especially true of liberal-parliamentary regimes, whose public law requires stabilization of political conflicts and considerable police and war powers even to begin to have the slightest chance of functioning at all. Law cannot itself form a completely rational and lawful system; the analysis of the state must make reference to those agencies which have the capacity to decide on the state of exception and not merely a formal plenitude of power.

In *Political Theology* Schmitt claims that the concepts of the modern theory of the state are secularized theological concepts. This is obvious in the case of the concept of sovereignty, wherein the omnipotent lawgiver is a mundane version of an all-powerful God. He argues that liberalism and parliamentarism correspond to deist views of God's action through constant and general natural laws. His own view is a form of fundamentalism in which the exception plays the same role in relation to the state as the miracles of Jesus do in confirming the Gospel. The exception reveals the legally unlimited capacity of whoever is sovereign within the state. In conventional, liberal-democratic doctrine the people are sovereign; their will is expressed through representatives. Schmitt argues that modern democracy is a form of populism in that the people are mobilized by propaganda and organized interests. Such a democracy bases legitimacy on the people's will. Thus parliament exists on the sufferance of political parties, propaganda agencies and organized interests which compete for popular 'consent'. When parliamentary forms and the rule of 'law' become inadequate to the political situation, they will be dispensed with in the name of the people: 'No other constitutional institution can withstand the sole criterion of the people's will, however it is expressed.'[11]

Schmitt thus accepts the logic of Weber's view of plebiscitarian democracy and the rise of bureaucratic mass parties, which utterly destroy the autonomy of the old parliamentary notables. He uses the nineteenth-century conservative Juan Donoso Cortés to set the essential dilemma in *Political Theology*: either a boundless democracy of plebiscitarian populism, which will carry us wherever it will (i.e. to Marxist or fascist domination) or a dictatorship. Schmitt advocates a very specific form of dictatorship in a state of exception – a 'commissarial' dictatorship, which acts to restore social stability, to preserve the concrete orders of society and to restore the constitution. The dictator has a constitutional office. He acts in the name of the constitution, but takes such measures as are necessary to preserve order. These measures are not bound by law; they are extralegal.

Schmitt's doctrine thus involves a paradox. For all its stress on friend–enemy relations, on decisive political action, its core, its aim, is the maintenance of stability and order. It is founded on a political non-law, but not in the interest of lawlessness. Schmitt insists that the constitution must be capable of meeting the challenge of the exception, and of allowing those measures necessary to preserve order. He is anti-liberal because he claims that liberalism cannot cope with the reality of the political; it can only insist on a legal formalism which is useless in the exceptional case. He argues that only those parties which are bound to uphold the constitution should be allowed an 'equal chance' to struggle for power. Parties which threaten the existing order and use constitutional means to challenge the constitution should be subject to rigorous control.

Schmitt's relentless attack on 'discussion' makes most democrats and radicals extremely hostile to his views. He is a determined critic of the Enlightenment. Habermas's 'ideal speech situation', in which we communicate without distortion to discover a common 'emancipatory interest', would appear to Schmitt as a trivial philosophical restatement of Guizot's view that in representative government, 'through discussion the powers-that-be are obliged to seek truth in common'.[12] Schmitt is probably right. Enemies have nothing to discuss and we can never attain a situation in which the friend–enemy distinction is abolished. Liberalism does tend to ignore the exception and the more resolute forms of political struggle. But Schmitt's reasoning is left with the exception and nothing else. In a 'total state', with a relatively established balance of political forces, his doctrine has nothing much to teach us. There is something of a contradiction between his concept of the political and his concept of the 'total state': by making everything political, the 'total state' infects the sphere of politics with the complex necessities of economic management and social organization. Schmitt can see the 'total state' only as a destruction of liberalism, the end of the division between the state and civil society. But such a state reduces the scope of the either/or by vastly broadening the agenda of public business. The state is no longer the 'sovereign' body of political struggle, but increasingly a vast complex of ill-co-ordinated public service agencies.

In such a complex public-service state, regulation and arbitration become essential, as does the need for a jurisprudence which takes into account the character of a state concerned primarily with practical problems of social organization. These problems are difficult to treat as matters of 'exacting moral decision', although that is what the contemporary New Right tries to do. They are matters of investigation, balancing advantages, paying regard to outcomes – matters which require 'discussion'. Such discussion will never be a seeking for truth in common; it is an approach to solving problems which can seldom have a 'truth'. It is a mixture of analysis and evaluation concerned with the existing state of affairs.

In reality, Schmitt's view of 'discussion' presupposes a high-bourgeois polity of a type which has never existed. It treats parliament as a kind of collective-reasoning agency. His acceptance at face value of the liberal-democratic rationale for parliament, however, is neither naive nor just polemical. He insists that institutions require a principle or rationale which commands support, that they cannot thrive or survive with only the claim that there is no alternative. The question 'what else?' is hardly a rallying call. Schmitt had as much contempt for the Weimar Republic's assembly as Weber did for the pre-1914 Reichstag. Both Schmitt and Weber judged parliamentarianism in terms of liberal-democratic rhetoric, and both found the practice wanting. Schmitt also found the rationale wanting. Weber wanted to marry parliamentarism and effective plebiscitary democracy to make the chamber an effective training ground for leaders. Such a function presupposes a chamber in which debate and genuine autonomy for its members still have a place.

In terms of modern political theory, parliament has ceased to play a crucial role. Schmitt and Weber could both be taken to task for seeing in the behaviour and nature of parties the failure of parliament, because parliaments function only as a certain focus of the party system, and can never work better than the system itself. Effective parliaments presuppose parties which can compromise because they operate within a consensus, which are strong enough to marginalize non-consensus parties. Schmitt rightly recognized that such a party system did not then exist in Germany. Where such a system does exist, parliaments can be one effective instrument among others in party governments, political management, and a limited forum for trading between the consensus parties. Such parliaments function very differently from Schmitt's view of parliamentarism. But they also function very differently from representative government in classic liberal-democratic theory.

In the Weimar Republic the state of exception was close to being the norm. Thus the constitutional status and political function of the exception powers of the president were a serious matter of political debate.

Schmitt used these practical debates to make general and challenging points about the nature of sovereignty and law. In most of the post-1945 Western democracies the state of exception in the form Schmitt knew it has become a marginal political problem. Political stability has permitted complacency in political theory and, indeed, has required it as one of its conditions. But stably functioning party systems exist for reasons that have little to do with constitutional doctrine, and no amount of formally liberal measures can compensate for the decline of such a doctrine. Despite growing strains and a less consensual political climate than obtained in the 1950s, nowhere in the West have parties reached the stage of antagonistic competition typical of the Weimar period. Parliamentary democracy has ceased to function as classic liberal-democratic theory supposes it to do. No one expects it to provide the forum for 'discussion' which Schmitt derided. But parliamentary institutions have ceased also to oversee effectively the workings of modern big government. The 'total state' may have marginalized Schmitt's politics of the 'morally exacting' decision. But it has also marginalized existing methods of democratic control. Parliament has become a tool of party government, even more so of government in general; it has come to serve as a means of giving legitimacy and legality to the actions of the ramified mass of state agencies.

Neither liberal-democratic theories nor pluralist views of polyarchical competition in a stable party system can provide an account of the organizational forms necessary for more effective democratic accountability. Schmitt cannot do so either. But his views on the nature of sovereignty are helpful for recognizing certain contemporary problems of democratic control. Because Schmitt is no democrat, he recognizes and insists on things democrats often wish to forget. The modern state may restrict the scope for Schmitt's politics of either/or, imposing a mass of functions in which such 'political' thinking would be reactionary and counterproductive. But the state remains, nevertheless, a political association in Schmitt's sense. Governmental agencies concerned by and large with matters of social and economic organization operate through managerial imperatives, and are subject to at least some minimal legal regulation and political control. But they do not exhaust the state. Schmitt is valuable because he stresses that all legal orders have an 'outside', and that definite agencies within the state have the option (if not the formal constitutional right) to act extralegally. The consequences of contemporary states acting in this way are far greater than in Schmitt's day, the Nazi notwithstanding, because organizational capacity and military power are so much greater.

The entire apparatus of nuclear security has escaped democratic political control in that the technology involved so radically telescopes the time involved in operational decision-making, and so restricts it to a small circle of persons, that it does become a simple matter of the 'morally exacting' decision. In that sense we do have a very clear 'sovereign' and a perpetual prospect of the state of exception. Friend–enemy relations have not disappeared, even if the consequences of the superpowers pursuing them to the full are self-defeating. The effect of this condition on the rest of the polity is considerable. The nuclear-security apparatus reserves to itself considerable powers of control over economic resources, special police measures, and so on, and has a capacity for secret policy-making whose limits are difficult to determine. If we take Schmitt's claim that 'sovereign is he who decides on the exception' seriously, then most of our formal constitutional doctrines are junk.

Notes

1. Carl Schmitt, *The Concept of the Political*, translated and introduced by George Schwab, New Brunswick: Rutgers University Press, 1976, p. 37.
2. Ibid., p. 19.
3. Ibid., p. 37.
4. Ibid., p. 22.
5. Ibid.
6. Carl Schmitt, *Political Theory*, translated and introduced by George Schwab, Cambridge, MA: MIT Press, 1985, p. 6.
7. Ibid., p. 5.
8. Ibid., p. 13.
9. Ibid., p. 12.
10. Ibid.
11. Ibid., p. 15.
12. Carl Schmitt, *The Crisis of Parliamentary Democracy*, translated and introduced by Ellen Kennedy, Cambridge, MA: MIT Press, 1985, p. 97, n. 5.

2

Carl Schmitt in the
Age of Post-Politics

Slavoj Žižek

I

The basic paradox of Carl Schmitt's political decisionism – the rule of law ultimately hinges on an abyssal act of violence (violent imposition) which is grounded in itself; that is, every positive order to which this act refers, to legitimize itself, is self-referentially posited by this act itself[1] – is that his very polemics against liberal-democratic formalism inexorably gets caught in the formalist trap. Schmitt targets the utilitarian-enlightened grounding of the political in some presupposed set of neutral-universal norms or strategic rules which (should) regulate the interplay of individual interests (either in the guise of legal normativism *à la* Kelsen, or in the guise of economic utilitarianism).

According to Schmitt, it is not possible to pass directly from a pure normative order to the actuality of social life – the necessary mediator between the two is an act of Will, a decision, grounded only in itself, which *imposes* a certain order or legal hermeneutics (reading of abstract rules). Any normative order, taken in itself, remains stuck in abstract formalism, that is to say, it cannot bridge the gap that separates it from actual life. However – and this is the core of Schmitt's argumentation – the decision which bridges this gap is not a decision for some concrete order, but primarily the decision for the formal principle of order as such. The concrete content of the imposed order is arbitrary, dependent on the Sovereign's will, left to historical contingency – the *principle of order*, the *Dass-Sein* of Order, has priority over its concrete content, over its *Was-Sein*. This is the main feature of modern conservatism which sharply distinguishes it from every kind of traditionalism: modern conservatism, even more than liberalism, assumes the lesson of the dissolution of the traditional set of values and/or authorities – there is no longer any positive content which could be presupposed as the universally accepted frame of reference. (Hobbes was the first explicitly to posit this distinction between the principle of order and any concrete order.) The paradox thus lies in the fact that the only way to oppose legal normative formalism is to revert to decisionist formalism – there is no way of escaping formalism within the horizon of modernity.

For that reason, Schmitt's notion of exception is necessarily ambiguous: it stands simultaneously for the intrusion of the Real (of the pure contingency which perturbs the universe of symbolic *automaton*) *and* for the gesture of the Sovereign who (violently, without foundation in the symbolic norm) imposes a symbolic normative order – in Lacanese, it stands for *objet petit a* as well as for S_1, the Master-Signifier. This double nature of the foundational act is also clearly discernible in religion – Christ enjoins his followers to obey and respect their superiors in accordance with established customs *and* to hate and disobey them, that is, to cut all human links with them: 'If anyone comes to me and does not hate his father and his mother, his wife and children, his brothers and sisters – yes even his own life – he cannot be my disciple' (Luke 14: 26).

Do we not encounter here Christ's own 'religious suspension of the ethical'? The universe of established ethical norms ('mores', the substance of social life) is reasserted, but only in so far as it is 'mediated' by Christ's authority: first, we have to accomplish the gesture of radical negativity and reject everything that is most precious to us; later, we get it back, but as an expression of Christ's will, mediated by it (the way a Sovereign relates to positive laws involves the same paradox: a Sovereign compels us to respect laws precisely in so far as he is the point of the suspension of laws). When Christ claims that he did not come to undermine the Old Law, but merely to fulfil it, one has to read into this 'fulfilment' the full ambiguity of the Derridean supplement: the very act of fulfilling it undermines its direct authority. In this precise sense, 'Love is the Fulfilling of the Law' (Romans 13: 10): love accomplishes what the Law (Commandments) aims at, but this very accomplishment simultaneously involves the suspension of the Law. The notion of belief which fits this paradox of authority was elaborated by Kierkegaard; that is why, for him, *religion is eminently modern*: the traditional universe is ethical, while the Religious involves a radical disruption of the Old Ways – true religion is a crazy wager on the Impossible which we have to make once we lose support in tradition.

What is properly modern in Schmitt's notion of exception is thus the violent gesture of asserting the independence of the abyssal act of free decision from its positive content. What is 'modern' is the gap between the act of decision and its content – the perception that what really matters is the act as such, independently of its content (or 'ordering' – independently of the positive determinate order). The paradox (which grounds so-called 'conservative modernism') is thus that the innermost possibility of modernism is asserted in the guise of its apparent opposite, the return to an unconditional authority which cannot be grounded in positive reasons. That is why the properly modern God is the God of predestination, a kind of Schmittian politician who draws the line of separation between Us and Them, Friends and Enemies, the Saved and the Damned, *by means of a purely formal, abyssal act of decision, without any grounds in the actual properties and acts of those concerned* (since they are not yet even born). In traditional Catholicism, salvation depends on earthly good deeds; in the logic of Protestant predestination, earthly deeds and fortunes (wealth) are at best an ambiguous *sign* of the fact that the subject is already redeemed by the inscrutable Divine act – that is to say, he is not saved *because* he is rich or does good deeds, he accomplishes good deeds or is rich *because* he is saved. . . . The shift from act to sign is crucial here: from the perspective of predestination, a deed becomes a *sign* of the predestined Divine decision.

Schmitt's decisionism has its philosophical roots in Duns Scotus's reaction against the Aristotelian 'essentialism' of Aquinas: beyond Divine Reason there is the abyss of God's Will, of His contingent Decision which sustains even the Eternal Truths. And it is this gap in God Himself which opens up the space for modern tragedy. In political terms, the difference between classical tragedy and modern tragedy is the difference between (traditional) *tyranny* and (modern) *terror*.[2] The traditional *hero* sacrifices himself for the Cause, he resists the pressure of the Tyrant and accomplishes his Duty, cost what it may; as such, he is appreciated, his sacrifice confers on him the sublime aura, his act is inscribed in the register of Tradition as an example to be followed. We enter the domain of modern tragedy when the very logic of the sacrifice for the Thing compels us to sacrifice this Thing itself; that is the predicament of Paul Claudel's Sygne (from his Coufontaine trilogy), who is compelled to betray her faith in order to prove her absolute fidelity to God. Sygne does not sacrifice her empirical life for what matters to her more than that life itself, she sacrifices precisely that which is 'in her more than herself', and thus survives as a mere shell of her former self, deprived of her *agalma* – thereby we enter the domain of the *monstrosity of heroism*, when our fidelity to the Cause compels us to transgress the threshold of our 'humanity'. Is it not proof of the highest, absolute faith that, for the love of God, I am ready to lose, to expose to eternal damnation, my eternal Soul itself? It is easy to sacrifice my life in the certainty that I am thereby redeeming my eternal Soul – how much worse it is to sacrifice one's very soul for God!

Perhaps the ultimate historical illustration of this predicament – of the gap which separates the hero (his resistance to tyranny) from the victim of terror – is provided by the Stalinist victim: this victim is not someone who finally learns that communism was an ideological mirage, and becomes aware of the positivity of simple ethical life outside the ideological Cause; the Stalinist victim cannot retreat into simple ethical life, since he has already forsaken it for his Communist Cause. This predicament accounts for the impression that although the fate of the victims of the great Stalinist show trials (from Bukharin to Slansky) was horrible beyond description, the properly tragic dimension is missing: they were not tragic heroes, but something more horrible and simultaneously more comical – they were deprived of the very dignity which would confer on their fate the properly tragic dimension.

For that reason, we cannot use Antigone as the model for the resistance to Stalinist power: if we do this, we reduce the Stalinist terror to just another version of tyranny. Antigone maintains the reference to the big Other's desire (to accomplish the symbolic ritual and bury her deceased brother properly), as opposed to the tyrant's (pseudo-)Law – precisely the reference which is *lacking* in the Stalinist show trials. In humiliating the victim, the Stalinist terror deprives him of the very dimension which could confer sublime beauty on him: the victim goes beyond a certain threshold, he 'loses his dignity', is simultaneously reduced to a pure subject bereft of *agalma*, and rendered 'destitute', unable to recompose the narrative of his life. To put it in yet another way: terror is not the power of corruption which undermines the ethical attitude from outside; rather, it undermines it from within, by mobilizing and exploiting to its utmost the inherent gap of the ethical project itself, the gap that separates the ethical Cause *qua* real from the Cause in its symbolic dimension (values, etc.); or – to put it in a Schmittian way – the gap that separates the God of the pure Act of Decision from the God of positive Prohibitions and Commandments.

This, again, opens up the possibility of a Kierkegaardian connection: does not the Kierkegaardian suspension of the (symbolic) Ethical not also involve a move beyond tragedy? The ethical hero is tragic, whereas the Knight of Faith dwells in the horrible domain beyond or between the two deaths, since he (is ready to) sacrifice(s) what is most precious to him, his *objet petit a* (in the case of Abraham, his son). In other words, Kierkegaard's point is that Abraham is forced to choose not between his duty to God and his duty to humanity (such a choice remains simply tragic), but between the two facets of the duty to God, and thereby the two facets of God Himself: God as universal (the system of symbolic norms) and God as the point of absolute singularity which suspends the universal.

For that precise reason, Derrida's reading of (Kierkegaard's reading of) Abraham's gesture in *Donner la mort*,[3] where he interprets Abraham's sacrifice not as a hyperbolic exception but as something which all of us perform again and again, every day, in our most common ethical experience, seems inadequate. According to Derrida, every time we choose to fulfil a duty to one individual, we neglect – forget – our duty to all the others (since *tout autre est tout autre*, every other person is wholly other) – if I look after my own children, I sacrifice the children of other men; if I help to feed and clothe *this* person, I abandon other people, and so on. What gets lost in this reduction of Abraham's predicament to a kind of Heideggerian constitutive guilt of *Dasein* which can never use/actualize all its possibilities is the self-referential nature of this predicament: Abraham's deadlock lies not in the fact that, on behalf of the ultimate *tout autre* (God), he has to sacrifice another *tout autre*, his most beloved earthly companion, his son, but, rather, in the fact that, on behalf of his Love for God, he has to sacrifice that which *the very religion grounded in his faith orders him to love*. The split is thus inherent to faith itself; it is the split between the Symbolic and the Real, between the *symbolic* edifice of faith and the pure, unconditional *act* of faith – *the only way to prove your faith is to betray that which this very faith orders you to love*.

II

How does psychoanalysis interpret this theological background of the Schmittian politician, the figure of 'irrational' authority, the bearer of an unconditional injunction which can never be translated into a set of determinate demands? The proper way to address this question is to tackle the enigma of why Freud supplemented the Oedipal myth with another mythical narrative, that of the 'primordial father' in *Totem and Taboo* (*T&T*), whose lesson is the exact obverse of Oedipus: far from having to deal with the father who intervenes as the Third preventing direct contact with the incestuous object (and thereby sustains the illusion that his annihilation would give us free access to this object), it is the killing of the father – in short: the realization of the Oedipal wish – which gives rise to the symbolic prohibition (the dead father returns as his Name). And what occurs in today's much-decried 'decline of Oedipus' (decline of paternal symbolic authority) is precisely the return of figures which function according to the logic of the 'primordial father', from 'totalitarian' political Leaders to the parental sexual harasser –

why? When the 'pacifying' symbolic authority is suspended, the only way to avoid the debilitating deadlock of desire, its inherent impossibility, is to locate the cause of its inaccessibility in a despotic figure which stands for the primordial *jouisseur*: we cannot enjoy because *he* arrogates all the enjoyment. . . .

We can now see the precise nature of the crucial shift from Oedipus to *T&T*: in the 'Oedipus complex', the parricide (and incest with the mother) has the status of an unconscious desire – we, ordinary (male) subjects, all dream about it, since the paternal figure precludes our access to the maternal object, disturbs our symbiosis with it; while Oedipus himself is the exceptional figure, the One who actually *did it*. In *T&T*, on the contrary, the parricide is not the object of our dreams, the goal of our unconscious wish, something we dream about, entertaining its future prospect, but something which never really happens and thus, via its postponement, sustains the state of Culture (since the realization of this wish, the consummation of the incestuous link with the mother, would abolish the symbolic distance/prohibition which defines the universe of Culture); the traumatic event, rather, is that which *always-already has to happen the moment we are within the order of Culture*. So how are we to explain the fact that although we really did kill the father, the outcome is not the longed-for incestuous union? There, in this paradox, lies the central thesis of *T&T*: the actual bearer of Prohibition, that which prevents our access to the incestuous object, is not the living but the *dead* father – the father who, after his death, returns as his Name, that is, as the embodiment of the symbolic Law/Prohibition. Thus the matrix of *T&T* accounts for the structural necessity of the parricide: the passage from direct brute force to the rule of symbolic authority, of the prohibitory Law, is always grounded in a (disavowed) act of primordial crime.

Therein lies the dialectic of 'You can prove that you love me only by betraying me': the father is elevated into the venerated symbol of Law only after his betrayal and murder. This problematic also opens up the vagaries of ignorance – not the subject's, but the big Other's: 'the father is dead, but he is not aware of it' – that is to say, he does not know that his loving followers have (always-already) betrayed him. On the other hand, this means that the father 'really thinks that he is a father', that his authority emanates directly from his person, not merely from the empty symbolic place that he occupies and/or fills in. What the faithful follower should conceal from the paternal figure of the Leader is precisely this gap between the Leader in the immediacy of his personality and the symbolic place he occupies, the gap on account of which father *qua* effective person is utterly impotent and ridiculous (the great example here, of course, is the figure of King Lear, who was violently confronted with this betrayal and the ensuing unmasking of his impotence –

deprived of his symbolic title, he is reduced to an impotent raging old fool). The heretical legend according to which Christ himself ordered Judas to betray him (or at least, let him know his wish between the lines) is thus well-founded: there, in this necessity of the Betrayal of the Great Man which alone can assure his Fame, lies the ultimate mystery of Power.

However, how is this reversal possible? According to Freud, in the *T&T* matrix, there is still something missing: it is not enough to have the murdered father returning as the agency of symbolic Prohibition – in order for this prohibition to be effective, actually to exert its power, it must be sustained by a positive act of Willing. . . . All these intricacies pave the way for the last Freudian variation on the Oedipal topography, the one in *Moses and Monotheism (M&M)*. Here also we are dealing with *two* paternal figures; this duality, however, is not the same as the one in *T&T*: the two figures are not the pre-symbolic obscene/non-castrated Father-*Jouissance* and the (dead) father *qua* bearer of symbolic authority – that is, the Name-of-the-Father – but the Ancient Egyptian Moses, the one who introduced monotheism – who dispensed with the old polytheistic superstitions and introduced the notion of the universe as determined and ruled by a unique rational Order, and the Semitic Moses who is in effect none other than Jehovah (Yahweh), the jealous God who shows vengeful rage when He feels betrayed by His people.

In short, *M&M* reverses the topography of *T&T* yet again: the father who is betrayed and killed by his followers/sons is *not* the obscene primordial Father-*Jouissance*, but the very 'rational' father who embodies symbolic authority, the figure which personifies the unified rational structure of the universe (*logos*). Instead of the obscene primordial pre-symbolic father returning after his murder in the guise of his Name, of symbolic authority, we now have the symbolic authority (*logos*) betrayed, killed by his followers/sons, and then returning in the guise of the jealous, vengeful and unforgiving superego figure of God full of murderous rage.[4] It is only here, after this second reversal of the Oedipal matrix, that we reach the well-known Pascalian distinction between the God of Philosophers (God *qua* the universal structure of *logos*, identified to the rational structure of the universe) and the God of Theologists (the God of love and hatred, the inscrutable 'dark God' of capricious 'irrational' Predestination).

In contrast to the primordial father endowed with a *knowledge* about *jouissance*, the fundamental feature of this uncompromising God is that He says 'No!' to *jouissance* – this is a God who, as Lacan puts it, is possessed by a ferocious ignorance ['*la féroce ignorance de Yahvé*'[5]], by an attitude of 'I refuse to know, I don't want to hear, anything about your dirty and secret ways of *jouissance*'; a God who banishes the universe of traditional sexualized wisdom, the universe in which a semblance of the ultimate harmony between the big Other (the symbolic order) and *jouissance*, the notion of macrocosm as regulated by some underlying sexual tension of male and female 'principles' (Yin and Yang, Light and Darkness, Earth and Heaven...) still persists. This God is the proto-existentialist God whose existence – to apply to him, anachronistically, Sartre's definition of man – does not simply coincide with His essence (as with the medieval God of Aquinas), but precedes His essence. For that reason He speaks in tautologies, not only about His own *quidditas* ('I am what I am') but also, and above all, about what concerns *logos*, the *reasons* for what He is doing – or, more precisely, for His injunctions, for what He is asking us or prohibiting us to do: His inexorable orders are ultimately grounded in an 'It is so BECAUSE I SAY IT IS SO!'. In short, this God is the God of pure Will, of its capricious abyss which stands beyond any global rational order of *logos*, a God who does not have to account for anything He does; it is to F.W.J. Schelling that we owe the most piercing descriptions of this horrifying abyss of Will. Schelling opposed the Will to the 'principle of sufficient reason': pure Willing is always self-identical, it relies only on its own act – 'I want it because I want it!'. Ordinary people are horrified when they encounter a person whose behaviour displays such an unconditional Will: there is something fascinating, properly hypnotic, about it; it is as if one is bewitched by the sight of it.... Schelling's emphasis on the abyss of pure Willing, of course, targets Hegel's alleged 'panlogicism': what Schelling wants to prove is that the Hegelian universal logical system is in itself, *stricto sensu, impotent* – it is a system of pure *potentialities* and, as such, in need of the supplementary 'irrational' act of pure Will if it is to *actualize* itself.[6]

This God is the God who *speaks* to His followers/sons, to His 'people' – the intervention of *voice* is crucial here. As Lacan put it in his unpublished Seminar on *Anxiety* (1960–61), the voice (the actual 'speech act') brings about the *passage à l'acte* of the signifying network, its 'symbolic efficiency'. This voice is inherently meaningless, even nonsensical; it is a mere negative gesture which gives expression to God's malicious and vengeful anger (all meaning is already there in the symbolic order which structures our universe), but it is precisely as such that it actualizes purely structural meaning, transforming it into an experience of Sense.[7] This, of course, is another way of saying that God, through this uttering of the Voice which manifests His Will, subjectivizes Himself. The Ancient Egyptian Moses betrayed and killed by his people was the all-inclusive One of *logos*, the rational substantial structure of the universe, the 'writing' accessible to those who know how to read the 'great book of Nature', not yet the all-exclusive One of subjectivity who imposes His unconditional Will on His creation. And again, the crucial point not to be missed is that this God, although alogical, 'capricious', vengeful, 'irrational', is *not* the pre-symbolic 'primordial' Father-*jouissance* but, on the contrary, the agent of prohibition borne along by a 'ferocious ignorance' of the ways of *jouissance*.

The paradox one has to bear in mind here is that this God of groundless Willing and ferocious 'irrational' rage is the God who, by means of His Prohibition, accomplishes the destruction of the old sexualized Wisdom, and thus opens up the space for the desexualized 'abstract' knowledge of modern science. The paradox thus lies in the fact that there is 'objective' scientific knowledge (in the modern, post-Cartesian sense of the term) only if the universe of scientific knowledge is itself supplemented and sustained by this excessive 'irrational' figure of the 'real father'. In short, Descartes's 'voluntarism' (remember his infamous statement that two plus two would be five if such were God's Will – there are no eternal truths directly cosubstantial with the Divine Nature) is the necessary obverse of modern scientific knowledge. Premodern Aristotelian and medieval knowledge was not yet 'objective' rational scientific knowledge precisely because it lacked this excessive element of God *qua* the subjectivity of pure 'irrational' Willing: in Aristotle, 'God' directly equals His own eternal rational Nature; He 'is' nothing but the logical Order of Things.

The further paradox is that this 'irrational' God *qua* the prohibitory paternal figure also opens up the space for the entire development of modernity, up to the deconstructionist notion that our sexual identity is a contingent sociosymbolic formation: the moment this prohibitory figure recedes, we are back with Jungian neo-obscurantist notions of masculine and feminine eternal archetypes which thrive today. This point is absolutely crucial if we are not to misunderstand completely the gap which separates the 'proper' authority of the symbolic Law/Prohibition from mere 'regulation by rules': paradoxically, the domain of symbolic rules, if it is to count as such, has to be grounded in some tautological authority *beyond rules*, which says: 'It is so because I say it is so!'.

We can now see why, on the level of individual libidinal economy, Lacan calls this prohibiting God the 'real father' as the 'agent of castration': symbolic castration is another name for the gap between the big Other and *jouissance*, for the fact that the two can never be 'synchronized'. We can also see in what precise sense perversion enacts the disavowal of castration: the pervert's fundamental illusion is that he possesses a (symbolic) knowledge which enables him to regulate his access to *jouissance* – to put it in more contemporary terms, the pervert's dream is to transform his sexual activity into an instrumental purpose-orientated activity which can be projected and executed according to a well-defined plan. When one speaks of today's decline of paternal authority, it is *this* father, the father of the uncompromising 'No!', who actually seems to be in retreat; in his absence, in the absence of his prohibitory 'No!', new forms of the phantasmic harmony between the symbolic order and *jouissance* can thrive again – this is what the so-called New Age 'holistic' attitude is ultimately about, this renewal of Reason and Life Substance (Earth or macrocosm itself as a living entity) at the expense of the prohibitory 'real father'. A sign of how even the Church is not resistant to this shift in the fundamental attitude is the recent grass-roots pressure on the Pope to elevate Mary to the status of co-redemptrix: one expects the Pope to render the Catholic Church viable for the post-paternal third millennium by proclaiming a dogma which asserts that the only way for us sinful mortals to gain divine mercy is via our plea to Mary – Mary serves as mediator; if we convince her, she will speak on our behalf to Christ, her son.

III

This, then, is the *theological background* to Schmitt's assertion of political antagonism. However, the question remains: does Schmitt actually provide the adequate theoretical articulation of the logic of *political* antagonism? The answer is *no*: his assertion of the political involves a specific disavowal of the proper dimension of political antagonism, and it is precisely this disavowal which determines Schmitt's rightist political orientation.

Let us begin with a question: what is politics proper?[8] Schmitt's well-known answer (a social situation which involves the opposition between friend and enemy), radical as it may appear, is *not radical enough*, in so far as it already displaces the *inherent* antagonism constitutive of the political on to the *external* relationship between Us and Them. That is to say: politics proper is a phenomenon which appeared for the first time, in Ancient Greece when the members of *demos* (those with no firm determined place in the hierarchical social edifice) demanded a voice: against those in power, in social control, they protested the wrong they suffered, and wanted their voice to be heard, to be recognized as included in the public sphere – they, the excluded, those with no fixed place within the social edifice, thus paradoxically presented themselves as the representatives, the stand-in, for the Whole of Society, for the true Universality ('We – the "nothing", not included in the social order – are the people; we are All against others who stand only for their particular privileged interest'). So political conflict involves tension between the structured social body, where each part has its place, and 'the part of no-part' which unsettles this order on account of the empty principle of universality, of what Étienne Balibar calls *égaliberté*, of the principled equality of all men *qua* speaking beings.

Politics proper thus always involves a kind of short circuit between the Universal and the Particular: it involves the paradox of a singular which appears as a stand-in for the Universal, destabilizing the 'natural' functional order of relations in the social body. The political struggle proper is therefore never simply a rational debate between multiple interests but, simultaneously, the struggle for one's voice to be heard and recognized as the voice of a legitimate partner: when the 'excluded', from the Greek demos to Polish workers, protested against the ruling elite (aristocracy or *nomenklatura*), the true stakes were not only their explicit demands (for higher wages, better working conditions, etc.), but their very right to be heard and recognized as an equal partner in the debate – in Poland, the *nomenklatura* lost the moment it had to accept Solidarity as an equal partner. . . . The entire history of political thought is ultimately nothing but a series of disavowals of this political moment, of the proper logic of political antagonism; there are three main versions of this disavowal:

- *arche-politics*: the 'communitarian' attempt to define a traditional, close, organically structured homogeneous social space which allows for no void in which the political moment-event can emerge;
- *para-politics*: the attempt to depoliticize politics – one accepts political conflict, but reformulates it into a competition, within the representational space, between acknowledged parties/agents, for (temporary) occupation of the place of executive power. This para-politics, of course, has a series of successive different versions: the main rupture is that between its classical and modern Hobbesian formulation, which focuses on the problematic of social contract, the alienation of individual rights in the emergence of sovereign power. Habermasian or Rawlsian ethics are perhaps the last philosophical vestiges of this attitude: the attempt to de-antagonize politics by formulating the clear rules to be obeyed so that the agonistic procedure of litigation does not explode into politics proper;
- Marxist (or Utopian Socialist) *meta-politics*: the political conflict is fully asserted, *but* as a shadow-theatre in which events whose proper place is on Another Scene (of economic processes) are played out; the ultimate goal of 'true' politics is thus its self-cancellation, the transformation of 'administration of people' into 'administration of things' within a fully self-transparent rational order of collective Will. (More precisely, Marxism is ambiguous here, since the very term 'political economy' also opens up the space for the opposite gesture

of introducing politics into the very heart of economy: of denouncing the 'apolitical' character of the economic processes as the supreme ideological illusion. Class struggle does not 'express' some objective economic contradiction; it is the very form of existence of this contradiction.)

How does Schmitt stand with regard to these three standard versions of the disavowal of the political? Far from simply asserting the proper dimension of the political, he adds the most cunning and radical version of the disavowal, what we are tempted to call *ultra-politics*: the attempt to depoliticize the conflict by bringing it to its extreme, via the direct militarization of politics. In ultra-politics, the 'repressed' political returns in the guise of the attempt to resolve the deadlock of political conflict by its false radicalization – by reformulating it as a war between 'Us' and 'Them', our enemy, where there is no common ground for symbolic conflict: it is deeply symptomatic that, instead of class *struggle*, the radical Right speaks of class (or sexual) *warfare*. The clearest indication of this Schmittian disavowal of the political is the primacy of external politics (relations between sovereign states) over internal politics (inner social antagonisms) on which he insists: is not the relationship to an external Other as the enemy a way of disavowing the *internal* struggle which traverses the social body? In contrast to Schmitt, a leftist position should insist on the unconditional primacy of the inherent antagonism as constitutive of the political.

What we have in all these four cases is thus an attempt to gentrify the properly traumatic dimension of the political: something emerged in Ancient Greece under the name of demos demanding its rights, and from the very beginning (i.e. from Plato's *Republic*) to the recent revival of liberal 'political philosophy', 'political philosophy' was an attempt to suspend the destabilizing potential of the political, to disavow and/or regulate it in one way or another: bringing about a return to the pre-political social body, fixing the rules of political competition, and so forth. 'Political philosophy' is thus, in all its different forms, a kind of 'defence-formation', and perhaps its typology could be established via the reference to the different modalities of defence against some traumatic experience in psychoanalysis. Arche-, para-, meta- and ultra-politics thus form a kind of Greimasian logical square in which arche- and ultra- are the two faces of the traditionalist attitude (self-enclosed community versus its war with external enemies), and para- and meta- the two versions of modern politics (democratic formal rules versus the notion that this field of democratic game simply expresses and/or distorts another level of pre-political socioeconomic processes on which 'things really happen'); while on the other axis, both meta- and ultra-politics involve the notion of ineluctable struggle, conflict, antagonism, against the assertion of a harmonious collaboration in arche- and para-politics.

Today, however, we are dealing with another form of the denegation of the political: postmodern *post-politics*, which no longer merely 'represses' the political, trying to contain it and to pacify 'returns of the repressed', but much more effectively 'forecloses' it, so that postmodern forms of ethnic violence, with their 'irrational' excessive character, are no longer simple 'returns of the repressed' but, rather, embody the case of the foreclosed (from the Symbolic) which, as we know from Lacan, returns in the Real. In post-politics, the conflict of global ideological visions embodied in different parties who compete for power is replaced by the collaboration of enlightened technocrats (economists, public opinion specialists . . .) and liberal multiculturalists; through a process of negotiation of interests, a compromise is reached in the guise of a more or less universal consensus. The political (the space of litigation in which the excluded can protest the wrong/injustice done to them) foreclosed from the Symbolic then returns in the Real, as new forms of *racism*. It is crucial to perceive how 'postmodern racism' emerges as the ultimate consequence of the post-political suspension of the political, of the reduction of the state to a mere police-agent servicing the (consensually established) needs of market forces and multiculturalist tolerant human-itarianism: the 'foreigner' whose status is never properly 'regularized' is the *indivisible remainder* of the transformation of democratic political struggle into the post-political procedure of negotiation and multiculturalist policing. Instead of the *political* subject, the 'working class' demanding its universal rights, we get, on the one hand, the multiplicity of particular social strata or groups, each with its own problems (the dwindling need for manual workers, etc.), and, on the other, the immigrant who is increasingly prevented from *politicizing* his predicament of exclusion.[9]

Here one should oppose *globalization* to *universalization*: globalization (not only in the sense of global capitalism, the establishment of a global market, but also in the sense of the assertion of 'humanity' as the global point of reference of human rights, legitimizing violation of state sovereignty, and interventions – from trade restrictions to direct military action – in parts of the world where global human rights are violated) is precisely the name for the emerging post-political logic which progressively precludes the dimension of universality at work in politicization proper. The paradox is that there is no *universal* proper without the process of political litigation, of the 'part of no-part', of an out-of-joint entity presenting/manifesting itself as the stand-in for the universal. The Otherness excluded from the consensual domain of tolerant/rational post-political negotiation and administration returns in the guise of inexplicable pure Evil whose emblematic image is that of the Holocaust. What defines postmodern post-politics, therefore, is the secret solidarity between its two opposed Janus faces: on the one hand the replacement of politics proper by depoliticized 'humanitarian' operations (humanitarian protection of human and civil rights and aid to Bosnia, Somalia, Rwanda, North Korea . . .); on the other, the violent emergence of depoliticized 'pure Evil' in the guise of 'excessive' ethnic or religious fundamentalist violence. In short, what Rancière proposes here is a new version of the old Hegelian motto 'Evil resides in the gaze itself which perceives the object as Evil': the contemporary figure of Evil too 'strong' to be accessible to political analysis (Holocaust) appears as such only to the gaze which constitutes it as such (as depoliticized). Crucial is their speculative identity, that is, the infinite judgement: 'Humanitarian depoliticized compassion *is* the excess of Evil over its political forms.'

IV

One should link this problematic to the notion of excessive, non-functional cruelty as a feature of contemporary life, proposed by Balibar:[10] a cruelty whose figures range from 'fundamentalist' racist and/or religious slaughter to the 'senseless' outbursts of violence by adolescents and the homeless in our megalopolises, the violence one is tempted to call *id-evil*, a violence not grounded in any utilitarian or ideological causes. That is to say: what is striking in these cases is the 'primitive' level of the underlying libidinal economy – 'primitive' not in the sense of a 'regression' to some archaic stratum, but in the sense of the utmost *elementary* nature of the relationship between pleasure and *jouissance*, between the circle of the pleasure principle that strives for balance, for the reproduction of its closed circuit, and the ex-timate foreign body. The libidinal economy that sustains the infamous battle-cry '*Ausländer raus!* Foreigners out!' may be exemplified by Lacan's schema of the relationship between the *Ich* and *Lust*,[11] where the *Unlust* is defined in terms of (non-) assimilation, as 'what remains *unassimilable*, irreducible to the pleasure principle'.[12] The terms used by Freud and Lacan to describe the relationship between *Ich* and *jouissance* perfectly fit the metaphorics of the racist attitude towards foreigners: assimilation and resistance to assimilation, expulsion of a foreign body, disturbed balance. . . .

     In order to locate this type of evil in the context of the usual types of evil, one is tempted to use as the classificatory principle the Freudian triad of ego, superego and id:

- the most common kind of evil is *ego*-evil: behaviour prompted by selfish calculation and greed, that is, by disregard for universal ethical principles;
- the evil attributed to so-called 'fundamentalist fanatics', on the contrary, is *superego*-evil: evil accomplished in the name of fanatical devotion to some ideological ideal;
- in the skinhead beating up foreigners, however, one can discern neither a clear selfish calculation nor a clear ideological identification. All the talk about foreigners stealing work from us, or the threat they represent to our Western values, should not deceive us: on closer examination, it soon becomes clear that this talk provides a rather superficial secondary rationalization. The answer we ultimately obtain from a skinhead is that it makes him feel good to beat up foreigners, that their presence disturbs him . . . What we encounter here is *id-evil*, that is, evil structured and motivated by the most elementary imbalance in the relationship between the *Ich* and *jouissance*, by the tension between pleasure and the foreign body of *jouissance* at its very heart. Id-evil thus stages the most elementary 'short circuit' in the subject's relationship to the primordially missing object-cause of his desire: what 'bothers' us in the 'other' (Jew, Japanese, African, Turk . . .) is that he appears to entertain a privileged relationship to the object – the other either possesses the object-treasure, having snatched it away from us (which is why we don't have it), or poses a threat to our possession of the object.[13]

What one should propose here, again, is the Hegelian 'infinite judgement' asserting the speculative identity of this 'useless' and 'excessive' outburst of violence, which displays nothing but a pure and naked ('non-sublimated') hatred of Otherness, with the post-political multiculturalist universe of tolerance for difference in which nobody is excluded. Of course, we have just used the term 'non-sublimated' in its common meaning which, in this case, stands for the exact opposite of its strict psychoanalytic meaning – in short, what takes place when we focus our hatred on some representative of the (officially tolerated) Other is the very mechanism of *sublimation* at its most elementary: the all-encompassing nature of the post-political Concrete Universality which accounts for everybody at the level of symbolic inclusion, this multiculturalist vision-and-practice of 'unity in difference' ('all equal, all different'), leaves open, as the only way to mark the Difference, the proto-sublimatory gesture of elevating a contingent Other (of race, sex, religion . . .) into the 'absolute Otherness' of the impossible Thing, the ultimate threat to our identity – this Thing which must be annihilated if we are to survive. . . . That is the properly Hegelian paradox: the final arrival of the truly rational 'concrete universality' – the abolition of antagonisms, the 'mature' universe of the negotiated coexistence of different groups – coincides with its radical opposite, with thoroughly contingent outbursts of violence.

There are two further Hegelian aspects of this excessive violence. First, Hegel's fundamental rule is that the 'objective' excess (the direct reign of abstract universality which imposes its law 'mechanically', with utter disregard for the concerned subject caught in its web) is always supplemented by the 'subjective' excess (the irregular, arbitrary exercise of whims). An exemplary case of this interdependence between the objective and subjective excess is provided by Balibar,[14] who distinguishes two opposite but complementary modes of the excessive violence: the 'ultra-objective' ('structural') violence which is inherent to the social conditions of global capitalism (the 'automatic' creation of excluded and dispensable individuals, from the homeless to the unemployed) and the 'ultra-subjective' violence of newly emerging ethnic and/or religious (in short: racist) 'fundamentalisms'.

The second aspect is that this 'excessive' and 'groundless' violence involves its own mode of knowledge, that of the impotent cynical reflection – back to our example of 'id-evil', of a skinhead beating up foreigners: if he is really pressed for the reasons for his violence, and if he is capable of minimal theoretical reflection, the skinhead will suddenly start to talk like social workers, sociologists and social psychologists, citing diminished social mobility, rising insecurity, the disintegration of paternal authority, the lack of maternal love in his early childhood . . . in short, he will provide the more or less precise psychosociological account of his acts so dear to enlightened liberals eager to 'understand' violent youth as the tragic victim of social and familial conditions.

The standard enlightened formula of the efficiency of the 'critique of ideology', from Plato onwards ('They're doing it because they don't know what they're doing', that is to say, knowledge is liberating in itself – when the erring subject reflects upon what he is doing, he will no longer do it) is turned around here: the violent skinhead 'knows very well what he's doing, but he's doing it all the same'.[15] This cynically impotent reflective knowledge is the obverse of 'senseless' 'excessive' violence; we are dealing here with something akin to the well-known unpleasant scene from Terry Gilliam's film *Brazil*: in a high-class restaurant, the waiter recommends to his customers the best of the daily menu ('Today, our tournedos is really special!', etc.), yet what the customers get on making their choice is a dazzling colour photo of the meal on a stand above the plate, and on the plate itself, a loathsome excremental paste-like lump. In the same way, the symbolically efficient knowledge embedded in the subject's effective social *praxis* disintegrated into, on the one hand, excessive 'irrational' violence with no ideologico-political foundation and, on the other, impotent external reflection which leaves the subject's acts intact. So, in the guise of this cynically impotent reflecting skinhead who, with an ironic smile, explains to the perplexed journalist the roots of his senselessly violent behaviour, the enlightened tolerant multiculturalist bent on 'understanding' forms of excessive violence gets his own message in its inverted, true form. In short – as Lacan would have put it – at this point, the communication between him and the 'object' of his study, the intolerant skinhead, is perfectly successful.

The distinction between this excessive/'irrational'/'dysfunctional' cruel violence and the outbursts of obscene violence which serve as the implicit support of the standard ideological universal notion is crucial here: when, say, 'the rights of man' are 'not really universal' but 'in fact the rights of white male property-owners', any attempt to disregard this implicit underlying set of unwritten rules which effectively constrains the universality of rights is met with outbursts of violence. Nowhere is this contrast stronger than in the case of dealing with African-Americans in the USA: the old para-political democratic racism excluded Blacks from participating effectively in universal political life by silently enforc-ing their exclusion (via verbal and physical threats, etc.). The adequate answer to this standard exclusion-from-the-Universal was the great Civil Rights movement associated with the name of Martin Luther King: suspending the implicit obscene supplement which enacts the actual exclusion of Blacks from formal universal equality – of course, it was easy for such a gesture to gain the support of the large majority of the white liberal upper-class establishment, dismissing their opponents as dumb lower-class Southern rednecks. . . .

Today, however, the very terrain of the struggle has changed: the post-political liberal establishment not only fully acknowledges the gap between mere formal equality and its actualization/implementation, it not only acknowledges the exclusionary logic of 'false' ideological uni-versality, it even actively fights this logic by applying to it a vast legal-psychological-sociological network of measures, from identifying the specific problems of each group and subgroup (not only homosexuals but African-American lesbians, African-American lesbian mothers, Afri-can-American single unemployed lesbian mothers . . .) to proposing a set of measures ('affirmative action', etc.) to rectify the wrong. What such a tolerant procedure prevents, however, is the gesture of *politicization* proper: although the difficulties of being an African-American single unemployed lesbian mother are adequately catalogued down to their most specific features, the concerned subject none the less somehow 'feels' that there is something 'wrong' and 'frustrating' in this very effort to do justice to her specific predicament – what she is deprived of is the possibility of a 'metaphorical' elevation of her specific 'wrong' into a stand-in for the universal 'wrong'. The only way openly to articulate this universality – the fact that I, precisely, am *not* merely that specific individual exposed to a set of specific injustices – consists, then, in its apparent opposite, in the thoroughly 'irrational' excessive outburst of violence. Here the old Hegelian rule is confirmed once more: the only way for the universality to come into existence, to 'posit' itself 'as such', is in the guise of its very opposite, of what cannot but appear as an excessive 'irrational' whim.

Does all this mean that, in today's post-political conditions, Schmitt is no longer pertinent? Quite the contrary: *the reference to Schmitt is crucial in detecting the deadlocks of post-political liberal tolerance*: Schmittian ultra-politics – the radicalization of politics into the open warfare of Us against Them discernible in different 'fundamentalisms' – is *the form in which the foreclosed political returns in the post-political universe of pluralist negotiation and consensual regulation*. For that reason, the way to counteract this re-emerging ultra-politics is not more tolerance, more compassion and multicultural understanding, but the *return of the political proper*, that is, the reassertion of the dimension of antagonism which, far from denying universality, is cosubstantial with it. That is the key component of the proper *leftist* stance as opposed to the rightist assertion of one's particular identity: in the equation of *Universalism* with the militant, *divisive* position of one engaged in a struggle – true universalists are not those who preach global tolerance of differences and all-encompassing unity, but those who engage in a passionate struggle for the assertion of the Truth which compels them. Theoretical, religious and political examples abound here: from St Paul, whose unconditional Christian universalism (everyone can be redeemed, since in the eyes of Christ there is neither Jew nor Greek, neither man nor woman...) made him into a proto-Leninist militant fighting different 'deviations', through Marx (whose notion of class struggle is the necessary obverse of the universalism of his theory which aims at the 'redemption' of the whole of humanity) and Freud up to great political figures. When De Gaulle, for instance, almost alone in England in 1940, launched his call for resistance to the German occupation, he was at the same time presuming to speak on behalf of the universality of France, and, *for that very reason*, introducing a radical split, a fissure between those who followed him and those who preferred the collaborationist 'Egyptian fleshpots'.

To put it in Alain Badiou's words,[16] it is crucial here not to translate the terms of this struggle, set in motion by the violent and contingent assertion of the new universal Truth, into the terms of the order of positive Being, with its groups and subgroups, conceiving of it as the struggle between two social entities defined by a series of positive characteristics; that was the 'mistake' of Stalinism, which reduced class struggle to a struggle between 'classes' defined as social groups with a set of positive features (place in the mode of production, etc.). From a truly radical Marxist perspective, although there is a link between 'working class' as a social group and 'proletariat' as the position of the militant fighting for universal Truth, this link is not a determining causal connection, and the two levels are to be strictly distinguished: to be a 'proletarian' involves assuming a certain *subjective stance* (of class struggle destined to achieve the Redemption through Revolution) which, in principle, can be taken by *any* individual – to put it in religious terms, any individual, irrespective of his (good) works, can be 'touched by Grace' and interpellated as a proletarian subject.

The limit which separates the two opposing sides in the class struggle is therefore not 'objective', not the limit separating two positive social groups, but ultimately *radically subjective* – it involves the position individuals assume towards the Event of universal Truth. Again, the crucial point here is that subjectivity and universalism are not only not exclusive, but two sides of the same coin: it is precisely because 'class struggle' interpellates individuals to adopt the subjective stance of a 'proletarian,' that its appeal is universal, aiming at everyone without exception. The division it mobilizes is not the division between two well-defined social groups ('Us' and 'Them'), but the division, which runs 'diagonally' to the social division in the Order of Being, between those who recognize themselves in the call of the Truth-Event, becoming its followers, and those who deny or ignore it. In Hegelese, *the existence of the true Universal* (as opposed to the false 'concrete' Universality of the all-encompassing global Order of Being) *is that of an endless and incessantly divisive struggle*; it is ultimately the division between the two notions (and material practices) of Universality: those who advocate the positivity of the existing global Order of Being as the ultimate horizon of knowledge and action, and those who accept the efficiency of the dimension of Truth-Event irreducible to (and unaccountable in terms of) the Order of Being. This inherent split constitutive of the true Universal is what even such a radical thinker as Carl Schmitt was unable to endorse.

Notes

1. See Carl Schmitt, *Political Theology: Four Chapters on the Concept of Sovereignty*, trans. George Schwab, Cambridge MA: MIT Press, 1985.
2. See Jacques Lacan, *Le Séminaire, livre VIII: Le transfert*, Paris: Éditions du Seuil 1991.
3. See Jacques Derrida, *Donner la mort*, Paris: Galilée, 1995.
4. For a concise description of these shifts, see Michel Lapeyre, *Au-delà du complexe d'Œdipe*, Paris: Anthropos-Economica, 1997.
5. The title of Chapter IX of Jacques Lacan, *Le Séminaire, livre XVII: L'envers de la psychanalyse*, Paris: Éditions du Seuil, 1991.
6. See Slavoj Žižek, *The Indivisible Remainder*, London: Verso, 1996.
7. For a more detailed account of this distinction, see Chapter 2 of Žižek, *The Indivisible Remainder*.
8. I rely here on Jacques Rancière, *La mésentente*, Paris: Galilée, 1995.
9. See ibid., p. 162.
10. See Étienne Balibar, 'La violence: idéalité et cruauté', in *La crainte des masses*, Paris: Galilée, 1997.
11. Jacques Lacan, *The Four Fundamental Concepts of Psycho-Analysis*, New York: Norton, 1979, p. 240.
12. Ibid., p. 241.
13. For a further development of this theme, see Chapter 3 of Slavoj Žižek, *The Metastases of Enjoyment*, London: Verso, 1995.
14. See Balibar, *La crainte des masses*, pp. 42–3.
15. For a more detailed account of this reflected cynical attitude, see Chapter 3 of Žižek, *The Indivisible Remainder*.
16. See Alain Badiou, *L'être et l'événement*, Paris: Éditions du Seuil, 1988.

3

Carl Schmitt and the Paradox
of Liberal Democracy

Chantal Mouffe

In his introduction to the paperback edition of *Political Liberalism*, John Rawls, referring to Carl Schmitt's critique of parliamentary democracy, suggests that the fall of Weimar's constitutional regime was in part due to the fact that German elites no longer believed in the possibility of a decent liberal parliamentary regime. In his view, this should make us realize the importance of providing convincing arguments in favour of a just and well-ordered constitutional democracy. 'Debates about general philosophical questions', he says, 'cannot be the daily stuff of politics, but that does not make these questions without significance, since what we think their answers are will shape the underlying attitudes of the public culture and the conduct of politics.'[1]

I agree with Rawls on the practical role that political philosophy can play in shaping the public culture and contributing to the creation of democratic political identities. But I consider that political theorists, in order to put forward a conception of a liberal-democratic society able to win the active support of its citizens, must be willing to engage with the arguments of those who have challenged the fundamental tenets of liberalism. This means confronting some disturbing questions, usually avoided by liberals and democrats alike.

My intention in this chapter is to contribute to such a project by scrutinizing Carl Schmitt's critique of liberal democracy. Indeed, I am convinced that a confrontation with his thought will allow us to acknowledge – and, therefore, be in a better position to try to negotiate – an important paradox inscribed in the very nature of liberal democracy. To bring to the fore the pertinence and actuality of Schmitt's questioning, I will organize my argument around two topics which are currently central in political theory: the boundaries of citizenship and the nature of a liberal-democratic consensus.[2]

Democracy, homogeneity and the boundaries of citizenship

The boundaries of citizenship have recently provoked much discussion. Several authors have argued that in an age of globalization, citizenship cannot be confined within the boundaries of nation-states; it must become transnational. David Held, for instance, advocates the advent of a 'cosmopolitan citizenship', and asserts the need for a cosmopolitan democratic law to which citizens whose rights have been violated by their own states could appeal.[3] Richard Falk, for his part, envisages the development of 'citizen pilgrims' whose loyalties would belong to an invisible political community of their hopes and dreams.[4]

Other theorists, however, particularly those who are committed to a civic republican conception of citizenship, are deeply suspicious of such prospects, which they view as endangering democratic forms of government. They assert that the nation-state is the necessary locus for citizenship, and that there is something inherently contradictory in the very idea of cosmopolitan citizenship. I see this debate as a typical example of the problems arising from the conflict between democratic and liberal requirements. Schmitt, I submit, can help us to clarify what is at stake in this issue by making us aware of the tension between democracy and liberalism.

As a starting point, let us take his thesis that 'homogeneity' is a condition of possibility of democracy. In the preface to the second edition of *The Crisis of Parliamentary Democracy* (1926), he declares: 'Every actual democracy rests on the principle that not only are equals equal but unequals will not be treated equally. Democracy requires, therefore, first homogeneity and second – if the need arises – elimination or eradication of heterogeneity.'[5] I do not want to deny that, given its author's later political evolution, this assertion has a chilling effect. I consider, however, that it would be short-sighted to dismiss Schmitt's claim on the necessity of homogeneity in a democracy for that reason. It is my contention that this provocative thesis – interpreted in a certain way – may force us to come to terms with an aspect of democratic politics that liberalism tends to eliminate.

The first thing to do is to grasp what Schmitt means by 'homogeneity'. He affirms that homogeneity is inscribed at the very core of the democratic conception of equality, in so far as it must be a *substantive* equality. His argument is that democracy requires a conception of equality as substance. and cannot satisfy itself with abstract conceptions like the liberal one, since 'equality is only interesting and invaluable politically so long as it has substance, and for that reason at least the possibility and the risk of inequality'.[6] In order to be treated as equals, citizens must, he says, partake of a common substance.

As a consequence, he rejects the idea that the general equality of mankind could serve as a basis for a state or any form of government. Such an idea of human equality – which comes from liberal individualism – is, says Schmitt, a non-political form of equality, because it lacks the correlate of a possible inequality from which every equality receives its specific meaning. It does not provide any criteria for establishing political institutions: 'The equality of all persons as persons is not democracy but a certain kind of liberalism, not a state form but an individualistic-humanitarian ethic and *Weltanschauung*. Modern mass democracy rests on the confused combination of both.'[7]

Schmitt asserts that there is an insuperable opposition between liberal individualism, with its moral discourse centred around the individual, and the democratic ideal, which is essentially political, and aims at creating an identity based on homogeneity. He claims that liberalism negates democracy and democracy negates liberalism, and that parliamentary democracy, since it consists in the articulation between democracy and liberalism, is therefore a non-viable regime.

In his view, when we speak of equality, we need to distinguish between two very different ideas: the liberal one and the democratic one. The liberal conception of equality postulates that every person is, as a person, automatically equal to every other person. The democratic conception, however, requires the possibility of distinguishing who belongs to the demos and who is exterior to it; for that reason, it cannot exist without the necessary correlate of inequality. Despite liberal claims, a democracy of mankind, if it was ever likely, would be a pure abstraction, because equality can exist only through its specific meanings in particular spheres – as political equality, economic equality, and so forth. But those specific equalities always entail, as their very condition of possibility, some form of inequality. This is why he concludes that an absolute human equality would be a practically meaningless, indifferent equality.

Schmitt makes an important point when he stresses that the democratic concept of equality is a *political* one which therefore entails the possibility of a *distinction*. He is right to say that a political democracy cannot be based on the generality of all mankind, and that it must belong to a specific people. It is worth indicating in this context that – contrary to several tendentious interpretations – he never postulated that this belonging to a people could be envisaged only in racial terms. On the contrary, he insisted on the multiplicity of ways in which the homogeneity constitutive of a demos could be manifested. He says, for instance, that the substance of equality 'can be found in certain physical and moral qualities, for example, in civic virtue, in arete, the classical democracy of vertus [vertu]'.[8] Examining this question from a historical angle, he also points out that 'In the democracy of English sects during the seventeenth century equality was based on a consensus of religious convictions. However, since the nineteenth century it has existed above all in membership in a particular nation, in national homogeneity.'[9]

It is clear that what is important for Schmitt is not the nature of the similarity on which homogeneity is based. What matters is the possibility of tracing a line of demarcation between those who belong to the demos – and therefore have equal rights – and those who, in the political domain, cannot have the same rights because they are not part of the demos. Such a democratic equality – expressed today through citizenship – is, for him, the ground of all the other forms of equality. It is through their belonging to the demos that democratic citizens are granted equal rights, not because they participate in an abstract idea of humanity. This is why he declares that the central concept of democracy is not 'humanity' but the concept of the 'people', and that there can never be a democracy of mankind. Democracy can exist only for a people. As he puts it:

> In the domain of the political, people do not face each other as abstractions but as politically interested and politically determined persons, as citizens, governors or governed, politically allied or opponents – in any case, therefore, in political categories. In the sphere of the political, one cannot abstract out what is political, leaving only universal human equality.[10]

In order to illustrate his point, Schmitt indicates that even in modern democratic states, where a universal human equality has been established, there is a category of people who are excluded as foreigners or aliens, and that there is therefore no absolute equality of persons. He also shows how the correlate of the equality among the citizenry found in those states is a much stronger emphasis on national homogeneity, and on the line of demarcation between those who belong to the state and those who remain outside it. This, he notes, is to be expected, and if it were not the case, and if a state attempted to realize the universal equality of individuals in the political realm without concern for national or any other form of homogeneity, the consequence would be a complete devaluation of political equality, and of politics itself. To be sure, this would in no way mean the disappearance of substantive inequalities, but, says Schmitt:

they would shift into another sphere, perhaps separated from the political and concentrated in the economic, leaving this area to take on a new, disproportionately decisive importance. Under the conditions of superficial political equality, another sphere in which substantial inequalities prevail (today for example the economic sphere) will dominate politics.[11]

It seems to me that, unpleasant as they are to liberal ears, these arguments need to be considered carefully. They carry an important warning for those who believe that the process of globalization is laying the basis for worldwide democratization and the establishment of a cosmopolitan citizenship. They also provide important insights into the current dominance of economics over politics. We should indeed be aware that without a demos to which they belong, those cosmopolitan citizen pilgrims would in fact have lost the possibility of exercising their democratic rights of law-making. They would be left, at best, with their liberal rights of appealing to transnational courts to defend their individual rights when these have been violated. In all probability, such a cosmopolitan democracy, if it were ever to be realized, would be no more than an empty name disguising the actual disappearance of democratic forms of government and indicating the triumph of the liberal form of governmental rationality that Foucault called 'governmentality'.

The democratic logic of inclusion–exclusion

It is true that by reading him in this way, I am doing violence to Schmitt's questioning, since his main concern is not democratic participation but *political unity*. He considers that such a unity is crucial, because without it the state cannot exist. But his reflections are relevant to the issue of democracy, since he considers that in a democratic state, it is through their participation in this unity that citizens can be treated as equals and exercise their democratic rights. Democracy, according to Schmitt, consists fundamentally in the identity between rulers and ruled. It is linked to the fundamental principle of the unity of the demos and the sovereignty of its will. But if the people are to rule, it is necessary to determine who belongs to the people. Without any criterion to determine who are the bearers of democratic rights, the will of the people could never take shape.

It could, of course, be objected that this is a view of democracy which is at odds with the liberal-democratic one, and some would certainly claim that this should be called not democracy but populism. To be sure, Schmitt is no democrat in the liberal understanding of the term, and he had nothing but contempt for the constraints imposed by liberal institutions on the democratic will of the people. But the issue he raises is a crucial one, even for those who advocate liberal-democratic forms. The logic of democracy does indeed imply a moment of closure which is required by the very process of constituting the 'people'. This cannot be avoided, even in a liberal-democratic model; it can only be negotiated differently. But this in turn can be done only if this closure, and the paradox it implies, are acknowledged.

By stressing that the identity of a democratic political community hinges on the possibility of drawing a frontier between 'us' and 'them', Schmitt highlights the fact that democracy always entails relations of inclusion–exclusion. This is a vital insight that democrats would be ill-advised to dismiss because they dislike its author. One of the main problems with liberalism – and one that can endanger democracy – is precisely its incapacity to conceptualize such a frontier. As Schmitt indicates, the central concept of liberal discourse is 'humanity', which – as he rightly points out – is not a political concept, and does not correspond to any political entity. The central question of the political constitution of 'the people' is something that liberal theory is unable to tackle adequately, because the necessity of drawing such a 'frontier' contradicts its universalistic rhetoric. Against the liberal emphasis on 'humanity', it is important to stress that the key concepts of democracy are the 'demos' and the 'people'.

Contrary to those who believe in a necessary harmony between liberalism and democracy, Schmitt makes us see how they conflict, and the dangers the dominance of liberal logic can bring to the exercise of democracy. No doubt there is an opposition between the liberal 'grammar' of equality, which postulates universality and reference to 'humanity', and the practice of democratic equality, which requires the political moment of discrimination between 'us' and 'them'. However, I think that Schmitt is wrong to present this conflict as a contradiction that is bound to lead liberal democracy to self-destruction. We can accept his insight perfectly well without agreeing with the conclusions he draws. I propose to acknowledge the crucial difference between the liberal and the democratic conceptions of equality, while envisaging their articulation and its consequences in another way. Indeed, such an articulation can be seen as the locus of a *tension* that installs a very important dynamic, which is constitutive of the specificity of liberal democracy as a new political form of society. The democratic logic of constituting the people, and inscribing rights and equality into practices, is necessary to subvert the tendency towards abstract universalism inherent in liberal discourse. But the articulation with the liberal logic allows us constantly to challenge – through reference to 'humanity' and the polemical use of 'human rights' – the forms of exclusion that are necessarily inscribed in the political practice of installing those rights and defining 'the people' which is going to rule.[12] Notwithstanding the ultimate contradictory nature of the two logics, their articulation therefore has very positive consequences, and there is no reason to share Schmitt's pessimistic verdict concerning liberal democracy. However, we should not be too sanguine about its prospect either. No final resolution or equilibrium between those two conflicting logics is ever possible, and there can be only temporary, pragmatic, unstable and precarious negotiations of the tension between them. Liberal-democratic politics consists, in fact, in the constant process of negotiation and renegotiation – through different hegemonic articulations – of this constitutive paradox.

Deliberative democracy and its shortcomings

Schmitt's reflections on the necessary moment of closure entailed by the democratic logic has important consequences for another debate, the one about the nature of the consensus that can obtain in a liberal-democratic society. Several issues are at stake in that debate, and I will examine them in turn.

One of the implications of the argument presented above is the impossibility of establishing a rational consensus without exclusion. This raises several problems for the model of democratic politics, which has been receiving quite a lot of attention recently under the name 'deliberative democracy'. No doubt, the aim of the theorists who advocate the different versions of such a model is commendable. Against the interest-based conception of democracy, inspired by economics and sceptical about the virtues of political participation, they want to introduce questions of morality and justice into politics, and envisage democratic citizenship in a different way. However, by proposing to view reason and rational argumentation, rather than interest and aggregation of preferences, as the central issue of politics, they simply replace the economic model with a moral one which – albeit in a different way – also misses the specificity of the political. In their attempt to overcome the limitations of interest-group pluralism, deliberative democrats provide a telling illustration of Schmitt's point that 'In a very systematic fashion liberal thought evades or ignores state and politics and moves instead in a typical, always recurring polarity of two heterogeneous spheres, namely ethics and economics, intellect and trade, education and property.'[13]

Since I cannot examine all the different versions of deliberative democracy here, I will concentrate on the model developed by Habermas and his followers. To be sure, there are several differences among the advocates of this new paradigm. But there is enough convergence among them to affirm that none of them can deal adequately with the paradox of democratic politics.[14]

According to Seyla Benhabib, the main challenge confronting democracy is how to reconcile rationality with legitimacy – or, to put it differently, the crucial question that democracy needs to address is how the expression of the common good can be made compatible with the sovereignty of the people. She presents the answer offered by the deliberative model:

> legitimacy and rationality can be attained with regard to collective decision-making processes in a polity if and only if the institutions of this polity and their interlocking relationship are so arranged that what is considered in the common interest of all results from processes of collective deliberation conducted rationally and fairly among free and equal individuals.[15]

In this view, the basis of legitimacy in democratic institutions derives from the fact that those who claim obligatory power do so on the presumption that their decisions represent an *impartial standpoint* which is *equally in the interests of all*. If this presumption is to be fulfilled, those decisions must be the result of appropriate public processes of deliberation which follow the procedures of the Habermasian discourse model. The basic idea behind this model is that:

> only those norms, i.e. general rules of action and institutional arrangements, can be said to be valid which would be agreed to by all those affected by their consequences, if such agreement were reached as a consequence of a process of deliberation which has the following features:
>
> (a) participation in such deliberation is governed by the norms of equality and symmetry; all have the same chance to initiate speech acts, to question, interrogate, and to open debate;
> (b) all have the right to question the assigned topics of conversation;
> (c) all have the right to initiate reflexive arguments about the very rules of the discourse procedure and the way in which they are applied or carried out. There is no *prima facie* rule limiting the agenda or the conversation, nor the identity of the participants, as long as each excluded person or group can justifiably show that they are relevantly affected by the proposed norm under question.'[16]

Let us examine this model of deliberative democracy closely. In their attempt to ground legitimacy on *rationality*, these theorists have to distinguish between mere agreement and rational consensus. That is why they assert that the process of public discussion must realize the conditions of ideal discourse. This sets the values of the procedure, which are impartiality and equality, openness and lack of coercion, and unanimity. The combination of those values in the discussion guarantees that its outcome will be legitimate, since it will produce generalizable interests on which all participants can agree.

Habermasians do not deny that there will, of course, be obstacles to the realization of the ideal discourse, but these obstacles are conceived of as *empirical*. They are due to the fact that it is unlikely, given the practical and empirical limitations of social life, that we will ever be completely able to leave all our particular interests aside in order to coincide with our universal rational self. This is why the ideal speech situation is presented as a regulative idea.

However, if we accept Schmitt's insight about the relations of inclusion–exclusion which are necessarily inscribed in the political constitution of 'the people' – which is required by the exercise of democracy – we have to acknowledge that the obstacles to the realization of the ideal speech situation – and to the consensus without exclusion that it would bring about – are inscribed in the democratic logic itself. Indeed, the free and unconstrained public deliberation of all on matters of common concern goes against the democratic requisite of drawing a frontier between 'us' and 'them'. We could say – this time using Derridan terminology – that the very conditions of possibility of the exercise of democracy constitute simultaneously the conditions of impossibility of democratic legitimacy as envisaged by deliberative democracy. Consensus in a liberal-democratic society is – and will always be – the expression of a hegemony and the crystallization of power relations. The frontier that it establishes between what is and what is not legitimate is a political one, and for that reason it should remain contestable. To deny the existence of such a moment of closure, or to present the frontier as dictated by rationality or morality, is to naturalize what should be perceived as a contingent and temporary hegemonic articulation of 'the people' through a particular regime of inclusion–exclusion. The result of such an operation is to reify the identity of the people by reducing it to one of its many possible forms of identification.

Pluralism and its limits

Because it postulates the availability of a consensus without exclusion, the model of deliberative democracy is unable to envisage liberal-democratic pluralism in an adequate way. Indeed, one could indicate how, in both Rawls and Habermas – to take the best-known representatives of that trend – the very condition for the creation of consensus is the elimination of pluralism from the public sphere.[17] Hence the incapacity of deliberative democracy to provide a convincing refutation of Schmitt's critique of liberal pluralism. It is this critique that I will now examine, to see how it could be answered.

Schmitt's best-known thesis is certainly that the criterion of the political is the friend–enemy distinction. Indeed, for him, the political 'can be understood only in the context of the ever present possibility of the friend-and-enemy grouping'.[18] Because of the way this thesis is generally interpreted, he is often taken to task for neglecting the 'friend' side of his friend–enemy opposition. In his remarks on homogeneity, however, we can find many indications of how this grouping should be envisaged, and this has important implications for his critique of pluralism.

Let us return to the idea that democracy requires political equality, which stems from partaking in a common substance – this, as we have seen, is what Schmitt means by the need for homogeneity. So far, I have stressed the necessity of drawing a frontier between the 'us' and the 'them'. But we can also examine this question by focusing on the 'us' and the nature of the bond that unites its components. Clearly, to assert that the condition of possibility of an 'us' is the existence of a 'them' does not exhaust the subject. Different forms of unity can be established among the components of the 'us'. To be sure, this is not what Schmitt believes, since in his view unity can exist only on the mode of identity. But this is precisely where the problem with his conception lies. It is useful, therefore, to examine both the strengths and the weaknesses of his argument.

By asserting the need for homogeneity in a democracy, Schmitt is telling us something about the kind of bond that is needed if a democratic political community is to exist. In other words, he is analysing the nature of the 'friendship' which defines the 'us' in a democracy. This, for him, is, of course, a way of taking issue with liberalism for not recognizing the need for such a form of commonality, and for advocating pluralism. If we take his target to be the liberal model of interest-group pluralism which postulates that agreement on mere procedures can assure the cohesion of a liberal society, he is no doubt right. Such a vision of a pluralist society is certainly inadequate. Liberalism simply transposes into the public realm the diversity of interests already existing in society and reduces the political moment to the process of negotiation among interests independently of their political expression. There is no place in such a model for a common identity of democratic citizens; citizenship is reduced to a legal status, and the moment of the political constitution of the people is foreclosed. Schmitt's critique of that type of liberalism is convincing, and it is interesting to note that it chimes with

what Rawls says when he rejects the 'modus vivendi' model of constitutional democracy because it is very unstable, always liable to dissolution,
and declares that the unity it creates is insufficient.

Having discarded the view that grounds it in a mere convergence of
interests and a neutral set of procedures, how, then, should we envisage
the unity of a pluralist society? Isn't any other type of unity incompatible
with the pluralism advocated by liberal societies? On this issue, Schmitt's
answer is, of course, unequivocal: there is no place for pluralism inside
a democratic political community. Democracy requires the existence of a
homogeneous demos, and this precludes any possibility of pluralism.
This is why, in his view, there is an insurmountable contradiction
between liberal pluralism and democracy. For him, the only possible and
legitimate pluralism is a pluralism of states. Rejecting the liberal idea of
a world state, he affirms that the political world is a 'pluriverse', not a
'universe'. In his view: 'The political entity cannot by its very nature be
universal in the sense of embracing all of humanity and the entire
world.'[19]

In *The Concept of the Political* – taking as his target the kind of pluralism
advocated by the pluralist school of Harold Laski and G. D. H. Cole –
Schmitt argues that the state cannot be considered as one more association among others, which would be on the same level as a church or a
trade union. Against liberal theory, whose aim is to transform the state
into a voluntary association through the theory of the social contract, he
urges us to acknowledge that the political entity is something different
and more decisive. For him, to deny this is to deny the political: 'Only
as long as the essence of the political is not comprehended or not taken
into consideration is it possible to place a political association pluralisti-
cally on the same level with religious, cultural, economic, or other
associations and permit it to compete with these.'[20]

A few years later, in his important article 'Ethic of State and Pluralistic
State', again discussing Laski and Cole, he notes that the actuality of
their pluralist theory comes from the fact that it corresponds to the
empirical conditions existing in most industrial societies. The current
situation is one in which 'the state, in fact, does appear to be largely
dependent on social groups, sometimes as sacrifice to, sometimes as
result of, their negotiations – an object of compromise among the
powerful social and economic groups, an agglomeration of heterogeneous factors, political parties, combines, unions, churches, and so on . . .'[21]
The state is therefore weakened, and becomes some kind of clearing
house, a referee between competing factions. Reduced to a purely
instrumental function, it cannot be the object of loyalty; it loses its ethical
role and its capacity to represent the political unity of a people. While
he deplores such a situation, Schmitt none the less admits that as far as

their empirical diagnostic is concerned, the pluralists have a point. In his opinion, the interest of their theory lies in the 'appreciation of the concrete empirical power of social groups, and of the empirical situation as it is determined by the ways in which individuals belong to several of such social groups'.[22]

Schmitt, it must be said, does not always see the existence of parties as being absolutely incompatible with the existence of an ethical state. In the same article, he even seems willing to admit at least the possibility of some form of pluralism that does not negate the unity of the state. But he quickly rejects it, declaring that it will inevitably lead to the type of pluralism that will dissolve political unity:

> If the state then becomes a pluralistic party state, the unity of the state can be maintained only as long as two or more parties agree to recognize common premisses. That unity then rests in particular on the constitution recognized by all parties, which must be respected without qualification as the common foundation. The ethic of state then amounts to a constitutional ethic. Depending on the substantivity, unequivocality and authority of the constitution, a very effective unity can be found there. But it can also be the case that the constitution dwindles into mere rules of the game, its ethic of state into a mere ethic of fair play; and that it finally, in a pluralistic dissolution of the unity of the political whole, gets to the point where the unity is only an agglomeration of changing alliances between heterogeneous groups. The constitutional ethic then dwindles even further, to the point of the ethic of state being reduced in the proposition *pacta sunt servanda*.[23]

Schmitt's false dilemma

I think Schmitt is right to stress the deficiencies of the kind of pluralism that negates the specificity of the political association, and I concur with his assertion that it is necessary to constitute the people *politically*. But I do not believe that this must commit us to denying the possibility of any form of pluralism within the political association. To be sure, liberal theory has so far been unable to provide a convincing solution to this problem. This does not mean, however, that it is insoluble. In fact, Schmitt presents us with a false dilemma: either there is unity of the people, and this requires expelling every division and antagonism outside the demos – the exterior it needs if it is to establish its unity; or some forms of division inside the demos are considered legitimate, and this will lead inexorably to the kind of pluralism which negates political unity and the very existence of the people. As Jean-François Kervégan points out: 'for Schmitt, either the State imposes its order and its rationality to a civil society characterized by pluralism, competition and disorder, or, as is the case in liberal democracy, social pluralism will empty the political entity of its meaning and bring it back to its *other*, the state of nature'.[24]

What leads Schmitt to formulate such a dilemma is the way he envisages political unity. The unity of the state must, for him, be a concrete unity, already given and therefore stable. This is also true of the way he envisages the identity of the people: it also must exist as a given. Because of that, his distinction between 'us' and 'them' is not really politically constructed; it is merely a recognition of already-existing borders. While he rejects the pluralist conception, Schmitt is nevertheless unable to situate himself on a completely different terrain because he retains a view of political and social identities as empirically given. His position is, in fact, ultimately contradictory. On the one hand, he seems seriously to consider the possibility that pluralism could bring about the dissolution of the unity of the state. If that dissolution is, however, a distinctive *political* possibility, it also entails that the existence of such a unity is itself a contingent fact which requires a political construction. On the other hand, however, the unity is presented as a *factum* whose obviousness could ignore the political conditions of its production. Only as a result of this sleight of hand can the alternative be as inexorable as Schmitt wants it to be.

What Schmitt fears most is the loss of common premises and consequent destruction of the political unity which he sees as inherent in the pluralism that accompanies mass democracy. There is certainly a danger of this happening, and his warning should be taken seriously. But this is not a reason to reject all forms of pluralism. I propose to refuse Schmitt's dilemma, while acknowledging his argument for the need of some form of 'homogeneity' in a democracy. The problem we have to face becomes, then, how to imagine in a different way what Schmitt refers to as 'homogeneity' but that – in order to stress the differences with his conception – I propose to call, rather, 'commonality'; how to envisage a form of commonality strong enough to institute a 'demos' but nevertheless compatible with certain forms of pluralism: religious, moral and cultural pluralism, as well as a pluralism of political parties. This is the challenge that engaging with Schmitt's critique forces us to confront. It is indeed a crucial one, since what is at stake is the very formulation of a pluralistic view of democratic citizenship.

I obviously do not pretend to provide a solution within the confines of this chapter, but I would like to suggest some lines of reflection. To offer a different – resolutely non-Schmittian – answer to the compatibility of pluralism and liberal democracy requires, in my view, putting into question any idea of 'the people' as already given, with a substantive identity. What we need to do is precisely what Schmitt does not do: once we have recognized that the unity of the people is the result of a political construction, we need to explore all the logical possibilities that a political articulation entails. Once the identity of the people – or rather, its multiple possible identities – is envisaged on the mode of a political articulation, it is important to stress that if it is to be a real *political* articulation, not merely the acknowledgement of empirical differences, such an identity of the people must be seen as the *result* of the political process of hegemonic articulation. Democratic politics does not consist in the moment when a fully constituted people exercises its rule. The moment of rule is indissociable from the very struggle about the definition of the people, about the constitution of its identity. Such an identity, however, can never be fully constituted, and it can exist only through multiple and competing forms of *identifications*. Liberal democracy is precisely the recognition of this constitutive gap between the people and its various identifications. Hence the importance of leaving this space of contestation forever open, instead of trying to fill it through the establishment of a supposedly 'rational' consensus.

To conceive liberal-democratic politics in such a way is to acknowledge Schmitt's insight into the distinction between 'us' and 'them', because this struggle over the constitution of the people always takes place within a conflictual field, and implies the existence of competing forces. Indeed, there is no hegemonic articulation without the determination of a frontier, the definition of a 'them'. But in the case of liberal-democratic politics this frontier is an internal one, and the 'them' is not a permanent outsider. We can begin to realize, therefore, why such a regime requires pluralism. Without a plurality of competing forces which attempt to define the common good, and aim at fixing the identity of the community, the political articulation of the demos could not take place. We would be in the field either of the aggregation of interests, or of a process of deliberation which eliminates the moment of decision. That is – as Schmitt pointed out – in the field of economics or of ethics, but not in the field of politics.

Nevertheless, by envisaging unity only under the mode of substantive unity, and denying the possibility of pluralism within the political association, Schmitt was unable to grasp that there was another alternative open to liberals, one that could render the articulation between liberalism and democracy viable. What he could not conceive of, owing to the limits of his problematic, he deemed impossible. Since his objective was to attack liberalism, such a move is not surprising but it certainly indicates the limits of his theoretical reflection.

Despite these shortcomings, Schmitt's questioning of liberalism is a very powerful one. It reveals several weaknesses of liberal democracy, and brings its blind spot to the fore. Those deficiencies cannot be ignored. If we are to elaborate a view of democratic society which is convincing and worthy of allegiance, they have to be addressed. Schmitt is an adversary from whom we can learn, because we can draw on his insights. Turning them against him, we should use them to formulate a better understanding of liberal democracy, one that acknowledges its paradoxical nature. Only by coming to terms with the double movement of inclusion–exclusion that democratic politics entails can we deal with the challenge with which the process of globalization confronts us today.

Notes

1. John Rawls, *Political Liberalism*, New York, 1996, p. lxi.

2. I would have thought everybody should be able to understand that it is possible to use Schmitt against Schmitt – to use the insights of his critique of liberalism in order to consolidate liberalism – while recognizing that this was not, of course, his aim. However, it does not seem to be the case, since Bill Scheuermann, in *Between the Norm and the Exception* (Cambridge, MA, 1994, p. 8), criticizes me for presenting Schmitt as a theorist of radical pluralist democracy!

3. David Held, *Democracy and the Global Order*, Cambridge, 1995.

4. Richard Falk, *On Human Governance*, Cambridge, 1995.

5. Carl Schmitt, *The Crisis of Parliamentary Democracy*, trans. Ellen Kennedy, Cambridge, MA, 1985, p. 9.

6. Ibid.

7. Ibid., p. 13.

8. Ibid., p. 9.

9. Ibid.

10. Ibid., p. 11.

11. Ibid., p. 12.

12. I have put forward a similar argument about the tension that exists between the articulation of the liberal logic of difference and the democratic logic of equivalence in my discussion of Schmitt in *The Return of the Political*, London 1993, Chapters 7 and 8.

13. Schmitt, *The Concept of the Political*, p. 70.

14. For a critique of the Rawlsian model and its incapacity to acknowledge the *political* nature of the discrimination, it establishes between 'simple' and 'reasonable' pluralism, see Chantal Mouffe, 'Democracy and Pluralism: A Critique of the Rationalist Approach', *Cardozo Law Review* 16, 5, March 1995.

15. Seyla Benhabib, 'Deliberative Rationality and Models of Democratic Legitimacy', *Constellations*, 1, 1, April 1994, p. 30.

16. Ibid., p. 31.

17. This, of course, takes place in a different way in both authors. Rawls relegates pluralism to the private sphere, while Habermas screens it out, so to speak, from the public sphere through the procedures of argumentation. In both cases, however, the result is the elimination of pluralism from the public sphere.

18. Carl Schmitt, *The Concept of the Political*, trans. George Schwab, New Brunswick, 1976, p. 35.

19. Ibid., p. 53.

20. Ibid., p. 45.

21. Carl Schmitt, 'Staatsethik und pluralistischer Staat', *Kantstudien* 35, 1, 1930, translated in this volume, Chapter 11.

22. Ibid., pp. 195–208.
23. Ibid.
24. Jean-François Kervégan, *Carl Schmitt et Hegel. Le politique entre métaphysique et positivité*, Paris, 1992, p. 259.

4

Carl Schmitt and 'World Unity'

Jean-François Kervégan

Among those writers (philosophers, jurists, political scientists, theologians) who – in increasing numbers – are becoming interested in the thought of Carl Schmitt – not for what he was but because they consider that he may be useful in thinking about the present – there is an ongoing debate between two main schools of opinion. On the one hand, there are many who believe the central element in Schmitt's thought to be a religious, even a theological, one;[1] the recent publication of the *Glossarium* which Schmitt wrote between 1947 and 1951, and the rediscovery of long-neglected writings such as *Römischer Katholizismus und Politische Form* (1923), has given this school new impetus. On the other hand, we have those for whom the most original and most powerful of Schmitt's work is based on legal–political matters; it is from this perspective, then, that he should be analysed and ultimately contested.[2] The writer of this chapter is located firmly in the second camp. This is not to say that religious themes are absent from Schmittian thought, or that they do not appear genuine in it; it is obvious that exactly the contrary is true. But ultimately, it would appear that although he once defined himself as a 'theologian of law',[3] Schmitt applied to himself Albericus Gentilis's phrase *Silete theologi in munere alieno!* [Theologian, be silent on matters that don't concern you!], a formulation which he quite rightly makes the symbol of the modern dissociation of the political and the religious.[4] Carl Schmitt became caught up in the movement towards the secularization of thought (albeit uncomfortably and rather restively), and in that sense he is – despite himself – a modern writer, and in certain ways also a precursor of 'postmodern' thinking. As a thinker on matters of law, not just as a thinker about the political, Schmitt has something to say about our world, and he can help us to think about it, though maybe despite himself, and quite contrary to his own intentions. One of the problems which reveals the singular topicality of Schmitt, himself an enemy of today's world, is that of *political world unity*, a problem which – as Francis Fukuyama's theses simplistically but pertinently remind us – still besets us today.

At the heart of Schmitt's work, there is a remarkable contrast between texts written before and after the Second World War (or National Socialism) – so much so that they can be gathered into two completely independent groups. At the centre of the first group is a consideration of the link between the legal and the political at the heart of that specifically modern configuration which is the state; *Verfassungslehre* is the central monument of this period, with *Politische Theologie* and *Der Begriff des Politischen* providing the keys. Following his rallying to National Socialism, Schmitt distances himself from the themes and theses of this earlier work; this can be seen, after 1933, in the 'Reich-Staat-Bund'[5] conference, as well as in *Staat, Bewegung, Volk*, a brief pamphlet which, in the name of the 'Movement' and of the *Führerprinzip*, questions the 'state ethic' professed hitherto. Furthermore, from 1937–1938, Schmitt concerned himself primarily with questions of foreign politics and international public law.[6] The reasons for this new tendency are easy to discern; it is evidently in tune with the politics of Nazi Germany, even if one considers it to be more than simple theoretical caution. This distancing from previously emphasized themes is described with recourse to new concepts such as those of *Grossraum* and *Reich*, which are opposed to that of the state, concepts which would tend to be rendered obsolete.[7] After 1945 (though perhaps the break should be placed a little earlier, say in 1943) Schmitt developed a less legal, more historical and sometimes more philosophical proposal, although he does not acknowledge this; the main theme recurring through this is the 'nomos of the earth',[8] more precisely, the question of world order. One particular question features prominently in this writing – even underlies it: does history tend towards world political unification, for which the United Nations acts as crucible? And, above all, what is the significance of the belief, or the hope, that this unity will be realized? What are the philosophical and political presuppositions of such a belief?[9]

It would obviously be wrong to set the two Carl Schmitts (before and after National Socialism) in opposition without identifying a third: the Nazi Carl Schmitt of 1933 to 1942.[10] In fact, Schmitt's work – beginning with *Land und Meer*, which was itself anticipated in the various texts published from 1938 on the subject of spatial order [*Raumordnung*] – aims at resolving questions raised but left in the air in earlier texts. Leaving to one side the effects of the period 1933–37, over the course of which Schmitt's writings are aimed at attaining and then preserving positions of intellectual power at the heart of the Nazi regime,[11] it is possible to consider his legal and political philosophical thought as a whole as relating to the future of that specifically modern configuration – born of the process of 'secularization' required by the rupture of the unity of Western Christianity and the constitution of new modes of production, action and being – which is the state. On this matter, Schmitt's diagnostic, outlined from the end of the 1920s, is even clearer:

> Not so long ago, the European part of humanity lived in a period whose juridical concepts came from [geprägt waren] completely from the state and saw it as a model of political unity. The age of the state is waning. Henceforth any commentary is superfluous. . . . The state, as a model of political unity, and invested with an incredible monopoly on the political decision . . . has been dethroned.[12]

The problem faced by Schmitt between 1943 and 1945 – it had already emerged in his (politically overdetermined) consideration of Grossraum (1939) – is: if it is true that the age of the state, in its modern European form, has come to an end, what sort of configuration will replace it? Will it be a new political figure, or are we heading towards a superseding of the political? I will attempt to reconstruct the stages in the thought process which leads from Der Begriff des Politischen to the older Schmitt's anxious, disillusioned, nostalgic questioning of 'world order', at the time of the confrontation between the blocs and the political birth of the 'Third World'; I will underline its uncertainties and inadequacies, but also its clear-sighted – indeed, strikingly lucid – aspects.

I

Schmitt's work of the 1920s and early 1930s is driven by a conviction of the centrality of the state. If it appears necessary to distinguish conceptually between the state and the political, as the essay on the concept of the political suggests from the outset,[13] this is in order the better to measure and emphasize the historical importance of the monopoly on politics and the political held, throughout modern times, by the state. The most eloquent expression of this state-centred conviction, summarized in the formula 'any state is better than no state at all', is to be found in a 1929 conference, and appears in 1930 in the Kantstudien entitled 'Ethics of State and Pluralistic State' (see Chapter 11 below). The thesis of the article, which is simultaneously a warning to both the opponents and the supporters of the Weimar regime, is as follows: the weakening of this unique vehicle for political decision which, in modern politics, is the state, and, beyond that, the break with established normality, create 'an intolerable situation, as removing normal conditions removes with them the presupposition of any ethical or juridical norm'.[14]

In response to a questioning of the sovereignty and impartiality of the state, which finds its origin in parliamentarism – or, more precisely, in the *Parteienstaat* which its corruption enables[15] – Schmitt appeals to an 'ethic of state' whose absolute goal would be the re-establishment and supremacy of the state.

Reflection on the total state, which was developed from 1927 onwards, was to lead gradually towards a questioning of the grounds and the actuality of this 'ethic of state'. Indeed, at first, Schmitt would like to see in Mussolini's *stato totalitario* the restoration of the primacy of the state on organized social interests, and the assumption of its role of – contrary to the liberal vulgate – a 'superior' third party, not a 'neutral' one.[16] But he quickly convinces himself that the process of totalization *of the political* (not merely of the state sphere) implies a calling into question of the very foundations of the modern *Staatlichkeit*. In effect, in the total state – whether it be the 'total-through-weakness' state, which is the administrative-bureaucratic state of parliamentary democracies, a simple organ of arbitration between different social groups, or a 'total-through-strength' state, either fascist or Bolshevik[17] – it is awkward, even impossible, to distinguish between what is and what is not political. As a result, this configuration – which, in one way or another, takes over from the realm of objective reason to which the modern state has committed itself – tends to remove any precise delimitation between what comes under the jurisdiction of the state and what escapes it.[18] At this point it is necessary to refer to the article 'Die Wendung zum totalen Staat' (1931),[19] which enumerates the reasons for which the ethic of state which Schmitt has espoused hitherto are no longer at issue, and therefore prepares for the 1933 'conversion' to an ideology whose main representatives exhibit violently anti-state convictions. In acknowledgement of this new rallying, Schmitt writes: 'Today the political cannot be defined in terms of the state; rather, the state must be defined in terms of the political.'[20] The liberal nineteenth-century state aimed at minimizing its intervention in civil society and, above all, at a neutrality *vis-à-vis* contradictory private interests which run through it; it therefore supposed a clear delimitation between the political (state) sphere and the non-political (social) sphere. Institutions of parliamentary liberalism, which ensured a political voice for those social interests organized in parties, have progressively reduced the state to nothing more than the 'self-organization of society.'[21] In such a state, 'there is simply nothing which is not, at least potentially, political and state-based' – that is why this state should be considered a 'potentially total' state.[22] The rest of this article shows that the 'turning' from neutral state to (quantitatively) total state, and simultaneously from legislative state to administrative state,[23] not only corresponds to an extension of its intervention in economic, social and cultural fields, but also reflects a real change in nature. In effect, with this transformation, the fate of this state is sealed, if it is true that this depends on a new and original dividing up of the political and the non-political.

Schmitt begins his article 'Weiterentwicklung des totalen Staates in Deutschland', which appeared at the very moment when Hitler came to power (though it was written slightly earlier), by saying 'There is a total state. It is possible, with all kinds of alarmed or distressed clamour, to reject the "total state" . . . but for all that, the thing itself is not made to disappear.'[24]

There is a new element relating to the 1931 text which is evoked in the title itself: the article states that only a 'total revolution' can replace the 'total-through-weakness' state installed in Germany and elsewhere, and that such a revolution should install in its place a state which is 'total in the sense of quality and energy'.[25] Schmitt's commentary on the article when it was republished in 1958 emphasizes that the German state (of Weimar) had been engaged in such a process of evolution towards bureaucratic 'totalitarianism' by pressure from all kinds of parties and interest groups, and that it had therefore ceased to be 'a territory of objective reason'.[26] Developed with reference to both Hobbes[27] and Hegel,[28] this last expression (or others like it) is often used by Schmitt to refer to what is specific to the modern state – which is at the heart of what he would ultimately call the *Jus Publicum Europaeum*.[29] From this point of view, the total state in its two concurrent forms (administrative state and totalitarian state), marks the break with the political form around which all modern law is organized, and with European civilization's conception of itself. It remains, however, a particular state confronted with other potentially or actually total states familiar with the same process of the extension of 'politicity', so to speak. The question raised, then – implicitly at first – is of knowing what might replace the state and continue the bringing in of a new order. Schmitt's writings between 1937 and 1941 provide a provisional answer to this, which centres on the notion of 'large space' [*Grossraum*].

II

From 1936 to 1937, Schmitt dedicated himself almost exclusively to international law. This new direction is clearly linked to the tensions which were eventually to lead to the war, and Schmitt was to show himself to be an eloquent and subtle defender of the expansionist aims of National Socialist Germany; perhaps it was further motivated by oppositions he found at the very heart of the Nazi movement. In any case, the analyses he produced in this period show a theoretical interest which exceeds their immediate purpose.

From the 1920s onwards, Schmitt undertook a critique of the international order emerging from the First World War and the Versailles *Diktat*: most notably this concerns the League of Nations,[30] and the evolution of international law from a 'non-discriminatory' attitude to a 'discriminating' one – for example, in matters of the laws of warfare.[31] In general it consists of a demonstration of the political nature of certain categories and institutions in international law, and the suggestion of an appropriate (political) response. The League of Nations, for example, despite its global and humanist ideals, in effect represents British and American interests; it is therefore the effective tool of a subtle form of imperialism. A general conviction – or, if you prefer, a nationalistic bias – drives his writings: 'a people are beaten only when they bow down to foreign vocabulary, to foreign ways of representing law, and international law in particular'.[32] If one believes, with Quaritsch, that before he succumbed to Nazism Schmitt's thought fed on three sources – Catholicism, Statism and nationalism – it is necessary to acknowledge that the 1933 'conversion' brings the latter into the foreground.

The writings of 1937–39 (the pamphlet *Die Wendung zum diskriminierenden Kriegsbegriff*, and a group of articles continued in *Positionen und Begriffe*) develop and systematize the critique of what Schmitt henceforth crudely calls the 'Geneva League', and the questioning of the international order in place since 1918. Two aspects of his proposals, beyond their immediate polemic aim, should be emphasized.

The Treaty of Versailles introduced into international law (which had hitherto been founded on the legal parity of states) a fundamental modification which 'criminalized' the defeated (with the German Emperor considered a war criminal). This criminalization of the enemy was a break with the essential experience of modern international law: the renouncing of the traditional theme – also developed in the work of St Augustine and Thomas Aquinas,[33] as well as in the twelfth-century Gratian Decree (the founding text of canonical law) – of *bellum ex justa causa*. This renunciation can also be seen, hesitantly, in Grotius, who does indeed maintain the classical notion of a just war,[34] but tends to identify this with 'solemn public war' – that is, 'declared formally' by one state on another.[35] But it is by eighteenth-century writers that the idea of a just war is really sidelined. Considering that every sovereign is ultimately the judge of the justice of his own cause,[36] Vattel actually replaces the criterion of material legitimation with that of formal regularity: 'as far as its effects are concerned, war conducted formally should be considered just on both sides'.[37] Thus he incurs the consequences of the process of dissociation between law and theology which began at the end of the sixteenth century; what Schmitt was later (in *Der Nomos der Erde*) to call the *Jus Publicum Europaeum* is primarily a de-theologized state law. The attitude of the victors in 1918 put in question these fundamental aspects of modern international law, mainly the second. Indeed, it is not a question of re-theologizing law, which would be impossible in a world in which religion had become a private matter; rather, it was morality, in the place of theology, which would exert supra-legal control over international law, on a humanitarian basis. This 'moralization of law' – which Schmitt detects, for example, in Georges Scelle, whose system 'shifts between the two poles of individualism and universalism'[38] – leads to an abandoning of the 'non-discriminatory concept of the enemy' which international – or, rather, inter-state – law implements.

The discriminatory concept of the enemy, the version developed out of the old notion of the unjust enemy, classes him – for example, the instigator of a war of aggression – as a criminal who must be punished. Schmitt emphasizes that it was at the end of the nineteenth century that attack began to be thought of as a crime, not as the ultimately legitimate means employed by a state to promote its interests.[39] This succeeds in transforming international law into an annexe of penal law, and war into a matter of law and order, aimed at suppressing those responsible.[40] But above all, criminalizing the enemy succeeds in eliminating any limitations on acts of war, limits inscribed in modern laws of war. In other words, the introduction (or reintroduction) of a moral perspective into law presumes recourse to a new conception of the enemy, that of *total enemy*, and results in a transformation of 'limited' war, such as classic war between legally equal sovereign powers, into total war. The 1938 book on the 'turn towards a discriminatory notion of war' cites and criticizes in some detail the theories of Georges Scelle – a well-thought-of expert from the League of Nations – according to whom war is 'international crime' when it seeks to establish world order, and 'law enforcement' when it aims to restore this order.[41] According to Scelle, this doctrine follows from a conception of international legal order as an authentic constitution whose violation is proscribed, and no longer as resulting from conventions between states maintaining all their own sovereignty. On the basis of such principles, it is tempting to transform a people or state which radically disputes this order into an 'enemy of humanity'.[42] If this mark is overstepped, the door is open to a war of annihilation, founded on moral or penal arguments:

> Justified from a ideological-universalist point of view, a war of annihilation, precisely because of its ecumenical aspirations, first deprives the state (this

popular and spatial closed order) of the nature of the order it had hitherto; it transforms a war between states into an international civil war . . .; as a result, it deprives the concepts of war and the enemy of their dignity and honour, making a war conducted 'justly' the application [of a sanction] or a health measure, while one conducted 'unjustly' becomes the illegal and immoral resistance of a few delinquents, troublemakers, pirates and gangsters.[43]

One might be surprised at the audacity with which Schmitt implicitly describes Nazi Germany as the potential victim of a war of annihilation. Applied to other contexts, however, this analysis lacks neither lucidity nor relevance.

In parallel with the contamination of international law with moral or humanitarian concepts, there is an attempt at the relativizing or overtaking of the state, the subject and point of reference of classical international law. On this matter, it is enough for Schmitt to extend and enlarge the critique of the League of Nations he developed in the 1920s.[44] In effect, this Genevan institution conceals an ambiguity. On the one hand, it is a classical federation of states [Staatenbund] – an inter-state organism equipped with certain functions and aiming at certain predetermined goals. On the other hand, it aspires to being a universal organization, and forms the outline of a Weltstaat, a state encapsulating all humanity. If this plan for a political unification of humanity (very different from the Kantian idea of a federation of states peacefully administering law[45]) were to come about, the result would be a 'total depoliticization' and, as a result, a 'state void'.[46] But in actual fact, this plan for a *political* unification of all humanity conceals a fiction or a stratagem: the professed overtaking of the national state framework is a disguise for state (or, rather, imperial) interests whose representatives have appropriated the vocabulary of the universal, reinterpreted in moral terms, to combat the interests of other states. In brief, the League of Nations [Völkerbund] 'is not a society [Bund], but might well be a league [Bündnis]'.[47]

From 1932 onwards, the study of changes in the legal status of war and the critique of the political usage of humanitarian ideas refer as much to the United States, the prototype of a new kind of global power, as to France and Great Britain, traditional colonial powers. As a critique of American diplomacy and the legal foundations it establishes, a text such as 'Völkerrechtliche Formen des modernen Imperialismus' (1932) considers the possible ways and effects of a positive superseding of a system of international law centred both on the *state* and on *Europe*. The United States made a crucial contribution to this process in implementing a coherent imperialist policy, from the Monroe Doctrine of 1823 to the Briand–Kellog Pact of 1928, thereby separating the United States's political interests from their territory, in the classical sense of the word. According to the Monroe Doctrine, there is an area which concerns the security of the United States directly, at the heart of which the USA challenges any interference by a foreign power, and reserves exclusively for itself the right to almost unlimited intervention; moreover, the extent of this area is a matter of its judgement alone – so much so that it is able to go so far as to encompass the whole of the Western hemisphere. On the strength of this, the United States has established itself as 'arbiter of the earth',[48] perhaps before attaining global power. As far as the Kellog Pact is concerned, with its aim to outlaw war as a means of *national* politics, it implicitly grants its creators the right to distinguish between war which is just, and war which is not. Schmitt concludes from this that 'whoever has true power is also in a position to determine for himself [the meaning of] concepts and words';[49] it depends on the others – and he is doubtless thinking of Germany here – obtaining this power too. Far from simply criticizing 'American imperialism', Schmitt considers it a more authentic and more directly consequent expression of modern politics – whose essence, as Treitschke put it, is 'power, power and more power' – than the humanist liberal constructions on which the League of Nations draws; he observes, moreover, that having practically forced the creation of the League of Nations, the United States was careful not to take part in it. So, rather than heading towards a universalism, always a disguise for power politics (indeed, there is no other kind of politics), a new pluralism should be invented which should not be that of the classic territorial states, but should be based on the coexistence of several imperial powers, each equipped with its own Monroe Doctrine – that is, ultimately with the power to 'define, interpret and implement'.[50]

III

The theory of *Grossraum*, developed from 1939 onwards in a whole range of writings, continues the analysis of imperialism and the critique of universalism already under way in the 1932 article. The sovereign state implements both a territorial and, so to speak, land-based conception of the political, which correspond, in effect, to the conditions of continental Europe from the seventeenth century to the nineteenth. For reasons which at first glance seem economic or technical, but which are fundamentally political, this notion of the state is obsolete from then on, as is the way in which it has been recorded in international law. As a result – according to Schmitt's thesis, in any case – there is a need to substitute a problematics of 'large space' [*Grossraum*] for the thematics of the territorial state. The 'necessity for a relativization of the concept of the state, a necessity which has become historically inescapable,'[51] is not only a response to the extension of the technical possibilities for action by the political authorities, hitherto considered by Schmitt to be a decisive factor in the 'turning towards the total state', but is above all a transformation of its sphere of activity. In the place of a 'micro-spatial' [*kleinräumig*] notion of an enclosed *territory*, a corollary of the classical concept of the sovereign state, there should be the notion of a space (terrestrial, maritime, aerial) whose limits are undefined or, rather, flexible: not those of a state, but those of an empire [*Reich*]. This space, which has the potential to be 'large' – that is, to go beyond the limits of the state – should not be seen as an enlarged territory;[52] similarly, great powers and empires are not merely vast powerful states, even if at their core they are made up of a more or less classical state structure. In fact, the transition from the problematics of the state and the enclosed territory to that of imperial power and large space embodies (according to Schmitt) the lapse from juridical and political order of modern Europe – a lapse whose recognized harbinger within the state was the formation of the total State (in both senses of the term). From this point of view, the 'spatial revolution' in the twentieth century is a counterpart to the 'territorial revolution' which, four hundred years earlier, gave rise to the modern state.[53] It is not a case of a simple change in geopolitical scale, but a qualitative change in the political.

If, however, it is indeed true that European territorial order, embodied in the state, is at an end, it is no longer a choice between 'small space' and 'large space', nor between state and empire, but, rather, between *Grossraum* and 'universalism' – that is, according to Schmitt, between a Monroe Doctrine which has been brought back to its originary and authentic meaning, and its reinterpretation in terms of a liberalist, humanist, globalist ideology, which supplies its 'typical weapons' for the 'interventionism' of certain powers.[54] On the one hand, there would be an orientation towards the setting up of a number of major powers, with each quite clearly implementing its own Monroe Doctrine, ending up with a 'limited coexistence on a meaningfully divided earth [*sic*]'[55] between certain empires. On the other, universalist or globalist discourse – which, moreover, tolerates the formal maintenance of the 'micro-spatial' framework of the traditional state – conceals its unstated ambition for world domination based not on direct political control but on a combination of economic hegemony and interventionism justified in moral or humanitarian terms.[56]

There are two ways of reading Schmitt's texts on 'large space'; in my opinion they are not mutually exclusive. From one point of view, these writings are the product of a specific national and international political situation, and align themselves unashamedly with the (evolutionary) views of Hitler's regime. In 1939, Great Britain was the main adversary, with her assumed desire to maintain global politico-economic hegemony; in 1940, when victory in Western Europe appeared secure, but with the beginnings of a war with the United States looking probable, at least eventually, the latter became the proponents of a new global imperialism. In other respects, Schmitt, who until that point believed that 'we are living under the watchful eye of the Russians', of 'that extremist brother who forces you to see practical conclusions through',[57] has no hesitation in stating in 1939 that the German-Soviet pact is the model for the international order to come, as it establishes the coexistence of two empires, each exercising its domination on 'a domain of liberty and ethnic (*völkisch*)[58] independence'; some years later, Soviet imperialism and its attempts at conquering world hegemony were again to become the main enemy – not, it must be said, because of its imperialist nature but, rather, because its political strategy brings with it the destruction – or, rather, subversion – of the *Jus Publicum Europaeum* and of its 'classical concepts'.[59]

There is, however, another way of reading these texts on *Grossraum*. Without denying their short-term aspect – best exemplified in their variation in the designated arch-enemy – it is possible to see in them sketches of the broader perspective which would be Schmitt's in *Land und Meer*, and above all in *Der Nomos der Erde*. These texts enable the process of becoming conscious of the ways in which modern international law, as a form of inter-state law, became both 'linked to time' (to the period between the establishment of the modern State and 1914) and 'linked to space' (to the continent of Europe);[60] thus the thesis of the expiry of the *Staatlichkeit* appears as the *theoretical* dimension of a proposal whose *political* motivations are otherwise evident. From then onwards, a question is raised concerning the kind of political order that could replace that which had been organized and recorded by the *Jus Publicum Europaeum*, the Europe-based law of the modern world. In this respect, Schmitt's diagnostic lacks neither perceptiveness nor relevance.

IV

The 'geo-philosophical' thought of *Land und Meer*, a short book significantly subtitled *Eine weltgeschichtliche Betrachtung* ('An examination of world history'), breaks away from the style and tone of the (badly) politically committed writings of the preceding period; at the same time it introduces the style which would be Schmitt's in *Der Nomos der Erde*.

This is the thesis of the piece:

> All fundamental order is spatial order. To talk about the constitution of a country or continent is to talk about its fundamental order, about its nomos. Now, true and authentic fundamental order is, at its core, based on certain spatial delineations and limits, on certain dimensions and a certain partitioning up of the earth. The single action which begins every great period is therefore one of territorial appropriation [*Landnahme*] on a large scale.[61]

I have already emphasized the fact that a dynamic notion of space is crucially different from that of territory, which suggests the specific formulation – in the process of becoming obsolete – which was the European state from the seventeenth century to the nineteenth. Another matter should now be raised. Until his writing on *Grossraum*, and *Land und Meer*, Schmitt explains the formation of the modern state as a result of the need to get over the civil war which arose out of the division of Western Christianity due to the establishment of a 'superior third party', the sovereign State. From then on, Schmitt insists that another factor is involved. From an external rather than internal point of view now, the great appropriation of territory [*Landnahme*] which was the conquest of the New World effected the formation of an inter-state juridical order in Western Europe. From then on a dozen sovereign states, all involved in this conquest in one way or another, formed a 'Union of nations'; the concept of international law developed in the seventeenth and eighteenth centuries was to formalize the juridical statute, and would structure those relations (whether peaceful or belligerent) which exist between them.

What is the relationship between these phenomena? It was significant that the fierce competition in which the Europeans engaged on the oceans and beyond did not extend to the continent itself. Hence the fixation on imaginary 'amity lines' (the meridian line, for example) and the definition of different juridical regimes 'on this side' of those lines and 'beyond' them.[62] For example, once international 'European' law had restricted activities of sea warfare to those in single combat, any ship belonging to a rival nation was considered an enemy, and so could be 'fair game'. From this point of view, Schmitt was interested in the juridical status of *privateers*; in a way, these irregular fighters were the forerunners of the partisans of the revolutionary war, in that they were not constrained by the juridical norms recognized by their state, without actually being pirates or *outlaws*.[63] In turn, the discovery of the New World, and the extensive spatial and cultural expansion that ensued, brought with it (besides bloody rivalries) the growing consciousness of a crucial kinship of the 'civilized' colonizers; it is this relationship which represents the *Jus Publicum Europaeum*. In short, the condition for – and, at the same time, the reverse of – the enclosed, terrestrial, European, Christian territorial order which emerged in modern Europe was the opening of an undefined maritime space in which the juridical norms enforced on the continent were modified or suspended.[64]

The split between land and sea, between Europe and the New World, is the fundamental law, the nomos, of the modern age. It resulted in the appearance of a great world power, Great Britain, the only major non-continental European state, whose power rested on its domination of the seas. In effect, as the famous privateer Sir Walter Raleigh (quoted by Schmitt) observed prophetically: 'Whoever rules the seas rules the world of trade; whoever rules the world of trade possesses all the treasures of the world – and the world itself.'[65] The struggle between land and sea, a struggle in which world hegemony had hitherto been at stake, 'reflects the existence of two worlds, with opposing juridical convictions'.[66] And it is the confrontation of these two visions – of land and sea, of the nomos of the earth – which, according to Schmitt, best explains the political history of the last two centuries.

Great Britain was not only ruler of the seas, however; it was also the cradle of the Industrial Revolution. As Hegel observed in 1820, there is also a necessary link between these two facts.[67] The Industrial Revolution, though at first an English phenomenon, was to become a global revolution which brought with it the birth of new powers: the United States, Germany, and later Japan and Russia. However, the Industrial Revolution as a *technical* revolution not only produced a growth and migration of economic and political power; it also – and more importantly – provoked a new (and final?) 'spatial revolution', characterized mainly by the superseding of the old antagonism between land and sea. The end of the text – contemporary with the turning point of Stalingrad – solemnly draws up the death certificate of the modern political order:

> The land–sea divide, which up till this point formed the basis for the link between rule of the sea and world domination, becomes obsolete. Just as we see the surpassing ... of the nomos the world has known hitherto. On its ruins the new nomos of our planet is inexorably imposed.... Many saw in it only death and destruction, and expected to live to see the end of the world. In fact, we will only live to see the end of traditional relations between land and sea.[68]

As I have already suggested, it seems indisputable that for Schmitt, the relative questioning of the new world order has its starting point in his hope of seeing the 'thousand-year Reich' bring about 'a new law in new orders'.[69] The German defeat forced him to rethink this opinion. But the problem raised at the end of *Land und Meer* remains. If it is in fact the case that 'the Eurocentric order of international law existing hitherto is currently in decline', and that 'with it the old nomos of the earth is swallowed up',[70] then what will be the meaning and focus of the new nomos born out of the ruins of the old? In this context, the problem of political unity (or plurality) will be approached again. In fact this problem, raised in the Preface to *Der Nomos der Erde*, is not really dealt with; none the less it is always on the horizon. Presented as 'the bitter fruit of hard experiences', the book offers a 'historical retrospective gathering the image of that great period of *Jus Publicum Europaeum*',[71] and leaves open the question of what is to replace it. While the knowledge Schmitt is able to mobilize, and the richness of his detailed analyses, are impressive, where basic orientations are concerned he limits himself to systematizing views found in writings of the previous decade, replacing the militant rhetoric used in service of of the new order with the undeceived serenity of someone witnessing the end of a world. If we read the work carefully, the analysis resists undermining the ideology it was meant to serve; in effect, its thesis – the dissolution of the *Jus Publicum Europaeum* – is supported by arguments which do seem to me to be consistent.[72] These arguments can be divided schematically into three groups.

To start with, in a continuation of the texts of the 1920s, *Der Nomos der Erde* emphasizes the role of the state as a vector of modern international and national political order. It is not merely a response to religious wars and the subsequent discrediting of traditional legitimations of power; it is also – and primarily – the foundation-stone for a 'Eurocentric, globalizing spatial order',[73] based on the distinction between 'sovereigns' who share European territory and the open space of the seas and non-European land. In the second place – and this is the point of the most important developments – international law established a statute of rules of war, corresponding to Grotius's 'solemn public war' or Vattel's 'legitimate and formally conducted war'. This new law for war replaces the notion of a just war (that is, one whose causes are just) with that of the formally conducted war; with the recognition of the sovereign nature of states implying that the *jus ad bellum* should apply to them without any restrictions, the emphasis is shifted henceforth to the *jus in bello*. As a result, the *Jus Publicum Europaeum* functioned as an inter-state European law for three centuries around what Schmitt called 'eine Hegung des Krieges', a restriction and means of managing a war whose consequences are 'rationalization, humanization and juridification.'[74] The third line of argument is borrowed from writings of the preceding period: the dissolution of the *Jus Publicum Europaeum*, begun at the end of the nineteenth century[75] and completed – one of the rare issues on which Schmitt never vacillated – by the juridical resolution of the First World War, is a striking manifestation of the decline of the *Staatlichkeit*, and so of the political in its modern form. This dissolution gives rise to a resurgence in the thematics of the just war, with characteristics which, of course, are not identical to those with which medieval doctrine endows it. Among these characteristics Schmitt mentions the recourse to humanitarian concepts and legitimations, which are the new face of the *justa causa*, and the criminalization of the enemy, which authorizes the recourse to total war, war of annihilation.[76]

None of these themes is really new: they can already be found, notably, in *The Concept of the Political*. On the other hand, from this point Schmitt's thinking on the disintegration of European spatial order of the classical period emerges more clearly on the problem of world unity, previously considered to be phantasmagorical:[77]

> For a long time global development has been leading up to a clear dilemma between universum and pluriversum, between monopoly and polypoly, in short to the question of whether the planet is ready for the global monopoly of a single power, or whether there is an ordered pluralism of large spaces ... themselves ordered and coexisting, which determines the new international world law.[78]

The situation in place from 1945 onwards was characterized by tension between the 'universalism' embodied in the United Nations (whose – clearly imaginary – ground rule is the parity of member states, and whose Charter is based on humanist principles) and the plurality of 'large spaces' organized around a great economic or political power with aspirations towards imperialism: the United States, the Soviet Union, and perhaps others. The stated desire for achieving world unity based on human rights is thus confronted with the reality of the great powers and their interests, which, of course, they disguise in the language of universality (adopted by the 'free world' as well as by the 'socialist camp'). In the face of such an alternative, it is no surprise that Schmitt rejects the globalist view of a *Menschheitstaat*, a universal state with the UN as its crucible. Even in so far as he announces the collapse of modern Europe's pluralist state political order, he still needs to find new reasons for this denunciation.

V

These reasons are provided – dispersed, and perhaps not entirely coherently – by a series of texts from the 1950s and early 1960s, whose general subject is – in the words of the title of one of them – 'the new nomos of the earth'.[79] The question of the nature and characteristics of this new world order, destined to replace the *Jus Publicum Europaeum*, remains open, except for those aspiring to 'a unique world leader'.[80] In effect, three possibilities are offered, and it is worth examining them without bias. The first is one of global political union under the hegemony of one of the two superpowers – and it is clear that Schmitt is thinking of one of these in particular – opposing the other in that new type of conflict which is the Cold War; the second consists in a new equilibrium (the terms of which would not be specified) which would be guaranteed by the naval, aerial and spatial powers that make up the United States; finally, the third is that of a global order based on the coexistence of 'several autonomous blocs or large spaces which would establish between them an equilibrium and, thus, a global order'.[81] Evidently, Schmitt was most won over by this last option. His reasons for this preference are not clearly indicated – or in any case, not in this article; it is nevertheless possible to reconstruct its core reasoning, which can be divided into four points.

First, the aspiration to world political unity is founded on a network of beliefs which spring from what Schmitt calls technical thought: 'if it is true that technique and not politics is the destiny of humanity, it is then possible to consider the problem of unity as being settled.'[82] But this is a false premiss, since 'the central problem of world order is always a political problem',[83] not a technical one. Global technical unification, at least that of the developed world, is a recognized fact; but it is a typical and persistent illusion that one can conclude from this fact that there is a need for political unification – or, rather, for a unification achieved by transcending the political, conflict, and negativity. This point had already been emphasized in the 1929 conference on 'The Age of Neutralization and Depoliticization', consolidated by a reading of Ernst Jünger's *Der Arbeiter*. It is known that at the time the total state ('quantitative' or 'qualitative') seemed to him to be the political response to the challenge posed by modern technology. From then on, Schmitt places more emphasis on the fact that the belief or myth of unification by technique is shared by the two principal players in world politics: in response to Lenin's famous statement 'socialism is Soviets plus electricity' (which Schmitt quotes, omitting the first term!), there was that of US Secretary of State Henry Lewis Stimson, according to whom the world had become too small to contain two opposing political systems.[84] Technical progress is the only religion of the 'masses', and this religion is common to the two blocs: 'the enemies meet in a self-interpretation of their position in the universal history'.[85] But if such a belief feeds globalist and pacifist concepts, it is not in a position to overcome the conflictual nature of political commerce, which – and this is not a new idea – is less 'natural' to man than it is a mark of the spirituality of his existence: 'the enmity between men contains a tension which far transcends naturalness'.[86]

The second point does not need to be developed, as it returns to the categories of *Land und Meer*: the opposition between the capitalist and communist blocs (beyond their common adherence to the religion of technique) is a conflict between two world visions, the terrestrial and the maritime. More than ever the struggle of 'sea against land' is a topical one, and the emergence of new 'elements' (air, and then space) does not affect this basic fact of the political world order. Added to this is the fact that in Schmitt's view, for this order to be stable and lasting it must be based on land, as 'man is a child of the land, and will remain so as long as he remains man'.[87]

The third point in the argument, presented as a thesis, states that even if the current organization (dealing with the period of the Cold War) of the world is bipolar, 'there is always a third factor, and more realistically *several* third factors'.[88] With remarkable acuteness, Schmitt observes that from the mid 1950s onwards the political emergence of the 'Third World' was called on to alter the equilibrium of the blocs significantly, even to the extent that one or other of these blocs attempts to lean on it. In this way the monistic phase during which people believed (or pretended to believe) in the imminent realization of *one world*, and the dualist phase marked by the rediscovery of the unsurpassable nature of hostility and by the appearance of a new version of it (the 'world civil war'), were followed by a third 'pluralist, multipolar' phase.[89] This phase certainly includes 'the threat of chaos', but could also open the way to the constitution of a coherent system of co-ordinated 'large spaces' concurrently facing the crucial and eminently political problem of the appropriation and sharing out of the planet's resources:

> If you ask me what the nomos of the earth is today, I can give you a clear answer: it is the division of the earth into industrially developed zones and less-developed zones, linked to the question which immediately follows from it of who should take over them. This allocation is the true constitution of the earth today.[90]

But this thesis does not only provide an acute observation of the world's political course. In reality it is built on a philosophical or theoretical conviction which Schmitt himself presents as a *belief*. The 'religion of technicity' common to East and West is the (somewhat trivialized) heritage of a *philosophy of history*, that of the Enlightenment, according to which progress flows inescapably from man's ability to transcend his naturalness culturally. This progressive and secularized philosophy – whose indisputable confirmation appears in the form of the French Revolution and the Industrial Revolution, and whose faith in supra-political world unity is the final offshoot – has come to impose itself against any other vision of history, either theological or traditional; in this sense, 'the philosophy of history acquires a historical power'.[91] As Schmitt points out succinctly:

> I do not believe in this philosophical view of history . . . this philosophy of history, which crosses the Iron Curtain, is more philosophy than history. . . . History is stronger than any philosophy of history, which is why I do not consider the current duality of the world to be a prerequisite for its unity, but rather a transition towards a new plurality.[92]

It seems that through this *credo* Schmitt reaches the final principle of his judgements on the problem of world unity. Certainly they express the mistrust of the professed Machiavellian he is towards ideological constraints which conceal and at the same time serve the conflict between powers; in this sense the criticism of this subject, and of the points of view he describes, is expressed in the old opposition of the author of *Der Begriff des Politischen* to political humanism. But these judgements also come from a thinker for whom rationality could not have the last word on the human condition, because this last word does not belong to man. So will world unity be the victory of philosophy over politics, and over its horizon of transcendence? If so, Schmitt's disciples have every reason to celebrate: for it is nowhere to be seen.

Translated by Daniel Hahn

Notes

1. This is the thesis supported by, among others, G. Maschke (*'La rappresentazione cattolica. Carl Schmitts politische Theologie mit Blick auf italienische Beiträge'*, *Der Staat*, 28–4, 1989); R. Mehring (*Pathetisches Denken*, Duncker & Humblot, 1989); H. Meier (*Carl Schmitt, Leo Strauss, und der Begniff des Politischen*, Metzler, 1998; *Die Lehre Carl Schmitts*, Metzler, 1994); G. Meuter (*Der Katechon*, Duncker & Humblot, 1994); and to some extent H. Quaritsch (*Positionen und Begriffe Carl Schmitt*, Duncker & Humblot, 1991). For a critique of this perspective, see J.-F. Kervégan, 'L'enjeu d'une théologie politique: Carl Schmitt', *Revue de Métaphysique et de Morale*, 2–1995, pp. 201–20.

2. See especially H. Hofmann, *Legitimität gegen Legalität*, Duncker & Humblot, 1995; the collection *La politica olttre lo Stato: Carl Schmitt* (ed. G. Duso), Arsenale, 1981; O. Beaud, 'Carl Schmitt ou le juriste engagé', in Schmitt, *Théorie de la Constitution*, PUF, 1993, pp. 5–113, and 'L'art d'écrire chez un juriste', in *Le droit, le politique* (ed. C.-M. Herrera), L'Harmattan, 1995; J.-F. Kervégan, *Carl Schmitt, Hegel. Le politique entre spéculation et positivité*, PUF, 1992; C. Galli, *Genealogia della politica*, Il Mulino, 1996.

3. 'I am a theologian of juridical science' (*Glossarium*, p. 23). Schmitt is doubtless far closer to the truth of his work when, around the same time (1947), he states: 'Theologians aim to define the enemy as something which can be annihilated. But I am a jurist, not a theologian' (*Ex Captivitate Salus*, p. 89).

4. See *Der Nomos der Erde* [hereafter *Nomos*], pp. 92, 129–31. On the subject of secularization, see H. Blumenberg's classic book *Die Legitimität der Neuzeit* (1966), which Schmitt himself took issue with, politely, in *Politische Theólogie II*.

5. Text republished in *Positionen und Begriffe* [hereafter *PuB*], pp. 190–98.

6. The most significant piece of writing in this period is *Völkerrechtliche Grossraumordnung mit Interventionsverbot für raumfremde Mächte* [hereafter *Grossraumordnung*].

7. 'The raising of the state to the level of a universal concept–norm of political organization, for all time and all people, would probably soon come to an end with the age of the state itself' ('Staat als ein konkreter, an eine geschichtliche Epoche gebundener Begriff', 1941, in *Verfassungsrechtliche Aufsätze* [hereafter *VA*], p. 376).

8. This is the title of the first work Schmitt published after 1945, *Der Nomos der Erde* (1950).

9. A group of articles dating from the 1950s deals with this question; they were collected by G. Maschke in Part IV ('Um den Nomos der Erde') of the anthology *Staat, Grossraum, Nomos* [hereafter *SGN*] Duncker & Humblot 1995. One should also add *Theorie des Partisanes* (1963).

10. The thesis that Schmitt's intellectual engagement with Nazism came to an end following the attacks against him in 1936 by *Das Schwarze Korps*, the mouthpiece of the SS, is a pleasing one; the expression of this engagement certainly does become less extreme, but it lasts until the turning point of the war – that is, until the end of 1942: see the last lines of the article 'Die Formung des französischen Geistes durch den Legisten' (*SGN*, p. 210).

11. See 'Der Führer schützt das Recht' (1934), *PuB*, pp. 199–203; and 'Die deutsche Rechtswissenschaft im Kampf gegen den jüdischen Geist', *Deutsche Juristen-Zeitung*, XL-20 (15 October 1936), cols. 1193–9.

12. *Der Begriff des Politischen* [BP], p. 10; this is a passage from the Preface to the 1963 edition of the 1932 work.

13. 'The concept of the state presupposes the concept of the political' (*BP*, p. 20).

14. *PuB*, p. 145. This assertion refers to the decisionist thesis: 'any norm presupposes a normal situation' (*BP*, p. 46).

15. In any case, this is what Schmitt explicitly proposes during this period. One could well wonder whether the description of the ideal functioning of parliamentarism which Schmitt proposes is not predetermined by his desire to show its failure.

16. See 'Wesen und Werden des faschistischen Staates', *PuB*, pp. 109–15.

17. This distinction appears in 'Weiterentwicklung des totalen Staates in Deutschland' (1933), in *VA*, pp. 359–66.

18. 'In this total state everything is political, at least potentially, and making reference to the state is no longer sufficient for defining the specific, distinctive nature of the political' (*BP*, p. 24).

19. This is actually a slightly modified version of pages 73–91 of *Der Hüter der Verfassung*, which appeared in the same year, containing a detailed analysis of the mechanisms of what Schmitt was soon to call the 'total-through-weakness' state. It also reappeared in *PuB*, pp. 146–57.

20. *Staat, Bewegung, Volk*, p. 15.

21. *PuB*, p. 151.

22. Ibid., p. 152.

23. It is in this text that we find the distinction, systematized in *Legitimität und Legalität*, between juridical state, governmental state, legislative state and administrative state (see *VA*, pp. 263–71). This distinction is primarily for the purposes of taxonomy, but also clearly suggests historical periodizing.

24. 'Weiterentwicklung des totalen Staates . . .', *VA*, p. 360.

25. *VA*, p. 361.

26. Ibid., p. 365.

27. In *De Cive*, *civitas* is defined as '*imperium rationis*' (*Opera Latina*, II, p. 265).

28. The state is 'universal and objective liberty' (*Grundlinien der Philosophie des Rechts*, para. 33), 'the rational, in itself and for itself' (para. 258) or 'the reflection of eternal reason' (para. 272R).

29. See *Nomos*, p. 68. This work repeatedly describes the modern state as 'the Empire of ethical life and objective reason'.

30. See *Die Kernfrage des Völkerbundes*, and Chapter 6 of *The Concept of the Political*, entitled 'The World is not a political unity but a *pluriversum*'. There is a series of often very polemical articles, published in *PuB*, which deal with these same issues.

31. See 'The Decision of War and the Designation of the Enemy' (*BP*, pp. 45 ff.).

32. 'Völkerrechtliche Formen des modernen Imperialismus' (1932), *PuB*, p. 179.

33. See especially *Cité de Dieu*, IV, 15 and XIX, 7; and *Somme théologique*, II.ii, 40.

34. See *Le droit de la guerre et de la paix*, I, 2.

35. See ibid., I, 3–4 and III, 3.

36. 'Whenever a cause is in doubt, the arms of both parties should be thought of as equally legitimate, at least as far as external effects are concerned, until the cause is resolved' (*Le Droit des Gens*, III, 3, para. 39).

37. *Le Droit des Gens*, III, 12, para. 190. On Grotius and Vattel, see *Die Wendung zum diskriminierenden Kriegsbegriff* [hereafter *Die Wendung*], pp. 39–40.

38. *Die Wendung*, p. 15.

39. *Nomos*, pp. 88, 92–3, 248–55.

40. See 'Über das Verhalthis der Begniffe Kreig und Feind' (1938): 'According to the Geneva Pact, it is the aggressor who is defined as the enemy.... The concepts of international law defined in this way visibly move towards categories of penal and criminal law' (*PuB*, p. 245, or *BP*, p. 103).

41. See *Die Wendung*, p. 37. Schmitt refers to the *Précis de Droit des Gens*, vol. II, Paris, 1934, p. 47.

42. *Die Wendung*, p. 45.

43. *Die Wendung*, p. 43 (n. 45).

44. See *BP*, pp. 56–8.

45. The essay on lasting peace (beginning of the second definitive article), as well as the *Rechtslehre* (para. 61) expressly distinguish the *Völkerbund*, or 'permanent Congress of States', which these texts advocate, from a *Völkerstaat*, a global state.

46. *BP*, p. 56.

47. Ibid., p. 57. See also the second appendix, *BP*, p. 103. Note that in German the League of Nations is referred to as a 'Bund' ('Society') rather than as a 'League', as in English.

48. *PuB*, p. 174.

49. Ibid., p. 179.

50. *PuB*, p. 178.

51. 'Raum und Grossraum im Völkerrecht' (1940) [hereafter 'Raum und Grossraum'], in *SGN*, p. 261.

52. 'A large space is not merely a small space enlarged' ('Raum und Grossraum', *SGN*, p. 260. See also *Grossraumordnung*, *SGN*, p. 315.

53. See *Grossraumordnung*, *SGN*, p. 314.

54. Ibid., p. 285. See also 'Grossraum gegen Universalismus' (1939), *PuB*, pp. 295–7.

55. *Grossraumordnung*, *SGN*, p. 296.

56. 'A global market results in a global international law [*Weltvölkerrecht*] which exceeds the sovereignty of the state and hence attains a legitimacy and a guarantee of the *status quo* whose reach is not just European but universalist' ('Raum und Grossraum', *SGN*, p. 248).

57. *BP*, pp. 79–80.

58. 'Raum und Grossraum', *SGN*, p. 260.

59. See 'Die Ordnung der Welt nach dem zweiten Weltkrieg', *SGN*, pp. 597–8.

60. 'Raum und Grossraum', *SGN*, p. 241.

61. *Land und Meer*, p. 41.

62. See *Nomos*, pp. 54–69.

63. See *Land und Meer*, pp. 22–9.

64. 'The meaning, the heart of the law of the Christian European peoples, can fundamentally be found precisely in the dividing up of the new territories' (*Land und Meer*, p. 43).

65. *Land und Meer*, p. 50.

66. Ibid., p. 51.

67. 'Just as the land, a solid *basis*, is a requirement for the principle of family life, so the natural element of industry, which gives it a life [facing] towards the outside, is the *sea*' (*Grundlinien der Philosophie des Rechts*, para. 247).

68. *Land und Meer*, p. 63.

69. 'The jurist's formation of the French spirit' (1942), SGN, p. 210. The passage ends: 'This time it is Germany which is the matrix for order. The guardians of the old order, driven mad, believe that measure is about to disappear, and law with it. In reality it is only the old measure, their legality, which is disappearing. And our new Empire is appearing.'

70. *Nomos*, Foreword.

71. *BP*, p. 17.

72. Notwithstanding, it seems indisputable (and is confirmed by a reading of the *Glossarium*) that Schmitt's own basic choices seem not to have changed after 1945.

73. *Nomos*, p. 120.

74. Ibid., p. 69. Schmitt emphasizes (*Nomos*, p. 44) the plurality of meaning of the verb *hegen*, which simultaneously means to enclose, to contain, to take care of, to preserve.

75. This process is related to the rise in the power of the United States, whose politics wavers between isolation and 'universalist-humanitarian' pan-interventionism (*Nomos*, pp. 200, 227). This observation continues to be a topical one. . . .

76. 'The growth in the technical methods of extermination reveals the abyss of destructive juridical and moral discrimination' (*Nomos*, p. 298).

77. 'The specific nature of the political brings with it a pluralism of states. . . . As long as such a thing as a state exists on earth, there will always be more than one state, and never a universal state embracing all of humanity' (*BP*, p. 54).

78. *Nomos*, p. 216.

79. 'Der neue Nomos der Erde' (1955), in SGN, pp. 518–22. The other important writings on this subject are 'Die Einheit der Welt' (1951), SGN, pp. 496–505; 'Nehmen – Teilen – Weiden' (1953), VA; 'Die geschichtliche Struktur des heutigen Weltgegensatzes von Ost und West. Bemerkungen zu Ernst Jüngers Schrift *Der gordische Knoten*' (1955), SGN, pp. 523–45; 'Gespräch über den neuen Raum' (1958), SGN, pp. 552–69; 'Nomos – Nahme – Name' (1969), SGN, pp. 573–86; 'Die Ordnung der Welt nach dem zweiten Weltkrieg' (1962), SGN, pp. 592–608; *Theorie des Partisanen* (1963); 'Gespräch über den Partisanen' (1970), SGN, pp. 619–36.

80. 'Der neue Nomos der Erde', in SGN, p. 522.

81. Ibid., p. 521.

82. 'Die Einheit der Welt', SGN, p. 497.

3. 'Die Ordnung der Welt nach dem zweiten Weltkrieg', SGN, p. 599.

84. 'Die Einheit der Welt', SGN, pp. 497, 503.

85. Ibid., p. 504.

86. 'Die geschichtliche Struktur des heutigen Weltgegensatzes von Ost und West', SGN, p. 533.

87. 'Gespräch über den neuen Raum', SGN, p. 569.

88. 'Die Einheit der Welt', SGN, p. 499.

89. 'Die Ordnung der Welt nach dem zweiten Weltkrieg', SGN, p. 602.

90. Ibid., p. 605.

91. 'Die Einheit der Welt', SGN, p. 505.

92. Ibid., pp. 504, 505.

5

Putting the State Back in Credit[1]

David Dyzenhaus

Political theorists of the Left agree with the central aim of Carl Schmitt's essay 'Ethic of State and Pluralistic State'. They wish to rescue the state from a situation of general 'discredit'. Like Schmitt, they suppose that this rescue will have much to do with finding a set of moral or ethical values which provide firm justificatory ground for a strong state. Hence they share Schmitt's suspicion of the dominant strand of liberal thought which demands that the state be 'agnostic' or neutral – that it limit its action with a principle against taking morally controversial positions.

This common ground explains the increasing interest on the Left in Schmitt and in the other political and legal theorists of Weimar who attempted to respond to the crisis of the European state in the late 1920s, a crisis which was at its deepest in Germany.

In the last years of the twentieth century, the situation of the state in the democracies of the West is, of course, very different from that of late Weimar. Nowhere is one of these democracies on the brink of a civil war between political factions. Nowhere is an advanced capitalist economy in danger of collapse.[2] Yet it is no exaggeration to say that the moral crisis of the state is as deep in these democracies as it was in Weimar. Here it suffices – to use Schmittian language – to recall the title of Will Hutton's book about the political economy of the United Kingdom: *The State We're In*.[3]

This moral crisis of the state is reflected in a consensus in the political centre – a centre which moves ever further rightwards – that the state's role in public life should be reduced to the management of those few essentials which are not best left to the private sphere. Here the presumption is one against the state, for it is assumed that in general, private actors will perform more efficiently.

This economic conservatism often goes hand in hand with the neutrality principle of liberalism; that principle shares with economic conservatism the view that the less the state is involved in the lives of individuals, the better. It is also the case, however, that in the New Right ideologies of Margaret Thatcher or Ronald Reagan one encounters an official attitude of extreme social conservatism – for example, hostile attitudes towards movements and measures which seek to bring about social equality.

Such official social conservatism does not undermine my claim about the moral discredit of the state – the general political aversion to organizing state action on the basis of an ethic of state. Indeed, such conservatism supports the claim when one notices that those in power who have hostile attitudes to social equality will usually shy away from state enforcement of their attitudes. They prefer, for the most part, a relentless hunt to eradicate any official support for social equality, and rely on old inequalities to reassert themselves in a 'spontaneous' private order, which differs from Hobbes's state of nature only in that the basic rules of criminal law are enforced.

The claim about moral discredit is also supported by the record of Bill Clinton's New Democrats in the United States of America. While his coming to power expressed a popular reaction to the worst excesses of New Right ideology, it has long been clear that he cannot move out of the shadow of general antipathy towards the state. It remains to be seen whether Tony Blair's New Labour can do better in the United Kingdom than Clinton's dismal record of retreat from any initiative that presupposes a positive moral role for the state in public life. But as I write, in the first few months in office of Blair's government, critics from the Left are already detecting the first signs of the paralysing grip on Labour of antipathy to state action on the basis of firm moral commitments.[4]

In short, while there is a consensus in public life today, at least among the main political players, it is an essentially negative consensus, a consensus against the state.

The moral discredit of the state is also reflected in contemporary liberal political philosophy, as liberals attempt to respond to the same phenomenon that animates Schmitt's 'Ethic of State and Pluralistic State' – the fact of pluralism. While civil war is not on the cards in the democracies of the West, liberal philosophers are still troubled by the fact that disaffected groups with increasing support are challenging the most fundamental values of liberal democracies. It is with this challenge that contemporary political philosophy grapples when it tries to deal with the fact of pluralism. Any attempt to contest those conceptions of the good life which go against the grain of liberal-democratic values invites the charge that liberalism is just one ideology among others, each of them seeking to enforce its partial idea of the good on the whole.

In this chapter, I ask what lessons can be learnt from Weimar by those who wish to respond to the present crisis of moral discredit in which the state finds itself. I will first set out the main features of Schmitt's position through an analysis of 'Ethic of State and Pluralistic State'. I will then argue that while Schmitt's diagnosis of the ills of the state is valuable, his solution should be rejected. If one is to find positive prescriptions from Weimar for the present, these will come not from Schmitt but, rather, from one of his main rivals, the social democrat Hermann Heller.

Schmitt's Ethic of State

Schmitt's arguments always require some excavation, and in 'Ethic of State and Pluralistic State' three of his points of focus provide the clues as to what lies beneath.

First, Schmitt, one of this century's most prominent antiliberals, seems to exclude liberalism from his critique of those political theories which seek to do without an ethic of state. If one takes liberalism to be represented in this essay by Kant, Schmitt – albeit a little grudgingly – concedes that Kant's political theory of the state meets the minimal criteria for a satisfactory theory. Kant presupposes that the state is a concrete state, which means that it is a political unity, a body supreme over all others in the sense that in situations of conflict which threaten unity, it can effectively decide how to resolve the conflict. Kant, according to Schmitt, thus rightly holds that the state is supreme judge, and excludes any individual right of resistance against the state.

Second, Schmitt's antiliberalism is often seen as entailing hostility to pluralism, since he finds one of the causes of the ills of the modern world in the plurality of views about the good among groups contesting for political power. Those ills are best exemplified in late Weimar, the backdrop of Schmitt's essay. He sees Harold Laski's and G.D.H. Cole's pluralism as the theory which invites civil war between groups because it denies the state a role as guarantor of political unity by making it just one more association alongside others. But while Schmitt's target in the essay is pluralism of the kind espoused by Laski and Cole, pluralism itself is not the target. He emphasizes at many points that the general social and political situation is, as a matter of fact, pluralistic; thus any response to the situation has to be a pluralistic one, although Laski's and Cole's pluralism is ill-conceived.

Third, Schmitt is usually thought to scorn the very enterprise of normative argument, since he takes such argument to be an attempt to conceal the reality of power politics. But while such scorn is evident in 'Ethic of State and Pluralistic State', he also suggests that the appropriate response to the fact of pluralism has to be pluralistic for ethical reasons.

It would be ethically wrong, it seems, to try to deal with the fact of pluralism by reshaping the empirical world, by imposing a monistic order on it. Indeed, Schmitt suggests that Laski and Cole are not pluralistic enough, since their position – perhaps unwittingly – is driven by a morally dangerous, imperialistic universalism and monism.

It would be a mistake, however, to take seriously Schmitt's apparent concession to Kantian liberalism: that it can found a genuine political unity. This concession, rather, goes the other way in that Schmitt thinks it significant that the pre-eminent liberal philosopher saw the necessity both to make the concrete state, not the individual, supreme judge of right and wrong; and to deny the individual any right of resistance against that judgement. In so far as liberals make this concession, they concede the necessity of the political. But they subvert that concession by denying the state any substantive basis for political unity. The last section of 'Ethic of State and Pluralistic State' is a polemic not only against Laski's and Cole's pluralism, but also against liberalism. Schmitt is not being sincere when he suggests that a state subjected to a liberal ethic or governed by agreed rules of the game can be an effective political unity. Rather, his position is that a liberal ethic, or any agreed rules of the game, are points on a continuum ending in the proposition *pacta sunt servanda* – contracts must be honoured: a proposition which, he says, cannot found an ethic of state.

Liberalism must degenerate into the kind of pluralism he decries because it wants the state to be agnostic, negatively confined and disciplined rather than positively motivated. To use Schmitt's term, liberalism seeks to 'relativize' the state, to reduce the active part of state activity to that which is left over once one 'subtracts' all 'contents', leaving 'absolutely nothing'. The state then becomes equated with its instrumental machinery, whose control is contested between those groups who strive for what passes for political power.

Such groups can decide to govern their contest by the existing rules of the game, or by devising new rules, or by a written constitution embodying liberal values. But on Schmitt's understanding, any of these pacts subsists only as a matter of temporary, terminable agreement; only as long as each group with power to resile from the pact finds it convenient to abide by it. Furthermore, such an agreement is no better than the status quo it maintains.

So when Schmitt says that a constitutional ethic can be very effective, he does not mean that the constitution itself can provide a substantive basis for authoritative decision-making. That substance cannot come about by agreement, but only because it is effectively imposed from above or emanates from below – from an already substantively homo-geneous people.

Schmitt makes two rather different arguments here. One has it that the subjection of the state to any set of ethical values is always in fact the result of a successful power grab by a group of people acting on an understanding of what serves their own interests. Schmitt's other argument is that to claim universality for a set of ethical values is politically dangerous. His position here is very similar to the one put forward some thirty years later by Isaiah Berlin in 'Two Concepts of Liberty', a classic of liberal pluralist thought. To act politically in the name of higher, universal concepts such as humanity or the individual involves more than an identification of one's own contingent interests with such concepts; it also involves a ready-made justification for riding roughshod over others who disagree with one on the basis that that they simply do not understand what is in their own best interests. Indeed, the closing sentence of 'Two Concepts of Liberty' would not be out of place in 'Ethic of State and Pluralistic State': ' "To realize the relative validity of one's convictions", said an admirable writer of our time, "and yet to stand for them unflinchingly, is what distinguishes a civilized man from a barbarian." '[5]

This last argument brings us to the second and third points of focus in 'Ethic of State and Pluralistic State' – Schmitt's sense of the right understanding of pluralism, and the role of moral or normative considerations in his work.

Schmitt clearly espoused a kind of pluralism at the international level. The flux of history has created different peoples whose sense of unity, what makes them into a people, depends on very different factors. These peoples are now largely organized into nation-states, often with very different core understandings of the good of political unity. One should resist the imperialist tendencies of a universalizing liberalism which seeks to subject all understandings of the good to its own ethical position by – to quote from Berlin – recognizing the 'relative validity' of different understandings.

But as one can see from 'Ethic of State and Pluralist State', Schmitt also seems to argue for a kind of pluralism internal to the nation-state. He says that there is a 'self-evident' 'internal complexity' to any state, and suggests that his understanding of statehood conduces more to the autonomy and freedom of the individual because 'experience tells us that there is no space for . . . [individual] freedom other than what a strong state guarantees'.

It is clear that Schmitt thinks that both internal pluralism and the space of individual freedom can be maintained only as long as there is a state in existence which can ensure the boundaries of both. Such a state has to be strong, which means that it can decide definitively on such boundaries – that is, it can decide without having to submit its decision to any of the mediatory procedures which Schmitt disparages and which, he thinks, typify the decision process of liberal democracy.

Note that while Schmitt supposes that some kind of internal complexity is inevitable, and thus some space for limited pluralism, he does not say anywhere that a state has to uphold a particular kind of pluralism. Nor does he ever suggest that the freedom and autonomy of the individual is or should be a universal value. Indeed, what goes wrong in Cole's and Laski's pluralism is the combination of pluralism with liberal individualism, since to place all associations on an equal footing at the same time as one makes the individual conscience the arbiter of social conflicts is what disables the state from action as a political unity.

Schmitt's point about freedom and autonomy is that if one values individual freedom and autonomy, one should see that a strong state is a necessary precondition of this value, as it is a necessary precondition of any value. In a work of the late 1930s in which he develops the theme of conflicting social groups carving up and devouring the once mighty Leviathan or state, Schmitt argues that Hobbes went badly wrong in starting his argument for a strong state with a premiss about individual freedom.[6]

Schmitt's view is that a strong state must be based on some set of values which can found the substantive homogeneity of the people, and only once such a basis is in place can space be opened up for either pluralism or values like freedom or autonomy.[7] To try to found a state on the value of individual freedom is to make the state a space for conflict between a plurality of groups, which leads to the pluralism of virtual civil war, the pluralism which Laski's and Cole's theory encourages.

As Schmitt argues rather more explicitly in other places, liberalism is constitutionally incapable of making the distinction of politics – the distinction between friend and enemy whose intensity is the only feature which distinguishes the political realm from others.[8] Liberalism suffers from this incapability because it tries to subject politics to ethics in its subordination of the state to negative ethical values, values which seek to limit rather than to enable state action in order to protect the individual from the state. And in seeing the issues of politics as essentially about the ethical governance of relationships between state and individual, liberalism blinds itself to the political – to the distinctions that constitute the differences between groups which vie for political power.

Liberalism's survival as a political order depends then on how long such groups are prepared to content themselves with fighting within the rules of the game over the spoils available in the liberal state. But that fight progressively weakens the state, as its instruments are increasingly colonized by a plurality of groups in the pursuit of their different conceptions of self-interest – the devouring of Leviathan. And so the temptation will grow for one of the groups to resile from the pact – from the agreement to abide by the rules of the game.

On Schmitt's account, then, it is a mistake to try to turn politics into ethics by subordinating the state to ethical norms, norms which he usually equates with the values of liberal individualism. But then we might well ask how he can argue for an 'ethic of state' – one that is capable of grounding the 'duty towards statehood' – as the way out of what he regards as the mess caused by the subjection of the state to ethics.

The answer is not that Schmitt is arguing against the importance of ethical values in the political life of a people. His argument is against the attempt to find universal ethical values to which politics must be subject. Ethics, properly understood, will emerge from politics in the sense that if the political distinction between friend and enemy is properly made, the values that happen to bind together any particular community of friends are, by definition, ethical. The fundamental decision which any political order takes will be one which establishes a normal situation out of a state of exception or political conflict, and the glue of that situation is its ethic.

One cannot say in advance, as liberals attempt to do, what these values are. Any content that succeeds in that it creates a normal situation will also create the norms – ethical and legal – of that situation. But one can say what the content cannot be – it cannot be liberal individualist ethics.

In my view, the value of Schmitt's position is that it correctly identifies the problems liberalism faces when it tries to deal with the fact of pluralism. There is no better illustration of this than in recent work by this century's most eminent liberal thinker, John Rawls. Indeed, a comparison between Schmitt's and Rawls's positions supports Leo Strauss's observation on Schmitt's most famous work, *The Concept of the Political*. Strauss said that Schmitt, despite his antiliberalism, remained trapped within liberalism's horizon: Schmitt presented a theory which, since it was the exact converse of its target, was no solution to the problems he had detected in liberalism.[9]

Liberalism's horizon

Rawls has recently begun to defend the liberal state in a self-consciously political fashion. The liberal state will not concede the space of politics to those who want to use that space to destroy it. In particular, the liberal state must defend its stance of neutrality between different individual conceptions of the good. Rawls now appears to suggest that what liberalism must primarily respond to is not the question of what rights individuals have against the state, but of how stability can be possible given the fact of pluralism.[10]

Contrary to initial expectations, the Enlightenment has not delivered us into an age where we can hope to discover a comprehensive basis in reason for ordering our common life.[11] What it has delivered us from is the substantively homogeneous communities where political conflict, conflict over fundamental values, was largely fought out as a matter of external affairs. It places us in the era of nation-states where political conflict characterizes internal politics, where groups with conflicting understandings of the good life struggle for power. Hence Rawls now seems to accept the Schmittian account of the Enlightenment as having given us not the era of sweet reason, but the era of choice between warring gods and demons. Moreover, he clearly shares Schmitt's view of the apocalyptic nature of that choice.[12]

Under his direction, liberalism now seems to be driven by the fear that to claim truth for one's position is to invite a clash of truth claims, which can only breed dissent and conflict. Liberalism, in seeking to set out the values of the domain of the political, must claim only that these are the values to which it is reasonable to assent. These 'freestanding' values together make up an 'overlapping consensus' about the basics of political and legal order.[13]

For Rawls, what these values stand free of is comprehensive positions or individual conceptions of the good life. While such positions perforce claim truth for themselves if they enter the space of public reason or constitutional discourse, the values which constitute that space claim only reasonableness. But the claim to reasonableness is far from modest. It operates to exclude the truth claims of comprehensive positions from the public realm, and requires them to contest each other only within the realm which Rawls calls the 'social'.[14]

Rawls thus claims only that his overlapping consensus is a solution to the problem of reasonable pluralism, not to pluralism itself. It is a consensus between individuals whom Rawls deems reasonable because they already hold to the values of the overlapping consensus. All others – the unreasonable sorts – are, Rawls says, to be 'contained', if they step out of line.[15]

The ideas of public reason and overlapping consensus thus discipline and confine the state. The overlapping consensus is a consensus about values whose greatness requires their protection from the state. Indeed, Rawls says that in an emergency situation, one in which it looks as if containment is not working, political liberalism might have to drop its claim to mere reasonableness and assert its truth in a conflict over political fundamentals.[16]

Here we see Rawls being tempted into the very battle of truth claims he wishes political liberalism to avoid. And it is difficult to know how it can be avoided, since the free and equal citizens who populate liberal society are citizens who might have, or might develop, views that challenge political liberalism. We must ask what such citizens share with liberals beyond the Hobbesian fear of the state of nature.

Rawls believes that political liberalism can promote civic harmony in the face of pluralism by removing or bypassing the most divisive political issues.[17] These are the issues which cannot be raised without insisting on the truth of a comprehensive doctrine.[18] Of course, if all comprehensive doctrines were to accept this discipline by public reason, we would have the end of politics, and thus of conflict. We would then have the sufficient convergence of comprehensive doctrines which Rawls desires. But this would be not, as he says, because they adopt a framework of deliberation,[19] but because they agree not to deliberate whenever there is conflict and controversy.[20] Citizens in Rawls's republic do not debate or deliberate on what political values should govern their lives. They abide by the values decreed to them, even if what they consider most important politically is put off-limits.[21] Indeed, the only time citizens speak is when the supreme court speaks in their name against a legislative decision, or against executive action, in the name of the higher law of 'We the people'.[22] Those against whom it speaks are exactly in the position of Hobbes's Foole – they should adopt the prudential stance of accommodating themselves to the court's pronouncements, or risk its sanctions.[23]

Political liberalism is therefore political in the Schmittian sense.[24] It asserts its truth against every radical challenge. But it is also political in just the contradictory way Schmitt thought liberalism had to be. At the same time as it asserts its truth, at least when it is hard-pressed by its enemies, it seeks to ban truth from politics, claiming that it is neutral between all positions. But this neutrality is between fully privatized moralities, the neutrality which liberalism aims to achieve.

The legitimacy which political liberalism claims is the legitimacy of a match between the values of the overlapping consensus and the values contained in the (constitutional) law of the society. That achievement would be what Schmitt feared – the end of politics. For it would bring about a society with the wrong kind of homogeneity – one of bourgeois individuals content to be passive consumers of the space accorded to them by the state. That is, liberal stability depends on liberal homogeneity which involves, by and large, getting rid of pluralism in politics.[25] However, Schmitt predicted that liberalism is prevented from achieving its own version of homogeneity because it must constantly re-create the conditions of pluralism plain and simple.

But Schmitt's own position is in many respects similar to political liberalism. He, too, wants a state populated by passive consumers rather than citizens. His talk of an ethic of state is of an ethic which, through its substantive content, imbues the lives of those who fit its criteria for friendship with meaning. Politics should be displaced from the internal affairs of nation-states to the international realm, since politics is ideally a matter between states. Its energy will come not from any internal conflicts but from the possibility (though not the inevitability) of war between states, a possibility kept alive by the fact that each political unity gets its sense of selfhood by defining itself against the others. Ideal politics is then a situation of mutual tolerance by each political unity of the others, which subsists only so long as no particular state goes on the offensive. Each state as a sovereign entity, decides for itself how to live within a terminable situation of mutual tolerance. It is terminable because there is no transcendent entity which can guarantee tolerance. For Schmitt, it seems that that fact reflects the absence of universal values. Once this is recognized, then at least, he thinks, the prime motive for ethical imperialism is removed. If war should break out, however, it takes place within the sphere of politics – a normative vacuum, because there is no supreme judge of right and wrong.

In Rawls's political liberalism, each individual is the sovereign entity, deciding for himself how best to live within the private or social sphere in a situation of mutual tolerance. Rawls wants that situation guaranteed by a state through the discipline of public reason, and that discipline is supposed not so much to displace politics as to suppress it altogether. The stability of that situation is supposedly based in the fact of an overlapping consensus, not a mere agreement terminable at the will of any party (which Rawls terms a *modus vivendi*).

As we have seen, Rawls cannot decide on the status of the values in the overlapping consensus. He is reluctant to claim truth or universal validity for them, though when push comes to shove – in a moment of crisis – he is willing to make an existential assertion of their truth. At that moment, it seems, the overlapping consensus reveals itself as a mere *modus vivendi*.

Rawls's indecision here makes it very difficult for liberalism to respond to the situation of moral discredit in which the state finds itself. In particular, it makes it difficult to see how political liberalism could respond to neo-conservatives, and this difficulty seems to be symptomatic of the trends which are pushing the political centre further to the right.

Like the German conservatives to whose ranks Schmitt belonged, neo-conservatives today give their priority to establishing order and stability. They also espouse a kind of libertarianism or *laissez-faire* ideology, especially in regard to the economic marketplace. The tension between their social conservatism and their libertarianism is resolved only once one realizes that the latter is predicated on the former. To free up the economy, the social, and the political from state control, to establish what Schmitt once called a 'qualitatively strong state',[26] one has first to put in place substantive homogeneity, on whatever basis seems available. Liberty seems to be a luxury which only the qualitatively strong state can afford.[27]

The tension in neo-conservatism results from the fact that in the wake of World War II it is, as Schmitt might have said, sociologically impossible to demote liberty entirely to luxury status. Neo-conservatives thus often suggest that they are the real supporters of liberty, by contrast with liberals, whose ideology brings about the weak 'quantitatively total' state – a state whose apparatus has been captured by conflicting social groups.

Liberals find it difficult to respond to this phenomenon because their commitment to neutrality deprives them of the opportunity to develop anything more than a negative state ethic. And political liberalism seems particularly ill-equipped to respond, because it is uncertain about even the epistemic status of its commitment. But Schmitt is no help out of this impasse, for the reason Strauss suggested. His state ethic is also essentially a negative one – it tolerates any content as long as that content is antiliberal.

I will now suggest that if political theorists on the Left are to find positive prescriptions for the future in Weimar legal and political theory, they should look first to the left wing of Weimar thought – especially to ideas put forward by the social democrat Hermann Heller.

Heller's vision of social homogeneity

Heller argued for the importance of homogeneity for the stability of political order, but his idea of homogeneity was one altogether different from Schmitt's concept of the homogeneity of the people. As we have seen, Schmitt's concept was of the substantive homogeneity of a group where the substance is given by making a distinction between friend and enemy. Heller, in contrast, argued for social homogeneity or a plateau of social equality sustained by a culture of commitments to maintaining and enhancing equality. In his view, such a culture is part and parcel of the legal and political institutions of democracy.

Heller regarded the question of the significance of social homogeneity for democracy as 'inexhaustible'.[28] For him the state is the decision unit in the plurality: the decisive authority in regard to the constitutive acts for a particular region. These acts are potentially of universal signifi- cance, since any social question can become a question for the state. Thus for him the fundamental question of politics is the establishment and maintenance of this unity.[29]

In his own view, the concept of people has to be understood, like all social concepts, as a cultural construct that will become a political one – the nation – when it sees itself as characterized by a unitary political will.[30] The first characteristic of a democratic people is the appointment by equals of representatives to an assembly. Second, its system of representation is magisterial, not sovereign – the representative, however autonomous his power of decision, is subject to the appointment and recall, direct or indirect, of the people. This, said Heller, is what marks off democracy from all other forms of rule. All forms of rule are bound by a social ethic to the people. But in democracy this bond is above all a legal one equipped with effective sanctions.

The appointment of representatives is the most important phase in the dynamic of the politics of state formation. The whole problematic of contemporary democracy lies in the fact that the legal form of the appointment of representatives is supposed to be fulfilled from below to above. Parties play an inevitable part in the process of building a unity in the plurality of individual wills.[31] And for Heller, it is here that the significance of social homogeneity for democracy resides:

> Democracy is supposed to be a conscious process of political unit-formation from bottom to top; all representation is supposed to remain juridically dependent on the community's will. The people in their multiplicity are supposed consciously to form themselves into the unity of the people. In order for the formation of the political unity to be possible at all, there must exist a certain degree of social homogeneity. So long as there is belief in and acceptance of such homogeneity, the possibility exists of arriving through discussion at political agreement with one's opponent, and so long can one renounce suppression by physical force, and so long can one debate with one's opponent.[32]

Heller rejected Schmitt's view that the only justification for parliamentar- ianism is the belief in public discussion, and in truth-finding through the competition of opinion. He regarded this view as a way of setting up parliamentarianism for the fall Schmitt desires. Rather, the intellectual foundation of parliamentarianism is not the belief in public discussion as such, but:

> it is the belief in the existence of a common foundation for discussion and thus in the possibility of fair play for one's internal political opponents, with

whom one thinks one can come to an agreement by excluding naked force. It is when this consciousness of social homogeneity disappears that it first happens that a party, which has until that time been one which debates, becomes a party which dictates.[33]

Note that Heller is not denying the worth of public discussion; indeed, it is crucial for his account of democracy that the structure of democratic institutions should enable such a discussion to take place. He is merely pointing out that belief in the worth of public discussion requires belief in the existence of a social and political foundation for such discussion which makes it possible to live with the result of that discussion, even when it is not to one's liking.

Thus Heller thought that the potential for forming a political unity depends on the degree of social homogeneity. It will cease to exist when all politically relevant sections of the people cease to recognize each other as part of the political unit, and when they are no longer capable of identifying themselves with the symbols and representatives of state. 'In that moment, the unity is cleaved and civil war, dictatorship, and alien domination become possible.'[34]

But for Heller, this social homogeneity can never mean that conflict will disappear. Belief in the transcendence of conflict amounts to mere prophecy. Indeed, he suggested that a properly functioning social democracy will bring many more conflicts to the surface of public life than a democracy severely constrained by liberal ideals.[35] Nevertheless, he put his faith in the resource which democracy, in a culture of social homogeneity, offers to work through such conflicts:

Social homogeneity is always a social-psychological state in which the inevitably present antitheses and conflicts of interest appear constrained by a consciousness and sense of the We, by a community will which brings itself into being. This kind of relative equalization of social consciousness has the resources to work through huge antithetical tensions, and to digest huge religious, political, economic and other antagonisms.[36]

But this sense of the 'We' should not, he emphasized, be equated with any kind of Rousseauian Romanticism and metaphysics that supposes the people as some a priori personification endowed with political will and ability to act.[37] He rejected both Rousseau's attempt to equate the state with the mere expression of the democratic people and the attempt at an equation of state with a romantic idea of nation. Rousseau's *volonté générale*, or general will, takes on a Romantic tinge in so far as it presupposes a pre-state political harmony and unanimity of will which has never existed in the always antagonistic and pluralistic reality of a people.[38]

Heller thus argued that to make sense of the idea of the *Rechtsstaat* one has to make the attempt to link together law, politics and democracy in one theory about legal order. He integrates his theory of the appropriate political organization of democracy and his account of legal order in a way that directly confronts concrete questions of appropriate institutional arrangements.

Heller regards legal order as a moral good in part because it provides us with a means to positivize values. But he departs from legal positivism in that he supposes that there must be a point to the process of positivization. That point comes from the realization that we have to make our order of values together – that the final court of appeal does not lie beyond our collective sense of what is right and wrong. But then law is not just an instrument of that collective sense. Rather, law is the way of ascertaining that sense in a process in which those charged with authoritative determinations of the content of the law are kept accountable. To put it differently: the legal order is not just an instrument of democracy but an essential part of its realization.

For Heller, the basis of legal order is in part a social one – the citizen's sense of both the actual level of social equality reached and the commitment of the society to social equality – and in part a political one – the sense of whether or not politics makes room for citizens to be authors of their own political and social order, so that citizens are able to influence both legislation and law reform. In the terms Heller uses to describe the citizen, this sense is one of the contingency of the concrete order established by law. It is contingent in that it is the result of politics, but of politics conducted within democratic institutions and thus subject to change. That is to say, this sense of contingency requires the institutions of the democratic *Rechtsstaat* as intrinsic elements of legal order. It is a sense which makes a touchstone of the validity of law the democratic process of its production, its implementation and execution through a system of the division of powers, and its openness to reform in the light of citizens' experience of it.[39]

Heller's view, then, is that the point of the democratic institutional structure of the *Rechtsstaat* is to make it possible for the values of social and political order to be positivized in a way that makes the powerful accountable to the subjects of their laws. Morality, in the sense of the values which the collectivity can legitimately require us to live by, is just the set of values that are concretized through the positive law. The subjects of the law become its authors first through the fact that it is their representatives who enact legislation. But their authorship does not end there – it continues through an appropriate process of concretization of the legislation.

What makes that process appropriate is that, both institutionally and substantively, the interpreters of the law must regard themselves as participating in a process of legislation which instantiates what Heller calls fundamental ethical principles of law. Most abstractly, these are the principles which promise both freedom and equality to all citizens. The ultimate check on delivery of such promises can be nothing other than the individual legal conscience – the individual citizen's sense of whether the law is living up to its promise.[40]

Indeed, Heller regards the seeds of modern democracy as sown with the appearance of two ideas: the idea that the law binds the rulers to the ruled, and the idea that the rulers must find an immanent justification for their rule. Legal process is not, then, empty form, but a process with a substantive point which both shapes it and is shaped by it. To forget this is to legitimate the abuse of legal form by those who want to use it as a cloak for their attempt to seize power.

In his view, politics is not a normative vacuum but the space one has when those institutions are in place which best allow for the emergence, contestation, and revision of fundamental values in the light of experience. The rule of law is then the institutional mechanism of democracy. Its justification is the same as the justification for democracy itself. And that justification requires both a fully argued commitment to the rightness of democracy and a recognition that social equality is as much a part of one's commitment to democracy as is the rule of law.

If it seems to democrats of the Left that it is high time to recredit the state, then it is also high time for them to explore their own resources in the social democratic tradition. Here I have tried to indicate how Hermann Heller's theory of the social nature of the democratic *Rechtsstaat* might be especially useful in this task.

Notes

1. This chapter is mainly a commentary on Schmitt's 'Ethic of State and Pluralistic State', and the unsourced references are to the version in this volume (chapter 11). At times, I draw on earlier work, especially on my *Legality and Legitimacy: Carl Schmitt, Hans Kelsen and Hermann Heller in Weimar* (Oxford: Clarendon Press, 1997). I thank Cheryl Misak for comments on a draft.

2. If one takes a more global approach, one can argue that the situation of both civil war and economic collapse is endemic, just quarantined in other parts of the world. But I will confine my focus here to the democracies of the West.

3. London: Vintage, 1996, revised edition.

4. See, for example, David Marquand, 'Blair's Split Personality', *The Guardian*, 16 July 1997, p. 17.

5. 'Two Concepts of Liberty', in Isaiah Berlin, *Four Essays on Liberty* (Oxford: Oxford University Press, 1969), pp. 118, 172. The person quoted is, I believe, Joseph Schumpeter.

6. Carl Schmitt, *The Leviathan in the State Theory of Thomas Hobbes: Meaning and Failure of a Political Symbol*, trans. George Schwab and Erna Hilfstein (Westport, CT: Greenwood Press, 1996).

7. Carl Schmitt, 'Weiterentwicklung des totalen Staates in Deutschland', in Schmitt, *Verfassungsrechtliche Aufsätze aus den Jahren 1924–1954: Materialen zu einer Verfassungslehre* (Berlin: Duncker & Humblot, 1988).

8. See especially Carl Schmitt, *The Concept of the Political*, trans. George Schwab (New Brunswick: Rutgers University Press, 1976).

9. Leo Strauss, 'Anmerkungenen zu Carl Schmitt, *Der Begriff des Politischen*', reprinted in Heinrich Meier, *Carl Schmitt, Leo Strauss, und 'Der Begriff des Politischen': zu einem Dialog unter Abwesenden* (Stuttgart: Metzler Verlag, 1988), pp. 99–125 (125).

10. John Rawls, *Political Liberalism* (New York: Columbia University Press, 1993), pp. xvi-xvii.

11. Ibid., p. xviii.

12. See ibid., p. xxvi:

> What is new about this clash is that it introduces into people's conceptions of the good a transcendent element not admitting of compromise. This element forces either mortal conflict moderated only by circumstance and exhaustion, or equal liberty of conscience and freedom of thought. Except on the basis of these last, firmly founded and publicly recognized, no reasonable political conception of justice is possible. Political liberalism starts by taking to heart the absolute depth of that irreconcilable latent conflict.

13. Ibid., p. 140.

14. Ibid., p. 220.

15. Ibid., pp. 37, 54, 60–61.

16. Ibid., pp. 152–6.

17. Ibid., pp. 150–51, 156–7.

18. Ibid., pp. 127–8.

19. Ibid., p. 156.

20. Compare Bruce Ackerman, *Social Justice and the Liberal State* (New Haven, CT: Yale University Press, 1980), p. 11; Charles E. Larmore, *Patterns of Moral Complexity* (Cambridge: Cambridge University Press, 1987), pp. 55–68. Rawls seems to endorse Larmore's similar position at p. 192 n. 24 of *Political Liberalism*. For an excellent critique of Rawls on these lines, see Bernard Manin, 'On Legitimacy and Political Deliberation', *Political Theory* 15 (1987), p. 338.

21. 'Faced with the fact of reasonable pluralism, a liberal view removes from the political agenda the most divisive issues, serious contention about which must undermine the social bases of cooperation': Rawls, *Political Liberalism*, p. 157. Rawls admits that among these are what people will rightly regard as 'the highest things': ibid., p. 4.

22. See ibid., p. 233, adopting Bruce Ackerman's views in 'Constitutional Politics/ Constitutional Law', *Yale Law Journal* 99 (1989), pp. 453 ff. (464); and *We the People: Foundations* (Cambridge, MA: Harvard University Press, 1991) vol. 1, pp. 6–10.

23. As Charles Larmore, who coined the term 'political liberalism', frankly puts it:

> The liberal freedoms set limits to democratic government, and in particular to the form it usually takes, majority rule. Nor is this ranking a mere makeshift. On the contrary, democracy is made subordinate to liberal principles precisely because the value of democratic institutions is held to lie chiefly, if not exclusively, in their being the best *means for guaranteeing* liberal freedoms.

See Larmore, *The Morals of Modernity* (Cambridge: Cambridge University Press, 1996), p. 182; original emphasis. It is worth noting that these remarks are penned in an essay responding to Schmitt's allegation of a contradiction between liberalism and democracy.

24. As Rawls seems to recognize: *Political Liberalism*, pp. 44–5, 152.

25. Indeed, Rawls is almost explicit about this. Political liberalism, as we have seen, is not neutral in its consequences, but he claims that it is still neutral in that it does not actively favour any one comprehensive doctrine over another: ibid., pp. 192–4. But the only comprehensive doctrines against which it will not tend to discriminate indirectly are different versions of liberal comprehensive doctrines. That is, while political liberalism does not target for political action reasonable but illiberal groups, these will find it harder

to survive in the social climate which political liberalism fosters. See ibid., pp. 197–200 for Rawls's tentative remarks on these points. It follows that one cannot hang on to what Rawls calls neutrality of aim while dropping a claim to neutrality of consequences, since the consequences he admits require individuals to regard their comprehensive views as fully private individual choices.

26. Schmitt, 'Weiterentwicklung des totalen Staates in Deutschland'.

27. For the classic statement of this view in the Anglo-American tradition, see Patrick Devlin, 'Morals and the Criminal Law', in *The Enforcement of Morals* (Oxford: Oxford University Press, 1965), p. 1.

28. Hermann Heller, 'Politische Demokratie und Soziale Homogenität', in Heller, *Gesammelte Schriften*, ed. Christoph Müller (Tübingen: J.C.B. Mohr [Paul Siebeck], 1992, 2nd edn), vol. 2, at p. 423.

29. Ibid., pp. 423–4.

30. Hermann Heller, *Staatslehre*, in Heller, *Gesammelte Schriften*, vol. 3, pp. 258–62.

31. Heller, 'Politische Demokratie und Soziale Homogenität', pp. 425–6.

32. Ibid., p. 427.

33. Ibid., p. 425.

34. Ibid., p. 428. Although see ibid., pp. 431–2 for some rather odd remarks by Heller on the 'negro question'. On the one hand, he seems to equate the exclusion of Blacks from the political process in the United States of America with the exclusion of slaves from the *polis* by Plato. On the other hand, he says that the negro question is partly about the 'anthropological' basis of homogeneity. This apparent but perhaps not untypical racism is completely at odds with his views on the general issue of ethnicity and state.

35. See Hermann Heller, *Die Politischen Ideenkreise der Gegenwart* in Heller, *Gesammelte Schriften*, vol. 1, p. 377.

36. Heller, 'Politische Demokratie und Soziale Homogenität', p. 428.

37. Heller, *Staatslehre*, pp. 262–4.

38. Ibid., pp. 266–7.

39. Hermann Heller, 'Bürger und Bourgeois', in Heller, *Gesammelte Schriften*, vol. 2, pp. 625–41.

40. Heller, *Staatslehre*, pp. 333–9. Heller argues that it is a necessary paradox of the democratic *Rechtsstaat* that the legal conscience's ethical right of resistance is something which has weight but no legal recognition.

6

From Karl to Carl:
Schmitt as a Reader of Marx

Jorge E. Dotti

The hermeneutic conflict which emerges from the writings of Carl Schmitt indisputably makes them a useful source of suggestions for a contemporary critical position. The following pages are a response to our conviction that for this reason a Schmittian interpretation of Marx's significance is a key issue.

I

At the centre of this Schmittian interpretation is the view that Marx shares the cultural assumptions, and especially the metaphysical principle, underlying the bourgeois way of life he is criticizing: the elimination of all transcendence, and the consequent reduction of the social dynamic to the horizontal relation between free producers of commodities, who exchange their products in the economic market. In one of his very first works, Schmitt was already suggesting reading *Das Kapital* rather as an example of a 'critique of the time' ('Kritik der Zeit'), unable to free itself from the paradox that in his search for meaning, Marx is presuming the validity of the very premises being criticized.[1] This common ground consists in a progressive philosophy of history, an outlook Marx inherited from his doctrinary mentor, Hegel.

As we shall see, for Schmitt the juncture at which these two thinkers meet is the key to understanding not only the internal conceptual structure of Marxism, but also its political success, by which I mean its multifaceted implementation as *real socialism*. And it is precisely on the subject of philosophy of history that the crux of Schmitt's interpretation is to be found; it is an interpretation that focuses on the political side of

Marxism and puts the strictly economic details of Marx's system to one side, without becoming aware of its complications, and even accepting the validity of its explanation of surplus-value.

Marx's underlying philosophy is a Hegelian transformation of history into an immanent process, a dialectical *epos* of a god-like reason which dominates the process of the growing rationalization of history. It is on such a basis that Marx offers an economic dynamic as the real referent of what Hegel theorizes as the speculative Logos; and at the same time he concentrates all of humanity's moral characteristics in the proletariat, replacing the previous, Enlightened identification of humanity with the *tiers état*. Read carefully by the doctor of philosophy in Berlin and Paris in the turmoil of the 1840s, Hegel endorses this decisive move to breathe the power of revolutionary politics into what was soon to become a Marxist theory of history and society. For Schmitt, the 'production process' is a secular form of Hegel's all-pervading *Logos*, and 'class' is the new subject which constructs history in obedience to the objective laws of a movement whose dialectical drive is similar to that of the Hegelian Spirit, and whose result (not an ethical state but a communist society) represents the total implementation of reason *on earth*.[2]

However, this does not by any means exhaust the defining role of Hegelian thought in Marxist doctrine. On the one hand, then, it favours Marx's positivist side, which we see in his presentation of his concepts as the result of a scientific vision of social reality which is axiologically neutral or free of ideology. On this front, Marx's conclusions are similar to Hegel's: the elimination of political decisions and the recourse to an impersonal process leading towards the rational aims of history. On the other hand, however, there is a strong streak of the political [*das Politische*] in Marx; Hegel is also the main influence on the doctrinary evolution of this side of his thinking. It is in the key concept of the proletarian dictatorship that Schmitt finds the political in Marx, albeit in a tense relation with the cast-iron laws with which Marx tries to justify the scientific nature of his theses.

For Schmitt, therefore, both of these trends present in Marx, positivist neutralization and revolutionary politicity, have their philosophical matrix in Hegel.

Concerning the first, the Hegelian dialectic ignores absolute negations as well as affirmations, and does not concern itself with thinking about radically exceptional situations which require definitive decisions. Everything can be processed, everything can be absorbed dialectically in the general process accomplished by the subject-substance; any anomalous or exceptional situation which appears to deviate from the pattern predetermined by the logical Idea is merely a predictable state within an all-inclusive dynamic. All cases of negation (differences, moments of alienation or negativity) find their true meaning in the light of universal rationality, when they succumb to the systematicity of the whole. From this perspective, revolution (conceived in Hegelian terms) is legitimate when it is not radically revolutionary, when it is conditioned speculatively and cannot represent anything unpredictable, nor the birth of anything absolutely novel. As a result, dictatorship – a construct vital to any act of revolution at the time of its eruption – is just a moment in the general procedure of the Objective Spirit, and ends up being systematized within an organic development. The Jacobins and Napoleon are necessary characters who fulfil a function which is predictable in the light of the rationality of the whole.[3]

However, Hegel also endorses philosophically the central motive of Marx's politics: the hyperpoliticity of the class struggle and its revolutionary culmination as the proletarian dictatorship.

This is presented as an exceptional break in the regular course of history, an exception which occurs when the stage reached by history is in turn also a dictatorship which hinders and slows the progressive nature of the general movement. The dictatorship which must be replaced is that of the bourgeoisie – that is, the state – which, by being dictatorial, can be challenged only by a non-conciliatory opposition; in other words, it demands to be replaced by another dictatorship: the proletarian dictatorship. The exercising of proletarian power in the form of a dictatorship is therefore the exception to the regular progression of history which, with revolutionary violence, eliminates the bourgeois state whenever this restricts rational development. Proletarian dictatorship removes bureaucratic centralization, which restricts liberty and monopolizes coercive forces to the gain of the exploiting class. This move in the process towards communism can be justified as the exceptional revolutionary intervention of the new bearer of the historical dialectic: the Western urban proletariat.[4]

Thus Marx combines the organicism of historical development, as he found it described in Hegel (rather than in other comparable versions so typical of the nineteenth century), with the reinstating of groundbreaking political decisions such as those of a *volonté générale* or a *pouvoir constituant*, although this revolutionary moment lies in a far more complex system of philosophy of history and economy than the Rousseaunian elements to be found in the Jacobins' ideology. For Schmitt:

> from the perspective of a theory of the state, the proletarian dictatorship (where proletariat is identified with the people), in the transition to an economic state in which the state [perishes], presupposes the concept of dictatorship, as it is found at the very base of the theory and practice of the National Convention. For a theory of the state relative to the transition

towards the elimination of the state, Engels's appeal in his speech on the road to be taken (to the Communist League in March 1850) also applies, when he said it is the same as [in France in 1793].[5]

Marx presents the conflict which gives all political significance to its theories as the confrontation between two dictatorships: that associated with the past and exploitation, and that of the class of the future, the universal subject whose liberation is the liberation of all those who have been exploited. A historical identity which has been constructed philosophically with Hegelian tools justifies the proletariat in its dictatorial act – using the disruptive power of an exceptional decision to interrupt the regular course of history, when this course has reached a stage where those forces which had previously driven it are now getting bogged down and becoming a hindrance to historical development.[6]

Schmitt encapsulates the problem of the dictatorship within the new sociopolitical and cultural context born of the irruption of the masses and the collapse of the classical liberal articulation between electors and a parliamentary representation which is formally independent of them, and obedient only to the dictates of dialogical rationality. Faced with contemporary industrial dynamism, the Parliament of a John Stuart Mill or a Guizot loses its historical background and its doctrinary support. At the same time there is a breakdown in the synthesis between liberalism and democracy, and between the logic of limited sovereignty and that of the identification of rulers and ruled. The conjunction of these two crises revitalizes the matter of the dictatorship, which Schmitt expounds as a regime which is clearly antiliberal but not antidemocratic, since it respects and even empowers the homogeneous nature of the people, which is the essential feature of democracy.

It is as a result of this total collapse of traditional legitimacy, and the precariousness of the compromise of liberalism and democracy at the dawn of the age of the masses, that Schmitt draws attention to the similarity between those called 'reactionaries' and those called 'revolutionaries', provided that both are aware of the irregular nature of the situation which, in historical terms, emerged in 1848 and reached its climax in the Russian Revolution. Both groups of intellectuals saw the need for a dictatorship as the extreme measure called for by a severe crisis, the justification for which is always an ex-post one, in the sense that the constitution which legitimizes the new regime is one which this same regime has imposed and is attempting to bring into effect. The perception of a dictatorship as the force behind the establishment of something radically new therefore unites revolutionaries and counter-revolutionaries, though for the former it marks the complete collapse of the existing bourgeois order, while for the latter it indicates that an order has been restored by the elimination of socialist or anarchist chaos. But there is a philosophical strand common to both groups.[7]

The text which is the most central to understanding the development of Schmitt's reading of Marx is his writing on parliamentarism.[8] Proletarian dictatorship is undeniably an heir to the pedagogical dictatorship typical of the Enlightenment: the Enlightened elite considers itself justified by reason to take extreme and exceptional decisions, in order to put into practice measures which those compelled to obey them would certainly accept if only their capacity for reason were as developed as that of the Enlightened. In this sense, proletarian dictatorship is a tool of rationalism. Except that – crucially – it is a tool not of an intellectual rationalism (that of the *Verstand*) but of a dialectical one, that of the Hegelian *Vernunft*. According to Schmitt, this diversity of views allows Marx to invoke a type of scientificity which is not neutralizing but combative; that is, he presents a scientific explanation for the social conflict which is in reality no more than the metaphorical disguising of a desire for power and cultural hegemony in the broadest sense.

While the positivist ideal of science is to be found only in 'popular Marxism', which rests on the invocation of the mechanistic inevitability and on an unhistorical predictability, the superior, dialectical scientificity nourishes the security with which this doctrine invokes violence, taking to the extreme the Enlightened equation of knowledge and power, and the related fictionalizing of potential consent. The 'final, conceptually decisive argument, the ultimate evidence behind socialist beliefs derives from Hegel, whose philosophy makes it possible to link theory and practice, since an understanding of the historical dynamic allows intervention, whatever it may be, in order to help this very dynamic when it is obstructed and/or becomes catastrophic'.[9]

If the conceptual axis of Marxism were seen through a positivist scientificity, proletarian dictatorship would be distinguishable from an Enlightened dictatorship only in secondary ways. The matter of authoritarian imposition legitimized pedagogically can certainly be found in Marx, but for Schmitt this is only generic, not specific.

> If the scientific foundation of socialism resided in this side of the question, then the spring into the reign of liberty would be no more than a spring into the reign of absolute technicity [*Technizität*]. It would be a question of the old rationalism of the Enlightenment, with another of those attempts – prevailing since the eighteenth century – to reach a kind of politics characterized by a mathematical and physical exactness, different only in the fact that the strong moralism still prevalent in the eighteenth century would have been given up from a theoretical point of view. As occurs in every kind of rationalism, the result would be the dictatorship of the rationalist elite.[10]

But the proletariat and its dictatorial vanguard correspond to another way of understanding history: dialectical comprehension:

> Precisely what is fascinating about the philosophical-metaphysical plan of the Marxist philosophy of history and sociology is not naturalistic scientificity but the way in which Marx retains the [Hegelian] thought about the dialectical development of human history, and his way of considering this history as a single concrete process characterized by reference to its antitheses, producing itself through some immanent, organic force.[11]

In other words, Schmitt is reclaiming a Marxist politicity which is at odds with Marx's economicism, of which the German jurist takes no account, as his interest lies in historical dialectics. Communist liberty can be reached and established through a string of antitheses between conflicting subjectivities, not in a more or less mechanical connection of stages within a conciliatory process of neutralization of the political. The weight of the historical task of communism therefore resides less in an imperative of technological development than in a dialectic whose own significance is ambiguous. It does contribute towards a neutralization of the political, if this dialectical process is understood in Hegelian terms as being conciliatory, but it also revitalizes the friend–enemy (or proletarian–bourgeois) confrontation by allowing the intervention of a dictatorial will which would be entirely meaningless if history were reduced to the impersonal sequence of various factors based on an inflexible rational system.

Although Schmitt distanced himself from the *métier philosophique*, his observations point suggestively to the metaphysical core of this dialectical schema. In order for the dialectic to function politically and legitimize the proletarian dictatorship, Marx had to claim for himself (by a peculiar personal interpretation of Hegelian thought) the thesis of self-consciousness as a driving force of history. The philosophical principle which identifies knowledge of what is with actual and objective (not ideological) self-consciousness (that is, with knowledge of the historical sense of personal subjectivity) finds in that self-awareness the justification for subjective intervention in the historical process. History as class conflict is self-productive, a kind of peculiar autopoiesis; and being aware of the dialectical nature of this production is equivalent to controlling the process itself cognitively, a position from which one assumes the authorization to interfere in it: 'The scientificity of Marxist socialism rests on the principle of a Hegelian philosophy of history.'[12]

There is certainly a difficulty in linking dialectical development with dictatorship, for this seems to be a break in the proper sequence of historical stages, a sort of 'mechanical intervention' (Schmitt's adjective is unfortunate) in an organic process of evolution. Apparently organic development and dictatorship are mutually exclusive, and the revolutionary specificity of proletarian dictatorship is threatened by its reduction to a mere predictable moment in an all-regulating system:

> In any case, Hegel's philosophy does not allow for a dictatorship in the sense of a moral decision which interrupts both development and debate. The opposite terms also influence each other, and become incorporated into the development. The either/or of moral decision-making, the decided and decisive disjunction, has no place in this system. Even that which the dictator dictates becomes another moment in the debate and in the development which unequivocally continues to advance. As always, that which is dictated by the dictator becomes assimilated into the peristalsis of the World-Spirit. . . .
> In this system, the proletarian dictatorship can never become an essential negation of something which itself is essential, but the elimination of an insignificant right.[13]

But this is not all that Hegel bequeaths to his young readers. In him can be found the claim to a 'conscious action' (to the transformation of what a human being is *an sich* into his consciousness *für sich*), an activist element which cannot be reduced to spontaneous and unconscious conciliation, and which the *Junghegelianer* would develop into revolutionary practice and, as such, 'educative', but on a different level to that of Enlightenment.[14] The aim of consciousness (the becoming aware of truth as a self-manifestation of truth itself), an Enlightened bequest originally received by Hegel and radicalized through Young-Hegelian interpretation, this proto-dictatorial side of Hegelianism, pulls against the conciliatory goals of the Hegelian system. The increasing class-consciousness opens a political dimension in Marx's discourse, and here it should be emphasized that Schmitt's interest lies precisely in the class struggle as it appears to be supported theoretically in the role played by self-consciousness in Hegel's philosophy of history.[15]

At this point the Schmittian interpretation of the politicity of Marxism is enriched with a new element. Marx's contribution is neither the notion of a class confrontation nor the hatred of the bourgeois. Both these were already familiar territory:

> What was new and fascinating in the Communist Manifesto was something else, the systematic concentration of the class struggle into a single ultimate struggle, at the level of a universal history, at a dialectical peak of the tension between bourgeoisie and proletariat. The oppositions between the different classes are simplified into a single, ultimate opposition.[16]

In our opinion, Schmitt admired Marx's theoretical processing, which involves the use of a conceptual Hegelian tool to group together, in sharp and definitive opposition, all the sense of the sequence of antith-

eses and conflicts which is characteristic of history, proposing an existential friend–enemy grouping with no hope of liberal conciliation: 'The
greatest tension in this moment of universal history comes about in this
way. Not only the real struggle but also the conceptual opposition
reaches its highest intensity through this logical simplification. Everything should be taken to an extreme, so that it is inverted, with dialectical inevitability.'[17] Marx stretches the opposition to this extreme point,
to the contradiction between two poles: at one we find maximum
wealth and inhumanity; at the other maximum poverty and simple
humanity. Without this Hegelian dialectization of history, it would not
be possible for Marxism to propose the present situation as the final
state prior to a struggle which brings about qualitative change. The
dialectic allows for an understanding of capitalism as a generator of its
own negation.'[18] Knowledge of the dialectical movement of history
provides this 'self-guarantee typical of Hegelian rationalism'.[19] The key
can be found in the role of the consciousness of history; that is, understanding is equivalent to knowing that what one has understood has
come to the end of its historic life: 'the fact that a period may be
understood in human consciousness is for the historical dialectic the
proof that the known period has come to an end historically'.[20] The
way is then open for a political intervention under the guidance of the
proletarian party.

This means, furthermore, that in Marx there is neither prophecy nor
scientificism. The 'strong moral pathos' and his 'hateful contempt for the
bourgeois' are characteristics of an age, and not exclusively socialist, let
alone unique to Marx. Rather, his contribution consists in transforming
the bourgeoisie, which had previously been the object for the resentment
of the aristocracy, of the literary world or of those whose point of view
was vaguely utopian, into the 'figure of universal history' containing
within it all inhumanity, the negation of humanity; which, as such, is set
against the bearer [Träger] of this characteristic – the modern industrial
proletariat – without hope of conciliation. The ontological consistency of
the proletariat has less to do with its actual position in contemporary
society than with its role as philosophical antithesis to that of the
bourgeoisie. The proletariat will attain a level of complete humanity only
if it destroys whoever is condemning it to infrahumanity, but to destroy
them it must set itself up as a universal class, the irreconcilable enemy,
'although the idea of class contradicts that of humanity'.[21]

Unravelling the real significance of the bourgeoisie is a question of
vital importance to Marx, as the proletariat can be defined only as the
negation of its enemy. Hence the Marxist recourse to the metaphysics of
progress and to the consciousness or knowledge of the whole movement,
possible only for those who find themselves situated historically at the

final stage. Concerning the crux of Hegelian Marxism, Schmitt insists that 'An appropriate consciousness is one criterion for starting a new stage in development . . . a period in decline becomes an object in the historic consciousness of a new age'.[22] A new age, which can only mark the death of the state, follows immediately behind the tough education of the people by their vanguard. The Enlightened dictatorship gives way to a more radical exercise in violence. Not only is Enlightenment *stricto sensu* left behind, but so is Hegelianism, both replaced by a call for the real and concrete 'bloody struggle'.[23]

At this point Schmitt begins to rethink a critical attitude to Marxism, having indicated the final characteristic which accounts for the element of politicity in Marx's theory – an element which theoretically justifies the application of violence, as in Sorel (who is not mentioned explicitly) – and the concretization of this philosophy of violence in the form of dictatorship, such as that of the Bolsheviks in Russia. This aspect is a product not of rationalism but of a *fin-de-siècle* vitalism. In this transition towards the immediate application of violence an irrational component becomes involved, one which marks the break with the rationalism underlying Marx's proletarian dictatorship.[24] With this new element, Marxism ceases to be a social theory with certain political elements, pressing for radical change and itself rooted in a philosophy of history, only to become the ideological motor behind a regime to which Schmitt is radically opposed.

II

To our understanding, Schmitt's reading of Marx is distinctive in its dual receptive attitude, which points in diametrically opposing directions: positive valorization of the dialectic *qua* method adequate to the human being's political conflictivity; and, at the same time, profound criticism of Marxist philosophy as a world-view which neutralizes the political (a criticism on which Schmitt's challenges to the Bolshevik regime and his warnings of the Soviet threat to the West both depend). We shall now look at the first aspect.

Dialectics are structured as a function of two closely linked driving forces. Above all there is the importance of the Hegelian method as that most suited to grasping the significance of contemporary reality. Secondly, we have the significance of this method, a revolutionary inheritance for posterity, in so far as it allows Marx to develop the proletariat–bourgeoisie opposition as a radical clash. It is this character of extreme existential conflict which gives this opposition connotations of the political – that is, of political conflict by Schmittian criteria, which would not exist were all of Marx's thought developed along lines laid down by his economicist inspiration.

Fortunately, we now have access to an excellent personal exposition of Schmitt's thoughts on the subject, illuminating the hermeneutical model – which aims at the 'understanding of the dialectical method' – by which the analysed texts are organized.[25] Without going into the details of Marx's critique of the Hegelian model of constitutional monarchy, it could be said that Schmitt understands that 'the arguments put forward by his teacher turn out to be, for Marx, no more than a vacuous apology and sophistic defence of the extant condition and structures.' Hegel is shown here to be 'an advocate of a saturated status quo, while Marx comes across as the radical revolutionary'.[26] The importance of Schmitt's commentary lies in the fact that he focused the analysis on the question of methodology – that is, on Marx's use of 'the Hegelian dialectics and method', having understood that linking this proposal to a conservative position was not the only option. For Marx, the dialectic was 'the most revolutionary of all philosophy produced by mankind', so it was a case of 'applying this method to reality, and in fact to political, current, concrete reality. According to this [Hegelian] philosophy, all Spirit [Geist] and all rationality are always present Spirit', not vague moral principles or utopian ideals, 'and all truthful historical knowledge is only a knowledge of the present'.[27]

Hegelian teaching that all historical discourse discusses the present in political terms becomes revolutionary when Marx suggests that the nineteenth-century state is by no means the reign of the Spirit made reality; rather, it is a mixture of archaic leftovers and a system of institutions functionalized to the dynamic intrinsic in a civil society. 'So it was a matter of rationally understanding the reality of this civil-society, whose existence is economic, as an instrument of the dialectical process', given that the economy has become the new tool with which the cunning of reason [List der Vernunft] propels history, displacing and neutralizing the politics hegemonized by the state. It is in Hegel's philosophy that Marx finds the path towards the economic. Despite his conservatism, 'old Hegel . . . had the strength to lead a young thinker to a polemical opposition, thus going very precisely to the heart of things'.[28] According to Schmitt, Hegel's influence on the young Marx had much more impact on the development of Marx's ideas than did the direct experience of the French bourgeoisie, which the future author of Das Kapital was to encounter later. In the final analysis, Marx is right to see in Hegel the key to modern conditions, as it was Hegel who first defined the bourgeois in essence, as a non-political human being motivated by the security of property;[29] the Hegelian text referred to by Schmitt is Die Verfassung Deutschlands (1802).

We cannot read the whole of this work of Schmitt's, nor the possible preparatory notes. A part of this Schmittian commentary on the young Marx's critique of Hegel has been lost, yet we can allow ourselves an observation: namely that Schmitt misses an element of Marx's text which reinforces his own proposal. By 1843, in his critical commentary on the Hegelian philosophy of the state, Marx is already describing a dialectical political confrontation between the 'people' as a subject characterized by its democratic right (democratic legitimization of the *pouvoir constituant*) and the modern individual divided into bourgeois and *citoyen*, whose dual nature is legitimized by the Legislative Power. The modern Parliament naively attempts to conciliate the social conflicts by means of formal legislation, and thus distorts the revolutionary impulse towards democracy, whose political tool is universal suffrage without any limitation on active and passive political rights. Schmitt does not recognize the politicity of the situation set up by a Marx who has not as yet formulated a theory of the proletariat. However, this possible oversight certainly does not alter the heart of Schmitt's interpretation. For the German jurist, Marx finds in the Hegelian dialectic, in the conception of history as an advancing of the consciousness of liberty, no longer a generic Enlightened concept, but a direct reference to contemporary reality as the distinguishing feature of all true philosophical thought. Great philosophers refer only to what is taking place around them, and Hegel captures the essence of the bourgeois world and its logic of motion.[30] It could even be said that Schmitt is unaware of the similarities between Marx's critique of Hegelian dialectics and his own polemics against both 'political Romanticism' and the abstraction of Kelsenian 'Normativism'.

In any case, it should be emphasized that cognitive access to current conditions, through Hegel, results in structural adjustment of the Marxist proletariat–bourgeoisie opposition to Schmitt's criterion of the political, as the intensity of the class struggle is such that it exceeds the bounds of the economic.[31]

Clearly the politicity of Marx's proposal is founded exclusively in the philosophical elaboration of a conflict characterized by an intensity which cannot be kept within its originary boundaries; that is to say, *contrario sensu*, Marx's vision has the existential conflict extended beyond its original nature as the only counterbalance to its economicism:

> Even [class] in the Marxist sense ceases to be merely economic and becomes a political entity when it reaches this decisive point, that is, when it seriously engages in the class [struggle] and treats the class enemy as a real enemy and fights it, whether this takes the form of one state against another or a civil war within a state'.

Only in this way does the proletariat become a historical subject capable of determining the personality of the political system it seeks to hegemonize; the division of the world into proletarian and capitalist states is the best test of the permanence of the political, which had previously been latent or cloaked in concepts and institutions which appeared to be exclusively economic. 'In any case, the driving force of the political is always extreme necessity', and the sovereign is defined by his capacity to impose the criteria of friendship and enmity on such conditions.[32]

III

Although we will not be dealing with this issue, it is worth mentioning that it is through Lukács that Schmitt reads Marx's reading of Hegel. Schmitt recognizes this explicitly.[33] The Hungarian thinker is the referent not only for the positive evaluation of dialectics, by virtue of the politicity inherent in it, but also in the war against cultural hegemony being waged by Marxism in the area of political, social and cultural interpretations of history, and in the consequent Schmittian denunciation of Bolshevism as a political enemy.

It is through Lukács, and through no other Western Marxist thinker, that Hegelian Marxism takes shape, as the affirmation of a substantial presumed continuity between the thinkers of dialectics as a comprehensive way of seeing the conflictual historicity of humanity, beyond the differences between Hegel's philosophical idealism and Marx's revolutionary mentality. When Lukács tries to justify theoretically the prolonging of this tradition under Lenin, and to legitimize it in practice, he also makes it possible for Stalin (and, with him, the reality of Russian socialism) to be presented as the almost natural heir to the revolutionary potential present in Hegelianism.

Schmitt brings out this aspect when he alludes to the movement of the 'Spirit of Hegel' from Prussia to Russia, his emigration to Moscow:

> There his dialectics retain their real strength in a new and concrete conception of the enemy, that of the class enemy; and the dialectical method goes through a significant change, as do other concepts such as legality and illegality, the state, and even the idea of compromising with the adversary as a [weapon] in this struggle.[34]

Against the unilateral and theoretically superficial reception of Hegelian philosophy by the Russian Dialectical Materialists,[35] Schmitt developed another strand of doctrinary continuity, which links Hegel with Dilthey and Freyer (we believe that Schmitt tacitly considered himself a part of this current, but that is another matter), and represents the alternative in the struggle for the legitimizing of political facts in the West in the last century.[36] It is precisely in the area of conflict over the interpretation of history that Schmitt establishes his greatest doctrinary opposition to Marxism and to its realization in the form of proletarian states. For Schmitt – we suggest – this construct, *der proletarische Staat*, is almost contradictory, since while the modern state (as it was theorized by European Public Law) is being established as a universal and impartial entity *vis-à-vis* the plurality of social elements, the proletariat is only a part within the whole, and cannot be the whole itself; in any case, even while the state privileges the political, any class position is, on the contrary, inevitably an economicist one.

A regime such as that in the Soviet Union, characterized by its dictatorial monopoly of the power in the carrying out of economic planning at any cost, can justify itself exclusively through a materialist philosophy of history. Although the structure of historical materialism is Hegelian, the ethics of German idealism have been replaced by the ideology of widespread electrification and communist ownership of the means of production. The confidence of Marxism that it has understood the course of history is the doctrinary guarantee of its political activism, without the West being able to set against it any equally forceful vision. For Schmitt there is no Western alternative to the inheritance of Marx, because the other current theories share with Marxism its basic economicist assumptions. Schmitt finds this common premiss condensed in the ideal of electrification, where the Leninist desire overlaps with the reality of the more developed Western countries.

Marx's theory is closely linked to industrialism as the characteristic ideology of the nineteenth century, and his vision of history is dependent on the belief that different periods are defined in their synchronic and diachronic specificity, taking as the main criterion the degree of productive development conditioned by technology: 'On a general level, Marxism seeks to think in economic terms, and as such he is stuck in the nineteenth century, which was essentially an economicist one.' Hence the absolute coherence of Soviet ideals to Marx's ideological foundations. The USSR is seen as a concrete realization of the utilitarian principle, which Schmitt formulates as *'cujus regio eius oeconomia'*.[37] The characters in this drama are linked by this materialist philosophy of history, notwithstanding the diversity of their origins or their ideological differences, which become mere doctrinary accessories. Capitalist or proletarian entrepreneurs, financiers and revolutionaries, positivist scientists and planning specialists, all belong to the same metaphysical family: that of economicism as opposed to the concept of the political. The Marxist struggles against the political, along with 'North American financiers, industrial technicians and anarchic-unionist revolutionaries', since they all ask that 'the non-objective control of the political over the objectivity of economic life be eliminated, there should only be technical-organiza-tional-sociological-economic duties, and not political problems'. Admin-istrationist thought reduces the state to a company, and eliminates 'the nucleus of the idea of politics, the inevitable moral decision'.[38]

This aspect of Marxist philosophy runs parallel to the politicity of the class struggle, and if, as we have seen, this links Marx to the great reactionaries, in their perception of the demand for dictatorship suitable for the time at which the urban masses break out, the economicist motive of technocracy sets Marx alongside the positivist and liberal thinkers, notwithstanding the differences that keep him apart from positivism and especially from liberalism. That is, he is prisoner to the idea of the necessity of a supra-personal, regular and objective process, which unfolds according to a tough legality, be these laws those of the dialectic movement or of market forces, both of which eliminate the specificity of history, *das Politische*.

To fight the Marxist monopoly of historical interpretation, Schmitt fights this metaphysics which, invoking the laws of the market or of the dialectic, eliminates the historical uniqueness and specificity of the political. The key to Schmitt's reception of Donoso Cortes (who, together with Hobbes, makes up his fundamental model of historical-political thought) lies precisely in this aspect of hermeneutic combativeness with an immediate practical application. It deals with the indication of a valid alternative to the hegemony imposed by Marxism on philosophers of history in the century of popular socialist revolutions: 'In actual fact, the Communist Manifesto is nothing but a part of the struggle towards an understanding of the events of 1848 and the situation in Europe at that time'.[39]

Marxism became strengthened through a continuous stream of revol-utionary events, in the context of the historical movement towards socialism. Within this picture of interpretative and political controversy, Schmitt makes reference to the scheme of the 'great parallelism' – that is, the possible analogy between the end of paganism and the birth of Christianity on the one hand, and the current ending of Christianity, now at the close of its historical life, and the beginning of a new atheist era, on the other. And although he recognizes that Marx rejects the logic of this parallelism, as it threatens to reduce the advent of communism to a mere spiritual rebirth,[40] none the less what Schmitt emphasizes is the ideological strength of a paradigm which – in its utopian vision as well as in that of historical materialism – has proved so successful in displac-ing the Christian view of history. The cultural significance of Schmitt's rediscovery of Donoso Cortes lies in its bringing into currency a model which, in so far as Donoso is conscious that he is standing at a juncture between Christianity and mass ideology, represents the real alternative to the ultimately technocratic model of Marx and his epigones.

Schmitt's dispute with Marx's legacy is a constant in his work, although it is more evident in some works than in others. His reconsideration of the sense of an aesthetic interpretation likewise bears witness to this. Upon reading *Hamlet*, Schmitt discusses the monopoly exerted by the Marxist vision of the history of art, in the space vacated by traditional (idealist) German aesthetics, as if making reference to the artist's social conditions and to the stage of economic development were the only way for history to broach the aesthetic dimension – that is, for what Schmitt calls the bursting of time into drama: 'For the Germans, there is nothing left but an eager choice between Dialectical Materialism and the appearances of aesthetic beauty.'[41]

Schmitt's last point of conflict with Marx and his theoretical and political heritage brings us back to the criterion of the political, according to which – as we have seen – Schmitt has already emphasized the significance of class struggle, in tension with – and almost in antithesis to – the technocratic vision of history to be found in Marx himself, as a metaphysical condition for the possibility of Marxist discourse. Now, however, in Schmitt's final verdict on Marxism, we find ourselves faced with the reversion of the political to total war. Taking the logic of the class struggle to its limit, its dynamic becomes one of war, through the transformation of political enmity into absolute enmity. This peculiar way of developing war is guerrilla or 'partisan' warfare, as Schmitt calls it.

Again, it is Hegelian philosophy which allows us to see the path of the spiritual and material movement that leads to the dialectical transformation of politics into war:

> After the war of liberation, Hegelian philosophy was dominant in Prussia, seeking a conciliation between revolution and tradition. It could have been considered conservative, and in fact that is just what it was. But this philosophy sought to conserve, among other things, a revolutionary element, and with the philosophy of history it provided a dangerous ideological weapon for the impending revolution, a weapon more dangerous than Rousseau's philosophy in the hands of the Jacobins. It is no secret that this historical-philosophical weapon fell into the hands of Karl Marx and Friedrich Engels; but these two German revolutionaries were thinkers rather than activists in the revolutionary struggle, and it was only thanks to a Russian professional revolutionary, Lenin, that Marxism as a doctrine acquired its universal historical significance.[42]

The text places before us the connecting theme of Schmitt's reading on the reversion of the political class struggle into this kind of absolute, non-political guerrilla warfare. Marx and Engels were aware of the birth of a new age as a step on the road to socialism, but it was the implementation of a revolutionary conflict in Russia that gave Marx's critique of the social order this absolutist, subversive dimension, which is characteristic of guerrilla warfare (with its irregularity, its politicity *qua* intense compromise with a revolutionary 'party', increased mobility, its attachment to the soil or tellurical nature) and is – we would insist – a particular realization of that absolute enmity which eliminates the political.[43]

In the last work published during his lifetime, dedicated to the *legal global revolution*, Schmitt recognizes that the young Marx had a conception of humanity which was that of German idealism (according to which the immortality of the species gives meaning to the life of the individual), but that this vision is nowhere to be found in Marxism. The very logic of this revolutionary proposal makes the partisan an actor in the dialectic between the human and the inhuman, in which the confrontation is so intense that it breaks the bounds of the political. When the political is torn to pieces by war-minded hyperpoliticization, and the absolute struggle of a revolutionary nature reaches a global level (according to the logic of partisan combat), the ruling criterion in human relations becomes the *'alles gilt'*, the free-for-all, the justification for any kind of attitude towards others. When the metaphysical premises are immanentist subjectivism and the renunciation of all transcendent regulation, it will always be possible to legitimize any kind of behaviour. So this total conflict develops according to the logic of extreme relativism – that is, it rests on the same metaphysics on which the result of liberal secularization is based: the doctrine of values. Schmitt thus proposes a conceptual and historical analogy between axiology (which is no more than the merchandising of ethics) and total war. Both the reduction of existential ethical dilemmas into questions of obviously interchangeable and negotiable values, and the absolute enmity which denies the adversary any political dignity, criminalizing it as representative of non-value and non-humanity, are the corollary of the neutralization of the political and its replacement by the intrinsically relativistic logic of commercial exchange. Totalitarianism and liberalism ('neoliberalism', as Schmitt would have said in the 1980s), the extreme version and the moderate version of a metaphysical and existential attitude which is substantially antipolitical, lead to a similar result: to depoliticization as a dehumanization of the other (who loses his identity and becomes no more than a common criminal). Even when their concrete historical realizations reveal differences and quite different nuances, the two historical constructs converge when they replace the *'amicus/hostes'* disjunctive with 'partner/criminal'.

This point of Schmittianism is worth emphasizing. Having eliminated the very category of political enmity, but not existential oppositions, the vision of the world currently prevalent concentrates on one extreme of the confrontation the features of humanity, rationality, truth, the reality of values, and so on, while condemning the opposite extreme as representative of non-humanity, the depths of wretchedness and immorality. It therefore justifies the free-for-all against this criminalized enemy, which is unworthy of respect in view of its in-, infra-, and antihumanity. As a result it is possible to justify any attitude which is taken by the spokesman for rational values towards a criminal, who has been excluded from the political, following the neutralization of the friend–enemy criterion by the logic of hypermoralism, economic exchange and guerrilla warfare.

Carried along by the logic of this metaphysics, Marxism encouraged the absolute conflictivity of global civil war, in a world predisposed to it by axiology and liberal pacifism. Thus the *Jus Publicum Europaeum* falls apart.[44]

IV

A brief summary of the central points of our reading of Schmitt as a reader of Marx brings us to the concluding section, which must needs concern itself with a current theoretical and practical contextualization of the questions raised.

Marx gives the proletarian class an identity dependent on an objective and impersonal process; but at the same time he grounds the proletariat's specificity (never mind the fact that this is more philosophical than sociological) in its revolutionary strength, which gives meaning to its historical action, irreducible to a mere link in a mechanical chain. The Marxist understanding of dialectics allows for a peculiar politicization of the proletarian class, a historical subject whose nature is essentially economistic. Dialectics are the heritage of Hegel, which Marx develops in a revolutionary way, so that history is not merely reducible to a strictly objective process, which can be adjusted by spontaneous and impersonal accords; it is, rather, a 'phenomenology' of class consciousness as a process of increasingly conflicting antitheses, until it reaches its most extreme and final confrontation, that of proletariat–bourgeoisie, in which a crucial role is performed by that same class consciousness which characterized the revolutionary subject. Resolution of such a conflict depends on the capacity of the proletariat and its party to replace, in whatever way it sees fit, a bourgeois dictatorship with a proletarian one.

As we understand it, the crux of Schmitt's interpretation is crystal-clear: since dictatorship is a political category, proletarian dictatorship marks the realm of the political in Marx's discourse.

Although we are not dealing with Lukács's influence on Schmitt, Lukács's thought is well known, and it allows us a further interpretative observation on Schmitt's reception of his writings. We believe that Schmitt highlights the figure of 'consciousness' in Marx as a politicizing element because he finds a deep affinity between it and the role played (in his own vision of the political) by 'will', a central category in decisionism, which should not be confused with the irrationalism, arbitrariness or aberrations which are often attributed to it. Our thesis is that the closeness between the role of the consciousness and that of will in the political illuminates an area in which Marx's thought (in tension within itself, we must stress) is in tune with Schmitt's. It is on the subject of antiliberalism.

The politicity of the category 'proletarian dictatorship' resides essentially in the noun, inasmuch as it refers to the exceptional response of a political will to an exceptional crisis, seeking thus to install a new order. The 'proletarian class', on the other hand, cannot separate itself from its theoretical debt to economicist metaphysics. In spite of this, however, it attains its political identity when it assumes (as a dictatorship) the same task that Schmitt describes in his conception of the political as the sovereign decision which creates order, faced with the extreme intensification of the existential conflict. Theorizing an extreme social opposition, a social conflict which breaks the barriers of regularity and predictability (that is, of capitalist economic order, according to Marx, and of bourgeois juridical-normative order, according to Schmitt) forms a piece of common ground between these two thinkers.

From this convergence, and notwithstanding their differences (which remain irreconcilable in so many key ways), both seem to strike a common chord in this kind of harsh realism in interpreting historical reality: in their intransigence when they are faced with naive resolutions of insoluble ideological conflicts through dialogue; in their capacity to avoid the trap of thinking without grasping the political turbulence, and seeking instead to navigate the calm waters of conceptual vacuity and/ or ambiguity, forgetting something that in fact neither Marx nor Schmitt ever forget: plurivocal and polemic political categories are always defined by those engaged in the struggle,[45] in the denunciation of the liberal distortion of homogeneity or democratic identity with which the consecration and crystallization of political and economic differences is hidden.

This leads them to reject the fundamental fiction of liberal contractualism, the utilitarian pact. It is Schmitt who sees in the decisionist origin of the republican and democratic order a complex net of decision and consent – that is, a political act which opens up to the labour dynamic and to its subject, the Marxist proletariat (in so far as it is able to leave behind – by virtue of its political free will – its economicist identity), some access to specifically human liberty, a superseding of *Homo faber* and *laborans* by *Homo politicus*, to use Hannah Arendt's terms.

Schmitt is fully aware that a mass society makes it necessary to rethink the question of democracy, in the face of what he considers the failure of liberal parliamentarism. The question arising in the 1920s concerned what kind of homogeneity would support the new democracy that should replace the liberal-democratic, usually parliamentary, state. He finds various models of collective identity inadequate: the invocation of a vague 'humanity', the reduction of citizenship to formal equality in the eyes of the law, the reference to the 'classist' economic substratum as the objective base of democratic homogeneity. In the context of the current collapse of traditional identities, it is not hard to find a note of contemporaneity in his proposal, given the richness of his thought (Schmitt has attained the resonance of a classic: one needs only to look at the number of publications on the subject over the last decade).

It is certainly true that there are moments in Schmitt's thought, where he describes the 'people' as a real alternative to abstract identities, which we find unsatisfactory and lacking in sensible reference, as it is not possible to sustain substantialist foundations of democratic identity. But Schmitt has also exposed the political as a mere 'form of ordering' in a desubstantialized, hypersecularized and relativistic world, as is currently the case – a fact from which any contemporary view should begin if it is not to be reduced to inane anachronism. Schmittian decisionism legitimizes the gesture of political will which has its source in itself, which justifies itself by virtue of the process of change it produces. In that sense, the way in which Schmitt understands and defends the political contributes to the claim of a new fiction which makes up democratic citizenship, which does not reduce it to a group of 'consumers' but which sees in it the direct protagonist of reform and varied articulations of an ideal of justice and equality, irreducible to confidence in the wisdom of the market acting without voluntaristic constraints.

In the face of conceptions of society as a system of fragments which neither have nor need any kind of global recomposition beyond the spontaneous harmony of exchange, nor any collective interest but that resulting from the search for personal gain in conformity with the laws of the market; the expansion of market relationships into all fields of social life; the related reduction of the notion of a 'crisis' to a mere dysfunction or provisional disorder which can be overcome by the objective dynamic of the economic system, the political in Schmitt gives meaning to the conflictivity inherent in human coexistence, which cannot be reconstituted in terms of automatic processes, but requires the intervention of the political will as a condition of the possibility of any kind of order, and therefore also of that democratic order, which seeks to develop itself as an overcoming of the crisis and of the injustices of the preceding system. The political is the logic of a profound transformation in the model of coexistence, because its existential horizon is conflict and because the metaphysics which sustain it are those of human liberty, a fiction that is perhaps still worth defending.

It remains a task of Judgement (of the *Urteilskraft* in Kantian, not necessarily Arendtian, terms) to mediate between the universal and the particular in politics – that is, the problem of proposing concrete and specific measures, following each particular case, through which the power of political decision is restrained within the boundaries separating democracy from despotism or, less dramatically, from authoritarian manifestations which history shows to be obsolete. A discourse such as the one we are attempting here can do no more than attempt a philosophical justification for what is a problem of practice. The open question, for legitimizing profound sociopolitical reforms, is to think it possible to articulate the degree of autonomy reached by personal consciousness with a new homogeneity or identity on which to base democratic demands, which are now renewing their tension with some liberal principles and neoliberal politics.

The Marxist class struggle, examined according to Schmitt's criterion of the political, does certainly seem unsustainable, as much because of its weakness as a theoretical category as because of the experiences it fostered, which historical memory – which makes up any political attitude – cannot but examine critically. The conflictivity inherent in Marx's proletariat cannot be proposed again, we believe – not only because of the conceptual breakdown of the substantialism which justified it, nor only because of the narrowness of the economicism which conditioned it, but also owing to the unacceptable effects arising from the historical realizing of the class struggle and proletarian dictatorship. Marx's idea of the revolutionary class submits it simultaneously to an economicist reductionism and to a hyperpoliticity which leads to the transformation of the political into war.

On the contrary, revitalization of the political, and the intellectual effort to propose an adequate categorization of contemporary democratization, find in Schmitt a source of suggestions at a high intellectual level, always bearing in mind the unacceptable corollaries which may emerge. The comparison of Marxian and Schmittian discourses attains its cultural significance in this hermeneutic and political context.

One first step in this direction should show that Schmitt analyses the significance of liberalism in depth, from the perspectives of both the philosophy of law and the history of ideas. We will not go into Schmitt's critique now; we simply note that it illuminates two aspects of the liberal manifesto: first, its unsurpassable limits, but also its unrestrainable contributions, an issue which leads directly to the question of human rights. A contemporary reading of Marxian and Schmittian positioning in the face of this subject cannot re-create the disdain shared by these two thinkers towards liberalism, despite the light their critiques throw on the antistate utilitarian character present in such an ideological framework, along with its ethical, progressive component.[46] A political positioning in the postmodern condition cannot, as a result, ignore either the inevitability of the ethical demands made by the notion of human rights or the limits of its liberal doctrinary support. This subject is particularly significant for Latin America but, we believe, our observation is not limited to that cultural context.

One further step, we contend, maintains that the current significance of liberalism should not be evaluated mainly on the basis of criteria of economic efficiency. The judgement on the neoliberal economy's ability or inability to resolve certain structural problems – not only in spite of but also by virtue of its success regarding other difficulties – depends not so much on a supposed objective consideration of determined data as on their political interpretation. This interpretation is grounded on a metaphysical position which, as Schmitt teaches, is always the key to any practical attitude. The question, then, should be raised primarily in the region of philosophical political principles, upon which the supposed objectivity of the domain of economics depends.

From this point of view, the third step we propose is a recognition that liberalism has already run the course of its conceptual productivity, and looks like a model which is closed in on itself and inadequate to give responses to social expectations which cannot be reduced to the defence of some (certainly indisputable) constitutional guarantees of personal liberty, and individual and collective security. The ideological productivity of liberalism cannot exceed the limit defined by its inability to reach the political. The specific significance of political decision-making is found at a level which is conceptually prior to that of the analytical philosophy of law, but none the less escapes the various versions of hypermorality and dialogic ethicity, all of which are rooted in the vagueness and generality of the concepts they propose as basic and universal ethical principles. The political conflictivity dismantles these systems, as they leave out of their schemes something which political thought believes, rather, to be an essential factor in human existence: radical crisis.

It is worth stressing that sustaining the theoretical draining of ethical-political liberalism does not in any way imply a renunciation of certain civilizing achievements, which such a current bore so noticeably. Less still does it entail a questioning of those civic liberties guaranteed by law. It simply consists in evaluating the lack of intellectual density in the liberal paradigm faced with the needs of the present. It is obvious that intensifying problems in the running of state institutions remain; hence the importance of maintaining some ideas of liberalism. But relative to the theoretical capability of neoliberalism or real *fin-de-siècle* liberalism to endorse political responses to current demands, their proposals either run directly contrary to a trend of significant changes, or – if they do tend towards novelty – they are equally trapped within utilitarian contractualism, whose paradigm is the actual horizontal movement of the exchange of equivalents (Marx continues to be an important reference point for the understanding of this logic).[47]

In contrast, the political brings about a unifying decision from top to bottom, corresponding to the wills which decide on its acceptance, in a two-way game of representation and participation. The political stimulates a mediation between transcendence and immanence, which is the alternative to the profit-through-exchange dynamics of the economic. The search for a novel kind of linking between what belongs to the private sphere of each human being, what is proper to society, and what constitutes the responsibility of the State, brings with it a rethinking of the notion of sovereignty, with a view to its responsible revitalization and with the assumption of a metaphysics which legitimizes the priority of the political over the economic, in a republican anticorporativistic sense.

A contemporary response to Schmitt motivated by and attentive to these elements sets in motion a hermeneutic mechanism which, in the light of earlier considerations, shows itself to be complex, certainly debatable, but – we would suggest – worth the attempt.

Translated by Daniel Hahn

Notes

1. Carl Schmitt, 'Kritik der Zeit', *Die Rheinlande* XXII, 1912, pp. 323–4, (324).

2. Carl Schmitt, *Politische Theologie. Vier Kapitel zur Lehre von der Souveranität*, Berlin: Duncker & Humblot, 1979 (reproduction of the 1934 edn), pp. 64–5; *Politische Romantik*, Munich–Leipzig: Duncker & Humblot, 1925 (second enlarged edn), pp. 95, 117–18. Marxism reduces all cultural manifestation to a 'reflection' of the economic connections, as can be seen in Sorel (ibid., pp. 56–7). Schmitt observes that in this Hegelian–Marxist system, real man is reduced to an instrument of a superior subjectivity who uses him. Seeing history as an opportunity for displaying such a secularized god is the Romantic leftover present in the ideas Schmitt is criticizing.

3. Carl Schmitt, *Die Diktatur. Von den Anfangen des modernen Souveranitätsgedankens bis zum proletarischen Klassenkampf*, Berlin: Duncker & Humblot, 1978 (fourth edn), p. 147n.

4. *Die Diktatur* pp. xv–xvi, 147–8n. See also Carl Schmitt 'Diktatur', in H. Sacher (ed.),

Staatslexikon im Auftrage der Görresgesellschaft, Freiburg: Herder, 1926, 1, cols. 1448–53, particularly 1452.

5. *Die Diktatur*, p. 205.

6. Ibid., pp. xv, xviii. Schmitt explains that from a juridical-normative point of view, dictatorship is a kind of normativeness belonging to the realm of the 'realization of law', and that this is where it gets its revolutionary strength (which essentially differentiates it from 'administrative' dictatorship). It is to that extent revolutionary, which serves to justify the use or implementation of liberal-democratic institutions as long as they help the advance towards socialism, and their elimination once the proletarian dictatorship has been put in place (ibid., pp. xiii–xiv, xviii).

7. *Die Diktatur* pp. 137–9, and especially 147–8n; *Politische Theologie*, pp. 76 ff.; *Der Begriff des Politischen. Text von 1932 mit einem Vorwort und drei Corollarien*, Berlin: Duncker & Humblot, 1963, p. 69.

8. *Die geistesgeschichtliche Lage des heutigen Parlamentarismus*, Berlin: Duncker & Humblot, 1979 (fifth edn – first edn pub 1923).

9. Ibid., pp. 64–6.

10. Ibid., p. 66.

11. Ibid.

12. Ibid., p. 68.

13. Ibid., pp. 68–9.

14. Ibid. Those who are able to get hold of the sense of history can propel and force forward those who are unaware; they are the 'vanguard of the spirit of the world' (p. 70). The rationality of the *totum* in an idealist system certainly threatens revolutionary activism, which can be legitimized only through the logic of exceptionality: 'However, those who, from the awareness of knowing their age well, demanded a political dictatorship in which, needless to say, they themselves would be the dictators, were themselves Hegelians' (p. 71). All these considerations of Schmitt's are strongly influenced by the Lukács of *History and Class Consciousness*, which is unfortunately an area we cannot go into here.

15. *Die geistesgeschichtliche Lage . . .*, p. 71.

16. Ibid.

17. Ibid., p. 72.

18. Ibid.

19. Ibid., pp. 72–3.

20. Ibid., p. 73.

21. Ibid., p. 74. With the increase in social struggles from 1848, European thought abandoned the triadic systems of the first half of the nineteenth century and began to search for clear and distinct polarities. Marx's polarity between the bourgeoisie and the proletariat:

> seeks to concentrate all the struggles of universal history into one final struggle against the ultimate enemy of humanity, so it unites all the world's bourgeoisies into a single bourgeoisie, and likewise all proletariats into a single proletariat, and thus manages to create a powerful friend–enemy grouping. The strength of its conviction in the nineteenth century came from its having followed its liberal-bourgeois adversary into the sphere of the economic, and had, so to speak, challenged it on its own territory and with its own weapons. (See *Der Begriff des Politischen*, p. 73)

On the political identity of the Marxist 'class', See ibid., p. 38.

22. Ibid., p. 75.

23. Ibid., p. 76.

24. Ibid., pp. 76–7.

25. Carl Schmitt, 'Hegel und Marx', in P. Tommissen (ed.), *Schmittiana IV*, Berlin: Duncker & Humblot, 1994, pp. 48–52 (49). This is a work Schmitt produced for a radio broadcast in 1931, which analyses Marx's text *Kritik der Hegelschen Staatsphilosophie*, published by D. Rjazanov in 1927 in the first MEGA volume. In *Marx–Engels Werke*, see vol. 1, Berlin: Dietz, 1972, pp. 201–333, entitled *Zur Kritik der Hegelschen Rechtsphilosophie. Kritik des Hegelschen Staatsrechts* (symbols of paragraph 261–313). Tommissen tells us that it is

not a complete text, and that the missing section may have been lost during the war or in Schmitt's move from Berlin; the text for the radio broadcast has also been lost (pp. 48, 49n.).

26. Schmitt, 'Hegel und Marx', pp. 49–50.

27. Ibid., p. 50.

28. Ibid.

29. Ibid., pp. 51–2.

30. Ibid., p. 52.

31. The fact that these statements have been overquoted does not diminish their power: 'Political opposition is the most intense and extreme kind of opposition, and every case of concrete opposition is more political the closer it gets to the extreme friend–enemy grouping': *Der Begriff des Politischen*, p. 30, p. 37. Nevertheless:

> religious, moral and other kinds of opposition can become intensified and turn into political oppositions, leading to the hostile friend–enemy grouping. But if it reaches the point of this hostile grouping, then the basic opposition is no longer purely religious, moral or economic but is now rather political. It is a question then of whether such a friend–enemy grouping is in fact possible, whether it is real, whichever human motives have been sufficiently strong as to provoke this.... Any religious, moral, economic or ethnic opposition, or indeed any other kind, becomes a political opposition when it is sufficiently forceful to group men effectively into friends and enemies. (ibid., pp. 36, 37)

32. Ibid., pp. 38, 39.

33. See *Der Begriff des Politischen*, p. 63 (where Schmitt mentions the 1923 *Geschichte und Klassenbewusstsein* and 1924 *Lenin*), and 'Hegel und Marx', p. 52, where no specific writings are mentioned but whose editor, P. Tommissen, refers to the essay 'Was ist orthodoxer Marxismus' of 1919, included in the book published four years later. We should recall that Schmitt removed any reference to Lukács and Marxism from the 1933 edition of *Der Begriff des Politischen*.

34. *Der Begriff des Politischen*, pp. 62–3.

35. See Schmitt's 'Observations' to his 'Die Lage der europäischen Rechtswissenschaft', a text from 1943–44, which did not come into circulation until 1950, when it was published independently, in *Verfassungsrechtliche Aufsätze aus den Jahren 1924–1954* (Berlin: Duncker & Humblot, 1958). On p. 428 Schmitt rejects the simplifying vision that 'made Savigny just a reactionary, and Hegel a precursor of Marx, Lenin and Stalin'.

36. Carl Schmitt, 'Die andere Hegel-Linie. Hans Freyer zum 70. Geburtstag', *Christ und Welt* X, 30, 25 July, 1957, p. 2.

37. Carl Schmitt, 'Das Zeitalter der Neutralisierungen und Entpolitisierungen' (1929), in *Der Begriff des Politischen*, p. 83.

38. *Politische Theologie*, p. 82. In the same way:

> The modern industrial businessman's image of the world resembles that of the industrial proletariat as one twin brother resembles another. They understand each other very well when they are engaged in a struggle together on behalf of economic thought. Socialism, to the extent that it has become the religion of the industrial proletariat of the large cities, sets against the macro-mechanism of the capitalist world a mythical antimechanism; the proletariat with a class consciousness is considered a legitimate dominator, because of its suitability, of this apparatus, and sees the private property of the capitalist businessman as an unsatisfactory residue of a technically backward age. The great businessman shares Lenin's ideal: 'a fully electrified world'. Strictly speaking, he is fighting for the correct method of implementing this. American financiers and Bolsheviks come together in the fight on behalf of economic thought, that is, in the fight against politicians and jurists. George Sorel is also a part of this group, and it is here, in economic thought, that we find one of the essential oppositions of our period, the opposition to the political idea proper to Catholicism. (*Romischer Katholizismus und politischer Form*, Theatiner, München, 1925 (second edn), p. 19–20).

In the *Dialogue on the New Space* we see the same figures, represented by the characters of Neumeyer the physicist-chemist, the North American MacFuture (the Bolshevist is missing); they are questioned by the old historian Altmann (Schmitt); see Carl Schmitt, *Gespräch über den Neuen Raum*, Berlin: Akademie V., 1994 (originally published in the volume in tribute to Barcia Trelles, from the Universidad Santiago de Compostela, 1958). See also 'La unidad del mundo', *Anales de la Universidad de Murcia*, 1950–51, pp. 343–355 (350).

39. Carl Schmitt, *Donoso Cortes in gesamteuropäischer Interpretation. Vier Aufsätze*, Cologne: Greven V., 1950; see p. 86: 'Today we accept the fact that the spiritual situation of 1848 is a current one, not only for a socialist and communist interpretation. It belongs to the darkening which took place during the second half of the nineteenth century in which non-socialist continuities, and with them significant names, had fallen into oblivion. The impact of new and tough experiences was necessary for creating awareness of this most profound continuity', the Catholic reading of events (p. 87).

40. Schmitt, *Donoso Cortes . . .*, pp. 96, 113.

41. Carl Schmitt, 'Was habe ich getan?', *Dietsland-Europa* II, 1957, 1, pp. 7–9; (9). Schmitt replies to those criticisms provoked by his *Hamlet oder Hekuba. Der Einbruch der Zeit in das Spiel*, Dusseldorf–Cologne: E. Diederichs V., 1956.

42. Carl Schmitt, 'Modern Theories on the Partisan', *Publicaciónes de la Cátedra General Palafox de Cultura Militar* III, 1962, pp. 327–59, (344–5). The same text can be found in *Theorie des Partisanen. Zwischenbemerkungen zum Begriff des Politischen*, Berlin: Duncker & Humblot, 1975 (second edn), p. 52. In order to complete the picture of Schmitt's views on the subject, see also Carl Schmitt and Joachim Schickel, 'Gesprach über den Partisanen', in J. Schickel (ed.), *Guerrilleros, Partisanen. Theorie und Praxis*, Munich: Hanser, 1970, pp. 9–29, 207, reissued in Schickel (ed.), *Gespräche mit Carl Schmitt*, Berlin: Merve, 1993, pp. 9–30, 88–91; and recently in Carl Schmitt, *Staat, Grossraum, Nomos. Arbeiten aus den Jahren 1916–1969*, ed. G. Maschke, Berlin: Duncker & Humblot, 1995, pp. 619–42.

43. 'Karl Marx and Friedrich Engels realized that revolutionary war could no longer be an old-style barricade war.' Above all, Engels saw that, thanks to universal suffrage, bourgeois society was capable of becoming communist:

> Lenin, on the other hand, insisted on the inevitability of violence and bloody revolutionary wars, civil as well as inter-state, and above all defended partisan war as a necessary stage in the totality of the revolutionary struggle. Lenin was the first to understand absolutely clearly that the partisan is an important player in national-civil and international war, and attempted to transform him into an effective tool for the central running of the Communist Party. (See 'Modern Theories . . .', p. 345; *Theorie des Partisanen*, p. 53.

In these pages we are not dealing with Schmitt's exposition of the post-Lenin development of the guerrilla.

44. The main text for this Schmittian motif, present from his very earliest works, is, we believe, Carl Schmitt, 'Die Tyrannei der Werte', in *Ebracher Studien: Sakularisation und Utopie. Ernst Forsthoff zum 65. Geburtstag*, Stuttgart-Berlin-Cologne-Mainz: Kohlhammer, 1967, pp. 37–62 (where the author adds a long introduction to his original 1959 text). On the relevance of the partisan war to this model of politicity, which is aggressive and not truly political, see *Theorie des Partisanen*, pp. 71–96. For his opinion on Marx associated with this subject, see Carl Schmitt, 'Die legale Weltrevolution. Politischer Mehrwert als Prämie auf juritsische Legalität und Superlegalität', *Der Staat* 17, 1978, pp. 321–39, (337 ff.).

45. The following *Marxist* observation by Schmitt, by way of example: In the context of a denunciation of the irrationalism into which economicist metaphysics sinks when it dissociates itself from the political, Schmitt criticizes the recourse to vaguely non-rationalist and vitalist authorities, as are found in Sorel, when he crosses Marx with Bergson to lay the foundations for his activism:

> Spiritualist explanations of material processes and materialist explanations of spiritual phenomena both seek to inquire into originary connections. Above all they establish an opposition between two spheres and, by means of a reduction in one or other, they transform this opposition into a nothing, a process which – if followed

through using the necessary methodology – ends in caricature. (*Politische Theologie*, p. 57)

46. We have chosen one of Schmitt's most significant texts on this matter, because it aligns itself expressly with Marx's position:

The bourgeoisie is the class of freedom of expression and of the press, and it attains these precise liberties not from some psychological or economic position, nor from some commercial thought or anything of the sort. It has long been known that the liberal idea of the right to liberty originated in North America. When, more recently, George Jellinek showed the North American origins of these liberties, his thesis barely surprised the Catholic philosophers of the state (as little, furthermore, as did Karl Marx, the author of the work on the Jewish question). For someone who, with some determination, is investigating the history of ideas, economic assumptions, freedom of trade, and free competition all just derive from a metaphysical nucleus. See *Politische Theologie*, p. 79.

47. Even though we have stuck to those works of Schmitt's which were published, it might be appropriate to turn to an observation in his personal journal, the entry from 31 May 1950, in which he recognizes Marx's understanding of the link in capitalism between physical object and social relation: Carl Schmitt, *Glossarium. Aufzeichnungen der Jahre 1947–51*, ed. E. Freiherr von Medem, Berlin: Duncker & Humblot, 1991, pp. 303–4. In these notes, Schmitt sees Marx as the precursor of the logic of annihilation, and even denies that he is a dialectical thinker; we should not omit the anti-Semitic observation that intellectuals of Jewish origin (such as Freud, Durkheim or Marx) used scientificity as a way of leaving behind the atavism of the ghetto (see pp. 189, 262). Unlike the case of those texts which have been analysed, the allusions to Marx in the journal are in the context of anti-Semitic statements, though without denying the recognition of the intellectual worth of the author of the *Judenfrage*. While we are on the subject, we will venture a hypothesis: although his privileged referent was Bruno Bauer, the metaphysical anti-Semitism of the young Marx also provided Schmitt with elements of his own theoretical positioning (see the quotation in the *Glossarium*, p. 61).

7

Carl Schmitt and Max Adler: The Irreconcilability of Politics and Democracy

Grigoris Ananiadis

One can always learn from Carl Schmitt. Schmitt's critique of liberalism – reviving as it does a tradition of political thought that goes back to Machiavelli and Hobbes – has a sobering effect inasmuch as it introduces conflict as a central category of politics. More to the point, his argument that every constitutional arrangement has a constitutive outside of power relations comes as a welcome reminder of the tragic dimension of politics which completely escapes the mainstream contractualism of the liberal tradition. It is this aspect of his thought that – starting with the Austro-Marxist Max Adler – has attracted so many theorists of the Left to his work.

Schmitt, however, is not the type of teacher who can be accepted on his own terms, unless, of course, one aspires to become counsellor to the Prince. This applies in particular to Schmitt's lesson on the political, that is, his conceptualization of conflict in terms of war. My main contention in this chapter is that despite his argument to the contrary, Schmitt's concept of the political is a derivative one that owes its polemical quality to the notion of sovereignty he is primarily concerned to defend. I hope to substantiate this claim by focusing on Schmitt's theory of dictatorship and democracy, which I compare to that of Adler. Such a comparison can serve not only to highlight my point, but also as a note of caution regarding the possible uses of Schmitt.

Adler and the distinction between social and political democracy

According to Adler, before the October Revolution the concept of democracy was more or less taken for granted by the socialist movement. Bolshevik theory and practice, however, had rendered it problematic, giving rise not only to heated political debate but also to great theoretical confusion. This confusion stemmed from a failure to differentiate between the procedural and the substantive meanings of the term, which Adler proposed to overcome by introducing the distinction between *social* and *political* democracy.[1] The former, in Adler's definition, is the ideal form of democracy, 'democracy according to its concept' (*SM*, p. 106), that is, self-determination of the people, or autonomy, and, as such, presupposes the substantive unity – indeed, the homogeneity – of the people. The designation 'political democracy', on the other hand, Adler reserves for 'all the other forms that come to be defined as democracy', inasmuch as they do not meet the homogeneity condition and, as a consequence, involve heteronomy or domination (*SM*, pp. 103–6; *PSD*, pp. 49–54; *DR*, pp. 132–8).

Contrary to the 'tragic *Weltillusion*' (*DR*, p. 134) of constitutional discourse and liberal theory, this condition can never be realized within the bounds of a class society:

> In the capitalist state, there is not as yet any popular unity, but only a population which represents neither an economic, nor a cultural, nor an ideological unity, but constitutes in each of those domains just a class fissure which is held together only through the compulsion of class domination. Even in the context of the most radical political equality, economic inequality gives rise to such oppositions that any sense of democracy, that is to say, of the formation of a unitary and general will, is necessarily vitiated. What remains is only the more or less *brutal* constitution of a majority. (*SM*, p. 108; emphasis added.)

Thus democracy in a class society can only be a political democracy, which is to say 'a democracy that *strictly speaking is no democracy* and must therefore be overcome if democracy is desired'. Social democracy, on the other hand, is 'a democracy that still does not exist but must be fought for' (*SM*, p. 106).

Adler's distinction between formal and substantive democracy prompted him to challenge the 'self-evidence' of the majority principle as the defining feature of democracy. To accept the majority principle as the essence of democracy, he argues, is tantamount to reducing democracy to a question of formal equality. At this level, however, it is impossible to come up with any rational ground justifying the subjection of a minority to the will of a majority. What is more, once democracy is situated in the context of its social determinations, it becomes obvious that as long as there remain irreducible 'vital interests' which divide the people, any resolution reached by the majority translates into a coercion of the minority or heteronomy, which in effect violates the principle of popular self-determination – the identity between rulers and ruled. Thus the majority principle reveals itself as a vehicle of power and domination, and the democracy it defines 'turns into its opposite' (DR, p. 138; SM, pp. 103–5). In the same spirit Adler further specifies that the protection of a minority in a *political* democracy is not a principle of democracy itself, 'but an exigency of opposition; its effectivity is entirely due to the power of the minority, that is to say, to the level of force [*Gewalt*], which – outside all forms of democracy – the minority in question is capable of amassing against the majority party' (SM, p. 167n.).

Adler concedes that resolutions by majority are indispensable for the functioning of democracy, but seeks to ground them on a solid foundation as opposed to the 'coarse numerical superiority of votes' (SM, p. 103). This foundation Adler identifies with the Rousseauian notion of the *volonté générale*, which he considers the true principle of democracy. In this respect Adler fully agrees with Rousseau's contention that voting is ideally a manifestation of the general will. In a classless or solidaristic society those in the minority would be bound by the resolutions of the majority not because they would be fewer in number or weaker, but because voting would have proven them to be in contradiction with the all-inclusive communal interest. In such a context, Adler specifies, majoritarian resolutions would no longer involve domination or heteronomy – that is to say, a violation of 'vital interests' – but mere differences of opinion as to how the common ends should be serviced. Thus, once the homogeneity condition is met – once, that is, 'the life interests and developmental possibilities of all are equally secured' – voting is divested of any antagonistic potential, and becomes 'a mere act of social administration' (SM, p. 104; PSD, 55–9, 67–85).

We can see from the above that Adler's choice of the adjectives 'political' and 'social' to designate the formal and substantive varieties of democracy respectively is far from accidental. For in his theoretical schema, true or homogeneous democracy is entirely apolitical or, rather, depoliticized. Adler himself is quite explicit about this when, for example, he qualifies political democracy as a 'conflict-concept' [*Kampfbegriff*] and social democracy as a 'peace-concept [*Friedensbegriff*] which issues out of the solidarity of the whole' (PSD, p. 51). This is the case because, in Adler's view, social democracy makes possible an ethical integration, a true shared *Sittlichkeit* that overcomes any divisive particularism.

The question, of course, arises: how does Adler theorize such an ethical integration; how – to put it in his own words – 'is this concept of the unity of the many in a single will possible?' Adler's solution to this Rousseauian puzzle is mediated by his own brand of Kantianism.[2]

> The common will is a sociological, not a psychological category; its sociological character consists precisely in the unification of the individual spheres, which goes beyond the individuals. It is only in this way that a comprehensive will, distinct from every individual will, is realized; and this process of unification is founded on the social *a priori* character of consciousness. (*SM*, pp. 109–10)

The problem with Adler's explication of social homogeneity consists in his underhand treatment of his transcendentalist assumptions regarding the 'consciousness in general' as sociological facts. Social democracy is in effect the reign of societalized consciousness at peace with itself, the reconciliation between *Sein* and *Sollen*; it is no less than the actualization of Kant's Kingdom of Ends. Needless to say, such a rationalist reformulation of the *volonté générale* takes Adler well beyond the '*misologie*' of Rousseau. For whereas the author of *The Social Contract* maintained an irreducible tension between *l'homme* and *le citoyen*, Adler's optimistic *Geschichtsphilosophie* announces the fusion of the two in the cultural figure of a *neuer Mensch* made possible by a classless society.

It is worth noting, in this respect, that Adler introduces a significant innovation *vis-à-vis* classical Marxism. In his view, social democracy or communism will not be without a coercive order. This *Zwangsordnung*, however, he considers to be essentially different from the 'order of domination' [*Herrschaftsordnung*], which he regards as coterminous with the (capitalist) state. Given its social and moral integration, the coercive order of a 'solidaristic society' is by definition autonomy. It denotes, in other words – in the deepest Rousseauian sense – the power of the community to force deviant members into freedom or the partaking of transcendental reason. That Adler would relegate hopeless cases to the *Krankenhaus* comes as no surprise (*PSD*, pp. 67–85).

Adler and Schmitt on dictatorship

It is in the light of this essentialist explication of the polysemy of democracy that Adler proceeds to consider the question of dictatorship. His aim is to retrieve the original sense of the Marxian formula of the dictatorship of the proletariat as a component of a substantive theory of democratization. To this effect, he sets out to dispel what he considers to be the main source of the confusion afflicting the post-October theoretical debates on the subject: the idea that dictatorship constitutes a negation of democracy.

This, according to Adler, would certainly be true of *social* democracy, inasmuch as the latter is by definition incompatible with any form of domination. It does not, however, apply in the case of *political* democracy, because 'even the most perfect parliamentarism does not preclude a privation of minority rights; on the contrary, inasmuch as a democracy is based on a majority decision, it legitimizes it' (*SM*, p. 166). Thus, to the extent that both involve majority domination, political democracy and dictatorship, far from being irreconcilable opposites, are 'merely two aspects of the same reality' (*SM*, p. 167). Strictly speaking, Adler argues, what does constitute a violation of political democracy is not dictatorship, but what he characterizes as 'terrorism' – the domination of a *minority* over the majority: 'In the case of terrorism the beneficiaries are just the few; in the case of dictatorship, the many; in short, terrorism coerces "aristocratically", whereas dictatorship coerces "democratically"' (*PSD*, p. 97). It is on this latter distinction that Adler bases his critique of Leninist vanguardism. The Bolshevik model – he says, rehearsing arguments similar to those of Rosa Luxemburg – should be rejected as a 'terroristic' rule of an elite over the proletariat and the people at large.

In his attempt to dissociate the concept of dictatorship from the connotation of plain arbitrary rule, Adler found a valuable aid in Carl Schmitt's *Die Diktatur* (1921).[3] In this important early work Schmitt reviewed the historical uses of the concept 'from the beginnings of the modern ideas of sovereignty to the proletarian class struggle'[4] with a view to clarifying its juridical content. Schmitt deemed such a conceptual elucidation imperative because, in his view, the diffusion of dictatorship as a vague political slogan was inversely proportionate to its systematic treatment by constitutional and state theory.

Schmitt arrives at the juridical specificity of dictatorship by contrasting it to despotism. Both involve the suspension of a legal order, but whereas despotism represents no more than arbitrary rule, dictatorship is, strictly speaking, norm-bound to carry out a clearly delimited political objective:

> The inner dialectic of the concept consists in the fact that the negated norm is precisely the one whose rule in the historico-political reality the dictatorship is supposed to secure. As a consequence, there can develop an opposition between the rule of the norm to be realized and the method of its realization. In terms of the philosophy of law the essence of dictatorship consists in the general possibility of a separation of the norms of law from the norms of the

realization of law [*Rechtsverwirklichung*]. A dictatorship which does not make itself dependent on the concrete realization of an outcome that corresponds to a normative idea – which, in other words, does not aim at making itself redundant – is an arbitrary despotism. (*D*, p. xvi)

Schmitt defines dictatorship generically as a state of exception [*Ausnahmezustand*] which can be differentiated according to the type of norm that is defended: 'What is to count as norm can be positively determined by an existing constitution or else by a political ideal' (*D*, p. xv). In any case, dictatorship involves 'not only action but also counteraction' against those who do not conform to the dictator's reference-norms (*D*, p. 136). The reason why the terms of Schmitt's definition remain at a high level of generality is because it is designed to cover two different types of dictatorship. The first is dictatorship in the classical sense of the term, which Schmitt, following Bodin, calls 'commissarial dictatorship'. This involves the suspension of a constitutional order, authorized by that very order, as an exceptional means for its protection from a particular threat. The second type of dictatorship, which makes its decisive historical appearance with the French Revolution, Schmitt designates as 'sovereign'. In this case, an established constitutional order is abolished as the first step towards the institution of a novel order. The fact, however, that a sovereign dictatorship places itself entirely outside the constitutional order it eliminates does not reduce it to a question of mere force that admits of no juridical categorization. For, Schmitt argues, such a dictatorship draws its legitimation from the people which, in its capacity of an originary *pouvoir constituant*, is constrained by no existing constitution (*D*, p. 137–9). The notion of sovereign dictatorship – joining, as it does, two concepts that monarchical political theory had kept well apart – embodies a peculiar dialectic which Schmitt will make much of. The dictator in this case owes his 'commission' to the constitutive power of the people; he is indeed the representative of the people's will, and in that sense his power is conditioned. The people, however, is as yet 'formless'; its will is indeterminate or 'unclear'. This is necessarily the case, for, had it been otherwise, the people's power would have been already *constituted* as opposed to *constituting*. Hence the need for the dictator's power to be absolute or sovereign: his brief to create a novel order or constitution is coterminous with 'forming' the people's will (*D*, pp. 137–46).

What attracted Adler to Schmitt's 'extremely lucid analysis' (*SM*, p. 165) is not difficult to gauge. In the first place, Schmitt's antiformalist treatment of the question of dictatorship introduced a political parameter eclipsed by positivist constitutional theory. By defining dictatorship as a '*concrete* exception', Schmitt draws attention to the fact that its 'content' depends on the existence of the opponent or enemy it is called to eliminate. The identity of such an enemy, however, is always concrete or factual, in the sense that it can never be specified juridically but only politically. Thus, in Schmitt's approach the constitutional order cannot be thought of independently of what lies 'outside' it. In Adler's case, as we have seen, this outside refers to the class division and antagonism occulted by formal constitutional equality.

Second, by defining dictatorship as a means to a determinate end, Schmitt in effect endorses Adler's position with regard to the intrinsic connection between political democracy and dictatorship: 'because its content is determined only by the interest in the result aimed for, . . . dictatorship cannot, generally speaking, be defined as the abolition of democracy' (D, p. xiv). Finally, Schmitt's explication of sovereign dictatorship as a juridical category that derives its legitimacy from a norm to be realized perfectly fits Adler's (broadly defined) dictatorship of the proletariat as a regime in transit towards social democracy. In the light of the Schmittian dialectic, the dictatorship of the proletariat can be construed as 'commissioned' to reconstitute the people's will on the basis of a homogeneous or classless society. It is instructive in this respect that Adler favoured the recuperation by the socialist movement of the popular democratic ideologies of the eighteenth- and nineteenth-century revolutions, stressing that the operative term should be 'the people' understood in the sense of *peuple*, not *Volk* (PSD, p. 127).

Adler was criticized at the time for his appropriation of Schmitt's concept of dictatorship on the grounds that the Marxist dictatorship of the proletariat is a 'sociological' concept, not a 'juridical' one.[5] Such a criticism involves a misreading of both Adler and Schmitt. Adler's attempt at a transcendentalist reconstruction of Marxism entailed a discursive conception of the social that did away with any rigid distinction between the 'economic', the 'ideological' or the 'juridical'.[6] The same, *ceteris paribus*, applies to Schmitt, whose juridical categories, notably that of the constitution, are always anchored in their substantive conditions of possibility.

Subsequent commentators on Adler's work tend to ignore the Schmitt connection, although it provides us with an invaluable interpretative key.[7] For it can be shown that what is involved here goes beyond an inconsequential conceptual loan or a merely external convergence. The concept of dictatorship occupies nodal points in the respective theories of Schmitt and Adler, where it performs symmetrically opposed polemical functions.

Adler's theory was developed in the context of the strategy debates of Austrian Social Democracy which culminated in the Linz Congress held in 1926. The draft programme bore the imprint of Otto Bauer who, considering socialism as an extension of democracy, rejected the Jacobin-ism practised by the Bolsheviks and insisted that socialism should develop into a hegemonic force on the ground of democracy. Bauer's strategy did not preclude the resort to emergency measures or defensive violence should the republican order be threatened by fascist counter-revolution. Such measures, he clarified, would admittedly constitute a dictatorship, but in a sense entirely opposite to the Leninist conception: it would be 'not a dictatorship *against* democracy, but a dictatorship *of* democracy'.[8] Bauer's principal contender at the Congress was Adler, who tried to alert the delegates against committing the Party to any particular state form, such as that of the parliamentary republic. The programmatic objective of the Party, he argued, should be the establish-ment of the dictatorship of the proletariat in the generic sense of the term, its particular form being a question not of principle but of tactical exigencies.

Schmitt's treatise was a similarly strategic intervention, styled as a defence of the Weimar Constitution.[9] The object of his critique was the way the liberal *Rechtsstaat* was prepared to deal with an internal emer-gency which, in continental constitutionalism, came under the rubric of the state of siege [*Belagerungszustand*]. In Schmitt's view, what had distinguished the 'political state of siege' from dictatorship proper since the early nineteenth century was its gradual subjection to legal regula-tion: 'The decisive point is that the empowerment to any course of action necessitated by the situation at hand is replaced by a series of circum-scribed powers, whereby it is not the Constitution in its entirety that is suspended, but only a number of particular constitutional liberties whose suspension, moreover, is not absolute, as it is subject to the specification of the permissible incursions' (D, p. 199). For Schmitt, what this mis-guided attempt to positively regulate the exception boiled down to was that the opponents of the constitutional order were still treated as *citizens* to be respected rather than as *enemies* to be eliminated.

According to Schmitt, the liberal state could afford to be liberal in its handling of emergencies as long as it was confronted with instances of disorder that affected public security but did not threaten the 'homoge-neity' of the state itself. This was the historical achievement of absolutist monarchy, which created 'sovereignty in the modern sense of state unity' by destroying feudal and corporate powers, and directly contraposing the state to the isolated – and therefore weak – individual. The growth, however, 'once more of powerful associations within the state' – of the organized proletariat in particular – jeopardized the very state unity that both liberal theory and practice took for granted. It was precisely this novel state of affairs, Schmitt concluded, that revealed the inadequacy – indeed, the 'fictitious' character – of the legally constrained state of siege and necessitated the restoration of dictatorship as a legitimate state tool (*D*, p. 201–5).

The decisionist political philosophy so characteristic of Schmitt's work can be seen as evolving in a number of steps out of his conceptualization of dictatorship in terms of an extension of 'the juridical [*das Staatsrechtliche*] into the political' (*D*, p. xv). The insights Schmitt gained in his *Diktatur* by focusing exclusively on the state of exception [*Ausnahmezustand*] are generalized in his *Politische Theologie*,[10] published a year later, into a fully fledged neo-Hobbesian theory of sovereignty. Here, what was previously a theory of the exception turns into its dialectical opposite, that is, into a theory of normality; for in Schmitt's reasoning, the exceptional is constitutive of the normal. The validity of any legal order, he argues, presupposes a 'homogeneous medium', a 'factual normality', as its immanent condition of possibility. Hence: 'sovereign is he who definitively decides on whether such a normal state truly obtains' (*PT*, p. 20). Accordingly, sovereignty comes into its own, revealing, so to speak, its full majesty at a time of crisis. Then, the sovereign's 'decision frees itself from any normative constraint and becomes in the true sense absolute' (*PT*, p. 19). In other words, whether or not the sovereign is constrained by law depends on the concrete situation at hand; and it is none other than the sovereign himself who, like Humpty Dumpty, gets to 'name' this situation as exceptional or normal. The implication of Schmitt's position is clear: the concept of sovereignty is, in effect, interchangeable with the concept of dictatorship. The sovereign and the dictator are one all along.

Schmitt seems to be aware that such a concept of sovereignty accurately depicts the condition of absolutist monarchy, which 'made the decision in the struggle of conflicting interests and coalitions and thereby founded the unity of the state' (*PT*, p. 62); and that, as a consequence, it is ill-suited for the condition of democracy: 'The unity that a people represents does not have this decisionist character' (ibid.). What was left here as an open problem, however, was resolved the following year by theoretical fiat. Indeed, the theory of democracy that Schmitt developed in *The Crisis of Parliamentary Democracy* (1923)[11] can be seen as an attempt on his part to endow the 'unity that a people represents' with a 'decisionist character'. Such a move requires, of course, the fashioning of 'the people' as a unitary subject. It is to this end that Schmitt, too, just like Adler before him, turns to the citizen of Geneva: 'The general will as Rousseau constructs it is in truth homogeneity. That is a really consequential democracy. . . . The democratic identity of governed and governing arises from that' (*CPD*, p. 14).

This identity, however, cannot be understood as a formal regulative idea; it can exist only *in concreto*. Hence the second requirement of

Schmitt's democracy: 'the elimination or eradication of heterogeneity' (*CPD*, p. 9). Thus democracy is always on the move and what, strictly speaking, characterizes it is not homogeneity but *homogenization*, with all that this might entail, be it Turkey's 'radical expulsion of the Greeks' or Australia's immigration policy to admit only 'the right type of settler'. Schmitt's democracy emerges in this light as decisionist in the most literal sense of involving an act of radical severance: a *de-cisio* or *Ent-scheidung*.

It is on this basis that Schmitt construes the incompatibility between liberalism and democracy. Liberalism's formal 'equality of persons as persons' (*CPD*, p. 13) stands in the way of democratic equality, which can only be substantive and concrete, that is, political. Universal and equal suffrage can, in his view, make sense only within *such* a 'circle of equals and does not exceed this equality' (*CPD*, p. 10), which is to restate that equality presupposes a factual homogeneity. It is precisely in the admixture of these antithetical principles that Schmitt locates the crisis of modern mass democracy. In his own words: 'As democracy, modern mass democracy attempts to realize an identity of governed and governing, and thus it confronts parliaments as an inconceivable and outmoded institution. If democratic identity is taken seriously, then in an emergency, no other constitutional institution can withstand the sole criterion of the people's will, *however it is expressed*' (*CPD*, p. 15; emphasis added). We have thus come full circle, as Schmitt's dispossessed sovereign/dictator is provided with a new abode from which to resume his eternal vigil against heterogeneity or the exception.

Adler's identification of political democracy with dictatorship corresponds to Schmitt's reasoning through and through. Let us consider how Adler restates his position in an excerpt from an intervention in the debate on the draft programme of the Linz Congress:

> It is true that political democracy seemingly functions as a voting mechanism on all issues which do not jeopardize the vital interests of the ruling strata; however, as soon as this happens it manifests its essential character as a *coercive mechanism*. Then – precisely by virtue of democracy – the majority abolishes the constitution, promulgates the state of exception and military law, appoints extra-ordinary commissars, . . . in short, it shows that *the essence* of political democracy is the dictatorship of one class over the other by virtue of the majority decision. And this is true of every democratic majority, i.e. not only of the bourgeois majority, which has existed until now, but also of the proletarian one, which, hopefully, will soon be realized.'[12]

We can clearly see that Adler, like Schmitt, defines the norm of democracy in terms of its exception. Democracy *is* dictatorship according to its 'inherent tendency', as he puts it elsewhere – a fact that is obvious whenever it comes down to a 'critical decision' [*Kampfentscheidung*] (*PSD*, p. 91). Adler is indeed explicit about the decisionist character of democracy. Thus he argues that the restriction of political equality or the disenfrachisement of a minority constitutes no curtailment of democracy, because '[o]ne cannot stipulate in advance what democracy should decide' (*PSD*, p. 106). It is in this paradigmatically Schmittian sense, that Adler designates dictatorship as an essential determination of the concept of (political) democracy.

The homology between Adler and Schmitt, however, does not end here; it runs through the entire structure of their respective arguments. For what also emerges quite clearly from the above is that the former's concept of class domination is isomorphic to the latter's concept of sovereignty. The concrete subjects which get to 'decide' at a time of crisis are, for Adler, always class subjects – or, to be more precise, majorities formed around a class core. Accordingly, the key issue becomes the replacement of the bourgeois – so to speak – sovereign by the proletarian one. This is precisely why Adler, too, is compelled to think of politics in terms of war: 'If in this way democracy and dictatorship constitute no opposites, this is certainly also the case with the concepts of democracy and civil war.'[13]

In his *Concept of the Political*, Schmitt lamented that the spirit of Hegel had evacuated Berlin, wandering instead 'to Moscow via Karl Marx and Lenin'.[14] It is this spirit, or the old Prussian conception of the state, that Schmitt attempted to revive, adapting it to the novel conditions of mass democracy. Schmitt's diagnosis captures a key feature of Marxism that characterized both its revolutionary and its social-democratic wings: the fact that it implicitly thought of politics in terms of the classical concept of sovereignty. Marxist theorists, from Bernstein and Kautsky through Adler and Laski to Lenin and Gramsci, differed in the answers they provided to a shared question: how would the working class 'become' the state? This is the type of question that Schmitt could fully appreciate; hence his fascination with Marxism.

Incidentally, it is worth noting that one Marxist thinker who stands out in this respect is Otto Bauer. Commenting on the German scene, the Austrian leader observed acutely that the collapse of the Prussian state did not automatically entail the loosening of its ideological grip. This is where Bauer located the major shortcoming of the divided German socialist movement. What – in his view – none of its component parts realized was that the ideology of 'Prussianism' could not possibly be rooted out 'as long as we simply translate the Prussian idea of the state in a different language, or adorn it with different colours, or put it in the service of a different class'.[15]

Schmitt's aporia: the politics of depoliticization

A widely held view places Schmitt's conception of the political at the epicentre of his theory, assuming that it is his affirmation of the ever-present possibility of war and the corresponding friend–enemy grouping that accounts for the specific contour of his reflections on the state and the constitution. Such an interpretation is admittedly plausible,[16] – at the cost, however, of underplaying Schmitt's chosen *rechtsphilosophisch* perspective and turning him into a mere 'sociologist' of *Machtpolitik*. A closer look at his juridico-philosophical assumptions can show, I believe, that, on the contrary, it is Schmitt's conception of the state and sovereignty that compels him to adopt such a reductive conception of politics. This is not an indifferent chicken-and-egg type of question, for – as we shall see below – determining which of the two terms is the accented one is crucial in order to highlight the aporetic character of Schmitt's theoretical endeavour.

It will be necessary in this respect to reconsider Schmitt's distinction between law [*Recht*] and the realization of law [*Rechtsverwirklichung*] which, as we have already seen, underlies his treatment of dictatorship. This distinction was first developed by Schmitt in an earlier work – *Der Wert des Staates* (1914)[17] – where he had set out 'to comprehend the state in its rationality [*Vernunftigkeit*]' (*WS*, p. 7). It is significant for our purposes that the first chapter of this book is devoted to a discussion of the relation between law and power, with a view to rejecting all attempts at a mere 'factual grounding' of law. Law, Schmitt argues, cannot be considered 'as an outcome of a particular division of social forces', nor can 'its concept be obtained for the philosophy of law by means of an explanation of historical events' (*WS*, p. 15). On those grounds, any power whatsoever would be justified, leaving the key question regarding the *rightness* or *justice* of law unanswered: in effect, as he puts it, it would be impossible to come up with any essential difference between the power of the murderer over his victim and the power of the state over the murderer. Equally unacceptable for Schmitt would be to establish the normative specificity of the state on the approval of its subjects, since in this instance, too, the source of the state's authority would be the merely factual superiority of a majority. Schmitt's own understanding of the majority principle is, incidentally, quite revealing about his subsequent appropriation of the Rousseauian 'general will': 'Contrariwise, as far as legal theory is concerned, a reference to the majority opinion, to the opinion of decent and fair-minded people, signifies a reference to something which is not valid of its own authority but indicates a content that corresponds to what should be [*was sein sollen*]' (*WS*, p. 18).

Schmitt's position is based on the affirmation of an insurmountable dualism, a proper chasm, between *Sein* and *Sollen*, normativity and facticity, ideality and reality, the abstract and the concrete. It is because of the radical antithesis of these two worlds that 'the sphere of *Recht* [justice/ law] is not exhausted in the area of the positive, actually valid, law'. When Schmitt speaks of the unbridgeable 'opposition between *Recht* and fact', he locates positive law definitively on the side of the factual. This is why *Recht* proper, or ideal law, should be regarded as an absolute end in itself, never a means to the accomplishment of other ends; power, in other words, should be totally excluded from the definition of *Recht*. Without this distinction, without acknowledging the independence and self-containment of the realm of *Recht*, there would, in Schmitt's view, be no room for 'juridical argumentation in its rightness [*Richtigkeit*]', only for 'the will of the state in its concrete factuality'(WS, p. 22).

This is the precise theoretical configuration in which Schmitt draws the distinction between law and the realization of law. Enclosed as it is in the sphere of absolute ideality, *Recht* possesses no will and entertains no ends of its own; as a consequence, it is inconceivable that it can in any way shape or affect factual reality by itself. The task of ordering reality according to the norms of *Recht*, which is precisely what *Rechtsver-wirklichung* stands for, can be undertaken only by an agent rooted in that very reality. This agent is, of course, the state, which is thus determined as the bearer of law, as a proper *Rechtssubjekt* 'in the most eminent sense of this word' (WS, pp. 38, 53):

> Out of the contraposition of the norm and the real empirical world follows the positing of the state as the crossing point of the one world into the other. In it as a construct, law as a pure thought turns into law as a wordly phenomenon. The state is accordingly the legal institution [*Rechtsgebilde*] whose meaning consists exclusively in the task to realize law.... (WS, p. 52)

In this passage, yet another distinction is implied, which merits our attention. This is the contrast between the ideal state, the state according to its concept or the state of jurisprudence, on the one hand, and the empirical, this-worldly state, on the other. Philosophically speaking, Schmitt argues, the concept of the state is a normative construct and, as such, it cannot be obtained by means of an induction from the empirical institutions that are designated by that name: 'The constitutive elements of the state concept can only be inferred from *Recht* ... in the coupling of the state with *Recht* [*Rechtsstaat*], the state is entirely enveloped and determined by *Recht*, it is fully elevated in the sphere of *Recht*' (WS, p. 50). We note that the original dualism of ideal and real is reproduced in the case of the very agent that is supposed to bridge them. As we shall see, this duplication is crucial for appraising Schmitt's decisionism.

The realization of *Recht* by the state is never, according to Schmitt, a straightforward and one-sided process of application, however gradual. Involving as it does *forming* reality in accordance with the precepts of abstract law, it is in turn affected by the contours of that reality: 'In the very moment that [the state] makes use of the empirical world in order to fashion something determinate out of it, the latter reacts upon it with the power that the given qualities of the servant exercise over the master or the material over the artist' (*WS*, p. 74). It is precisely in order to curb the resistance of its designated 'material' that the state is compelled to deploy 'empirical means' – force being the most important among them – which are otherwise foreign to the pure concept of law. It is on this basis that Schmitt reaffirms the dualism which, in his view, characterizes positive law throughout: 'Within every state ruling [*Satzung*] the idea of the law must be separated from the moments that bear on its realization and implementation' (*WS*, p. 76).

From this analysis Schmitt draws two far-reaching conclusions. In the first place, if ideal law is to inform the moulding of reality, it needs to be concretized or positivized in the sense of being provided with a determinate content that is commensurate with the exigencies of implementation and enforcement. Such a concretization, Schmitt stresses, can be achieved only by 'an act of sovereign decision'. Schmitt's qualification of this decision as sovereign is essential to his argument; it is therefore important to be clear about it. The point Schmitt is making is only secondarily that the decision in question issues from a supreme empirical authority. Primarily, the law-positing or instituting decision is 'sovereign' in relation to the supra-positive *Recht* – in relation, that is, to the very idea it is called upon to realize: 'Between every *concretum* and every *abstractum* there lies an insurmountable chasm, which no gradual bridging can fill. It is therefore necessary to bring to the fore in every positive law this moment of its being clearly decided upon, whereby coming up with any positive determination whatsoever is more important than specifying which its concrete content should be' (*WS*, p. 79). Under the pressure of reality, the concretizing decision is thus fully autonomized from *Recht* – or, to put it differently, *normalization* takes precedence over the *norm*. The profoundly theological character of this formulation is highlighted by Schmitt himself: 'The abandonment of timeless justice and the admission of a moment of indifference to content are the consequences of the *enanthropesis* of *Recht*, the sacrifice that must be made by reason of the dealings entered into with the powers of the real phenomenal world' (*WS*, p. 80).

Schmitt's ancillary conclusion pertains to the sovereign. The concretizing decision requires 'a similarly determinate and infallible instance' capable of actualizing it. It comes as no surprise that Schmitt models his sovereign on the figure of the Pope. In his view, the Catholic doctrine of papal infallibility constitutes 'an example of typical purity'. It is because 'the failings-prone humans must above all know and, indeed, do want to know where they stand' that the Pope is invested with the authority to decide irrevocably on all equivocal questions. 'Whoever grants the premiss of a divine law and of an ecclesiastical legal order', Schmitt writes, stressing the parallelism to his own schema, 'cannot help but admire this conclusion' (WS, p. 81). This parallelism, however – Schmitt is quick to add – in no way entails elevating the Pope into a judge of the sovereign's decisions. Indeed, Schmitt categorically refuses to admit any extra instance of authority entitled to 'protect the law' from possible abuses of state power. He dismisses out of hand the mistrust towards temporal power that led many philosophers, from Plato to Fichte, to advocate such a *potestas indirecta*, as undermining the notion of absolute sovereignty: 'No law can implement itself by itself; only humans can be appointed as guardians of the laws and whoever fails to trust the guardians will accomplish nothing by providing the laws with new guardians' (WS p. 83).

Thus, having set out – *contra* 'Thrasymachus' – to ground power on *Recht*, Schmitt ends up with a sheer affirmation of factual power: 'what the state ordains in a determinate form is right, and this only because it is precisely the state that ordains it' (WS pp. 46–7). This circle, however, is only apparently vicious. For along the way Schmitt has armed power with something it previously lacked: a claim to *Richtigkeit* or absoluteness. It is this claim to absoluteness that gives Schmitt's decisionism its cutting edge. We are now better placed to identify the object of Schmitt's critique which, strictly speaking, is not arbitrary power as such but its *'faktisch'* as opposed to a properly *'rechtsphilosophisch'* mode of conceptualization. Next to the sovereign we may thus discern the elusive figure of the *Rechtsphilosoph* himself. By providing power with a 'sense' or 'meaning' it is otherwise deemed to lack, the latter emerges as a true 'guardian' not of law from the abuse of power, but of power from the restriction of law.

Schmitt declares his analysis to be non-political in the sense of focusing on first principles and rising above partisan political ends: 'the political question regarding the *technique* of the concrete implementation [does not] belong in the philosophy of law' (WS, p. 83; emphasis added). It is clear, however, that in *Der Wert des Staates* he is already as political as he will ever be. In our view, the key to Schmitt's political position is precisely that he constructs his sovereign as a *pre-* or, rather, *meta-political* instance. (The sovereign is absolute primarily by virtue of his partaking in a transcendent realm of pre-established harmony.) If, however, this is the case – if, that is, politics do not bear on the construction of the sovereign – politics in turn cannot but be a *technical* matter of concretization or normalization.

It is understandable now why Schmitt deems dictatorship to be 'the critical concept of *Rechtsverwirklichung*' (D, p. xx). By suspending a legal order with a view to restoring the conditions of its applicability, dictatorship is the exceptional instance that reveals the unbridgeable chasm between abstract and concrete which legal positivism obscures by taking normality for granted. Yet, paradoxically, there is nothing 'exceptional' about it. However paradigmatic it might be in relation to positive law, dictatorship emerges in essence as just a *technical* moment of the overarching process of the realization of ideal law. This is precisely why Schmitt cannot and need not come up with any clear conceptual distinction between the dictator and the sovereign. The restoration of a 'homogeneous medium' for law, no less than its creation, is but an instance of the 'indifference' to norm inherent in any process of normalization. Hence a case can be made for either according to the 'matter' at hand.

We are now also in a position to appreciate better a significant change in relation to his original problematic that Schmitt introduces in *Die Diktatur*. This has to do with the chasm between abstract and concrete, which is henceforward relocated in a different theoretical context. In *Das Wert des Staates* Schmitt had designated the abstract as 'natural law without naturalism' [*Naturrecht ohne Naturalismus*]: (WS, p. 76). Although he chooses to leave this notion unclarified, we can safely assume that it refers to a transcendent (divine) justice which, contrary to the aspirations of Enlightenment thought, is rationally indeterminable. As we have seen, this is the justice the sovereign is called upon to concretize. The overall schema remains intact in *Die Diktatur*, the difference being that it is now the indeterminate popular or national will in its capacity of *pouvoir constituant* that functions as the abstract term to be realized. This is how Schmitt comments on the dialectic embodied in the concept of sovereign dictatorship:

> This logic, as developed by Sieyès, already anticipates the fully antirationalist philosophy of the nineteenth century, for which God, understood as something 'objectively indeterminate' [*ein 'objektiv Unklares'*], is the centre of the world, in the same way that the formless but always form-producing *pouvoir constituant* is the centre of state life. (D, pp. 143–4)

Schmitt's entire *Verfassungslehre*, published seven years later, can be unpacked out of these few lines.

In *Der Wert des Staates* Schmitt offered an explication of what he was subsequently to characterize as the 'classical' concept of the state, for which politics [*Politik*] was identical with policing [*Polizei*].[18] The crisis that resulted from the military collapse of the Wilhelmine *Obrigeitsstaat* and the eruption of mass politics rendered such an identification of politics with the state questionable, prompting Schmitt to adopt a different stance towards the 'political question'. The new approach was, of course, systematically spelled out in his *Concept of the Political*, but was in effect already implicit in *Die Diktatur* where, as we have seen, Schmitt inaugurated his exploration of the sliding of the juridical into the political. Schmitt's own retrospective account of this shift is worth quoting at some length:

> The classical profile of the state was shattered once its monopoly on politics was untenable. New, different subjects of political struggle asserted themselves, with or without the state, with or without state postures. This furnished theoretical thinking with a new ground for reflection. The distinction was now made between 'politics' [*Politik*] and the 'political' [*das 'Politische'*]. The question regarding the new bearers and the new subjects of the political became the key question of the entire problem-complex designated as 'political' [*des gesamten Problemkomplexes 'Politisch'*]. Here lies the origin and inception of the attempt to come to terms with the many new subjects of the political which became active in the political reality of state or non-state politics and brought about novel friend–enemy groupings.[19]

This is the logic underlying the famous opening line of *The Concept of the Political* ('The concept of the state presupposes the concept of the political'). The new departure, however, is compromised from the outset by the fact that Schmitt can think of the 'new subjects of the political' only in terms of his category of sovereignty. For Schmitt, a political subject is always a fully constituted, empirically given subject – a proper in-dividual – capable of a critical decision:

> In any event, that grouping is always political which orients itself toward this most extreme possibility. This grouping is therefore always the decisive human grouping, the political entity [*Einheit*]. If such an entity exists at all, it is always the decisive entity, and it is sovereign in the sense that the decision about the critical situation, even if it is the exception, must always necessarily reside there. (*CP*, p. 38.)

The crux of the matter lies in this metonymic sliding from 'grouping' through 'political entity' or unity to sovereignty. It is precisely this investment of the political subject with the attributes of sovereignty that accounts for Schmitt's reductive conception of the political in terms of war. The friend–enemy dichotomy that defines the political, in his schema, acquires its polemical necessity only on the assumption of a purified instance of absolute decision and command. In effect, the only *truly* political entities this schema allows for are the state and the potential antistate. This way, however, Schmitt remains trapped in the very 'unsatisfactory circle' (*CP*, p. 20) that he was supposedly trying to think his way out of: the concept of the state presupposes the concept of the political, yet the latter, premised as it is on a substantive notion of sovereignty, is *ab initio* fully 'statized'. In other words, Schmitt failed to change register; he never wrested the *political* from the classical notion of *Politik*.

Schmitt's project is directed against the depoliticizations and neutralizations he deems characteristic of liberal modernity.[20] Paradoxically, however, depoliticization – both as a condition and as an active engagement – emerges as the obverse side of his own affirmation of the political. Having the right of a *'hostis* declaration', it is always the sovereign who, affirming his supra-political status, decides which issue is political with a view precisely to cancelling or 'neutralizing' it, in the sense of rendering it ineffective – by force if necessary.[21] Transposed to the ground of democracy, this logic entails that it is the sovereign who decides no less a matter than who the people is (elimination of the internal enemy = homogenization) so as to apply his rule of law (homogenization = normalization). The end of politics is thus inscribed in Schmitt's theory as much as it is in Marxism – with a crucial difference: whereas in the case of Marxism it is associated with a utopian passage from the administration of men to the administration of things, in the case of Schmitt it defines the dystopia of the administration of men *as if they were things*.

In Schmitt's work we find a spectacular display of the aporia of modern politics: that is, of the fact that the state's condition of possibility – the political – is also the condition of its impossibility.[22] This inherent tension is disclosed by Schmitt, only to be denied. Despite his claims to philosophical or scientific detachment, this is a *political* denial effected by preserving sovereignty as an instance impervious to politics. It should be remembered, however, that Schmitt's sovereign is the guardian of the idea all along and that, conversely, it is the idea that confers on sovereignty its value. This is how Schmitt restates his position in *Römischer Katholizismus und politische Form* (1923), whose interwar English translation bore the apt – if misleading – title *The Necessity of Politics*:

> ... so long as even a ghost of an idea lingers on, the conception is admitted that, prior to the acknowledged reality of material things, something else was already in existence, something transcendental, and that recognition necessarily implies an authority from above.[23]

Thus it is ultimately the 'idea' that Schmitt wants to keep uncontaminated, beyond the reach of politics. The idea – be it transcendent justice or an equally transcendent popular will – cannot be the object of conflicting appropriations or negotiation, it can only be revealed or represented – hence the *necessity* of an authority from above. The proletariat, incidentally, is Schmitt's enemy because, though organized, it is none the less 'formless';[24] because, in other words, it fails to conform to Schmitt's idea.

Schmitt's central contention that there is an unbridgeable chasm between any norm or idea and its realization, that – involving, as it does, an element of untameable contingency – no juridical decision is directly deducible from its normative premises, is unobjectionable. Only a hard-nosed rationalist would reject an insight shared by innovative anti-essentialist thought, from Wittgenstein to Derrida. The problem arises when Schmitt designates this moment of undecidability as a 'moment of indifference'. The undecidable, in Derrida's words, 'is the experience of that which, though heterogeneous, foreign to the order of the calculable and the rule, is obliged – it is of obligation that we must speak – to give itself up to the impossible decision, *while taking account of law and rules'*.[25] The undecidable, in other words, is a tension-ridden experience through-out, and in that sense there is nothing indifferent about it. It is the irreducibility of this tension that opens up the possibility of critique and allows Derrida to maintain that '[j]ustice remains, is yet to come, *à venir . . .'*.[26] But this is precisely what Schmitt cannot tolerate, since it implies the priority of the political over the sovereign, ruling out his ultimate equation of justice with order and calculability, irrespectively of their content.

Notes

Unless otherwise indicated, all translations cited in the text are mine.

1. Adler developed his positions in a number of publications: Max Adler, 'Demokratie und Rätesystem' (1919), in N. Leser and A. Pfabigan (eds), *Max Adler. Ausgewälte Schriften*, Vienna: Österreichischer Bundesverlag, 1981 – hereafter *DR*; Adler, *La concezione dello Stato nel Marxismo* (1922), Bari: De Donato, 1979 – hereafter *SM*; Adler, *Politische oder Soziale Demokratie*, Berlin: E. Laub'sche Verlag, 1926 – hereafter *PSD*. On the development of Adler's political views, see A. Pfabigan, *Max Adler. Eine Politische Biographie*, Frankfurt: Campus, 1982.

2. Adler sums up his attempt at a transcendentalist reconstruction of Marxism in his *Das Rätsel der Gesellschaft*, Vienna: Saturn, 1936.

3. Carl Schmitt, *Die Diktatur*, Berlin: Duncker & Humblot, 1978 – hereafter *D*.

4. This is how Schmitt's treatise is subtitled.

5. See A. Gurland, *Marxismus und Diktatur*, Leipzig: Leipziger Buchdruckerei, 1930.

6. This is how Adler puts it: '*In no way* do economy and ideology constitute two distinct spheres, they are on the contrary two distinct instances of one and the same *spiritual* complex. And the economic instance itself emerges from the outset in quite determinate "ideological" forms, above all in determinate legal forms'. Max Adler, *Kant und der Marxismus* (1925), reprint, Aalen, 1975, p. 179.

7. An exception in this respect is R. Racinaro, who discusses the Adler/Schmitt connection, albeit in a positive light, his main concern being to interpret Adler in a Gramscian key, contra Kelsen. R. Racinaro, 'Introduction' to H. Kelsen, *Socialismo e Stato*, Bari: De Donato, 1978.

8. Otto Bauer, *Bolschewismus oder Sozialdemokratie?* (1920), in *Otto Bauer Werkausgabe*, vol. 2, Vienna: Europaverlag, 1975, p. 350.

9. For an assessment of Schmitt's politics that goes against the interpretation of his American apologists, see V. Neumann, *Der Staat im Bürgerkrieg. Kontinuität und Wandlung des Staatsbegriffs in der politischen Theorie Carl Schmitts*, Frankfurt: Campus, 1980; J. A. Estévez Araujo, *La crisi del estado de derecho liberal. Schmitt en Weimar*, Barcelona: Ariel, 1989.

10. Carl Schmitt, *Politische Theologie*, Berlin: Duncker & Humblot, 1985 – hereafter *PT*.

11. Carl Schmitt, *The Crisis of Parliamentary Democracy*, translated and introduced by Ellen Kennedy, Cambridge, MA: MIT Press, 1985 – hereafter *CPD*.

12. Max Adler, 'Zur Diskussion der neuen Parteiprogramms' (1926), in Leser and Pfabigan (eds), *Max Adler*, p. 220.

13. Ibid.

14. Carl Schmitt, *The Concept of the Political* (1927), translated and introduced by G. Schwab, New Brunswick: Rutgers University Press, 1976 – hereafter *CP*.

15. Bauer, *Bolschewismus oder Sozialdemokratie?*, p. 356.

16. For an excellent systematization of this view, see E.W. Böckenforde, 'Der Schlüssel zum staatsrechtlichen Werk Carl Schmitts', in H. Quaritsch (ed.), *Compositio Oppositorum. Über Carl Schmitt*, Berlin: Duncker & Humblot, 1988.

17. Carl Schmitt, *Der Wert des Staates und der Bedeutung des Einzelnen*, Tübingen: J. C. B. Mohr Verlag, 1914 – hereafter *WS*. This early work by Schmitt has not generally received the attention it merits, despite the fact that Schmitt himself underlines its significance as a prelude to his *Diktatur* (*D*, p. xx). Exceptional in this regard are the works of H. Hofmann (*Legitimität gegen Legalität*, Neuwied and Berlin: Luchterhand, 1964); M. Nicoletti ('Die Ursprünge von Carl Schmitts "Politische Theologie"', in Quaritsch (ed.), *Compositio Oppositorum*); and O. Beaud ('Carl Schmitt ou le juriste engagé', Preface to Schmitt's *Théorie de la Constitution*, Paris: Presses Universitaires de France, 1993).

18. Carl Schmitt, 'Introduction' to the 1963 edition of the *Begriff des Politischen*, Berlin: Duncker & Humblot, p. 10.

19. Carl Schmitt, 'Introduction' to the 1971 Italian edition of the *Concept of the Political*, in H. Quaritsch (ed.), *Compositio Oppositorum*, p. 271.

20. See Carl Schmitt, 'Das Zeitalter der Neutralisierungen und Entpolitisierungen', in *Der Begriff des Politischen*.

21. This would be 'neutrality' in the positive sense, as defined by Schmitt in 'Corollarium' 1. II. 3, in *Der Begriff des Politischen*, p. 101.

22. The reference works for the exploration of this aporia are Ernesto Laclau and Chantal Mouffe, *Hegemony and Socialist Strategy*, London: Verso 1985; and Laclau, *New Reflections on the Revolution of Our Time*, London: Verso, 1990.

23. Carl Schmitt, *The Necessity of Politics: An Essay on the Representative Idea in the Church and Modern Europe*, trans. E. M. Codd, with an Introduction by Christopher Dawson, Essays in Order no. 5, Catholic Book-a-Month Club, London: Sheed & Ward, 1931, p. 70.

24. Ibid., p. 71.

25. Jacques Derrida, 'Force of Law: The "Mystical Foundation of Authority"', in D. Cornell *et al.* (eds), *Deconstruction and the Possibility of Justice*, London: Routledge 1992, p. 24; emphasis added.

26. Ibid. p. 27. It should be stressed that this 'justice to come' cannot but be politically indeterminate. Schmitt's handling of the matter attests to the fact that affirming the undecidable is not necessarily associated with any particular ethical or political position. Such an affirmation is as compatible with an injunction to be open to 'the other' (Derrida) as with a call to his/her elimination (Schmitt). For a general discussion of this issue see Ernesto Laclau, '"The Time is out of Joint"', in *Emancipation(s)*, London: Verso, 1996.

8

Carl Schmitt versus Max Weber: Juridical Rationality and Economic Rationality

Catherine Colliot-Thélène

Besides Hobbes and Hegel, Max Weber is one of the greatest of the interlocutors Carl Schmitt chose for himself; he is a writer from whom Schmitt borrowed arguments and concepts essential to his own thought, and at the same time – and this is the thesis I mean to defend in this chapter – he is one of the privileged poles of Schmitt's polemic. This is certainly not immediately obvious. For though there are numerous references to Weber throughout Schmitt's writings, they appear in very varied contexts and are, upon first reading, more eulogistic than critical.

Carl Schmitt sees Weber as 'one of the main representatives of the most productive kind of secularization'.[1] In support of his own critique of certain aspects of the modern liberal state, he mentions Weber's characterizing of the kind of legitimacy suitable for legal or rational domination. He celebrates his radical subjectivist interpretation of the foundation of values as a lucid recognition of the conflictual dynamic to which all philosophy of values necessarily tends. There are so many elements which lead us to wonder: was Jürgen Habermas correct in stating some time ago that Carl Schmitt was a legitimate disciple of Weber?[2] For anyone who is seeking in Weberian sociology the conceptual tools for a better understanding of the present, it is undoubtedly a question worth asking.

Diverse as they are at first glance, Schmitt's references to Max Weber can none the less be easily divided into three distinct sections.

The first – the best known because it is the most explicit – concerns the positivization of law. In the Weberian concept of the legal and/or rational state, Carl Schmitt discovered the recognition of what was, in his view, a phenomenon characteristic of modern ways of exercising political power: the transformation of law into a simple formal procedure, into a technical mechanism modifiable to suit the short-term needs or varying interests of those in power. In *Legalität und Legitimität*[3] – a work which appeared in 1932, devoted to an analysis of internal contradictions within the Weimar constitution – Schmitt referred to Weber when he was illustrating the consequences of the collapse of original axiological justifications of the judicial state (which, for reasons which we will not go into here, he preferred to call *Gesetzgebungsstaat*, the 'legislating state'). The legislating state escapes the question of the founding of sovereign authority by confusing legality and legitimacy, a confusion which the Weberian formulas cited by Schmitt in such contexts attempt to clarify: 'This legality can count as legitimacy'; or 'The kind of legitimacy most current today is a belief in legality'.[4]

Carl Schmitt's proposal is slightly ambiguous here. There is no doubt that he is doing justice to Max Weber in his observations that the loss in the credibility of metajuridical axiomatics, at the head of which is that of the natural law of contractual theories, would pervert the particular rationalism under whose auspices the institutions of the modern state had first appeared. The pages of *Legalität und Legitimität* to which we are referring are, in a way, a gloss on the considerations developed by Max Weber in the last two sections of his *Sociology of Law*:[5] when a simple respect for formal procedure is sufficient to confer the status of a legitimate act on any command, whatever the circumstances, a barely disguised pragmatism is definitively substituted for the normative originary rationalism. However, this summarizing of Weber's analyses does not mean that Schmitt, like Weber, was prepared to confirm this process as irreversible.

Various passages from the *Glossarium*[6] bear witness to the fact that the relationship between legality and legitimacy in the modern state, like the subject of the positivization of law, continued to concern Schmitt until the 1950s. A draft of a letter to Madame Winckelman, dated 20 December 1947, refers to recent reflections on the Weberian concept of legitimacy, and comments that the real problem – since 1848 – is not the antithesis between positive law and natural law but, rather, the relationship between legality and legitimacy. A month later, on 19 January 1948, this time writing to Winckelman himself – who was the chief editor of Weber's work at the time, and was preparing a piece on the notions of legality and legitimacy[7] – Schmitt set himself against the normativist stance taken by Winckelman, with objections which also drew on the legality/legitimacy opposition on the one hand, and on the hackneyed question of natural law on the other.

But it is in a passage dated 16 March 1948 that the thread of these often allusive remarks emerges most clearly. Schmitt quotes a passage from the end of *Sociology of Law*, under the heading 'The Diagnostic and Prognostic of Max Weber':

> In any case, as a result of technical and economic development, it is inevitable that current law is destined to be conceived more and more as a rational technical mechanism which can be modified at any time for functional purposes, and is lacking in any kind of sacred content. This destiny may be hidden by the suppleness of belief of the current law, but it cannot be truly avoided.

And he adds this brief but revealing comment: 'Before 1933, who else but I spoke of this situation, and who else tried to do something about it?'[8]

The second line of confrontation between Carl Schmitt and Max Weber concerns the latter's stance in the debate on the foundation of values. This can be found in the postscript to the second *Political Theology* (1969), in a passage where, writing about Hans Blumenberg, Schmitt observes that Blumenberg also speaks the language of the philosophy of values: 'whose logic implies not only re-evaluations but also devaluations, denials of value, and even affirmations of the meaninglessness of values, and which can therefore be used to convey extreme aggressiveness' (*TP*, p. 171). He does not linger on this point, implicitly referring back to an earlier work, known as *Die Tyrannei der Werte*.[9] This is an extraordinary text, notably because it is the only one in which Schmitt explicitly uses analyses of Heidegger (a passage from 'The Word of Nietzsche: God is Dead') to support his own proposal. Here Heidegger characterizes the philosophy of values as a 'positivist ersatz of metaphysics', a desperate attempt to bring contemporary nihilism to an end and rescue the possibility of ethics.

In this context Schmitt mentions Weber (whom Heidegger does not mention), attributing to him the thinking through (to its final consequences) of the subjectivist logic of the philosophy of values – that is to say, he was not afraid to put forward ideas which others kept back: that the validity of values hinges entirely on their position and recognition by the individual, so that the antagonism between values and incompatible systems of values is the inevitable correlative of an ethics which speaks the language of values. In other words, Weber's description, at the end of the conference on 'The Vocation of Knowing', of the struggle between the old gods emerging from their tombs, is a faithful dramatic expression of the conflictual dynamic inherent in the philosophy of values and in the condition of modern man. Again the relationship between Schmitt and Weber comes across ambiguously; because although Schmitt singles Weber out from all those others who represent the philosophy of values (most notably Max Scheler and Nicolaï Hartmann) for carrying the logic inherent in the language of values to its conclusion, he is not prepared to recognize the ordinary regime in this near-permanent conflictuality, nor a normal kind of functioning of the political.

The third facet of Schmitt's confrontation with Weber is less well known. None the less, it seems to me to be crucial, in that it allows us definitively to resolve those ambiguous aspects of the two areas described above. Let us say in advance that in spite of Schmitt's unquestionable admiration for Weber, in spite of the tributes he frequently pays him, he does nevertheless consider him above all as an adversary. It is in his writings of the early 1920s, *Political Theology* (1922) and *Römischer Katholizismus und politische Form* ('Roman Catholicism and Political Form'),[10] that this emerges most clearly. These are the texts on which we will base the crux of our argument, supplementing them only occasionally with later texts.

The first three chapters of *Political Theology*, devoted to the sociology of the concept of sovereignty in relation to political theology, were published in a volume in tribute to Max Weber, edited by Melchior Palyi and published in Munich in 1923. The complete work also includes a fourth chapter ('The Philosophy of the State in the Counter-revolution [De Maistre, Bonald, Donoso Cortés]'). It is certainly by no means compulsory for every contribution to a tribute collection to deal with the writer to whom the book is dedicated; nevertheless, the conditions of publication of the first three chapters did result in certain commentators seeing the relation which Schmitt establishes between Catholicism and politics as a parallel to Max Weber's subject matter in *The Protestant Ethic and the Spirit of Catholicism*. As Jean-Louis Schlegel observes in his introduction to the French translation of this work: 'Perhaps it would not be an exaggeration to say that what Max Weber wanted to demonstrate in the economic field with Protestantism, Schmitt tries to do in the political sphere with Catholicism' (*TP* p. v).

Weber, in other words, proposed a theological (Protestant) genesis of modernity, with its gravitational centre in the capitalist economy, in opposition to which Schmitt would base his Catholic theological genesis on the political sphere. This interpretation seems unacceptable, since it ignores the very different natures of the types of mediation, established by each of these two writers, between religion and the formation of modern Western society. More specifically, G.L. Ulmen states that *Römischer Katholizismus und politische Form* was written 'as a response to the *Protestant Ethic and the Spirit of Capitalism*' – certainly not as a critique of Weber's thesis, but, rather, as a meta-critical counter-model, a Catholic counterbalance to Weber's work.[11]

The proposition, when it is properly understood, is actually more precise than this. In *Römischer Katholizismus* it is possible to see a meta-critical counter-model to *The Protestant Ethic*, provided one makes it clear that, compared to the sociologist, the jurist-theologian has a very different way of questioning the relations between religion and modernity. Although Weber did attach importance to religious determinations of lifestyle in the formation process of modern Western society, in effect there is nothing in his work which can in any way take the place of political theology.[12]

So in what sense can *Römischer Katholizismus* be interpreted as the Catholic's response to the Protestant? One thing is certain: in these two works, *Political Theology* (1922) and *Römischer Katholizismus* (1923), there are undeniable signs that Schmitt is thinking about Weber, and this thinking has an extremely polemical tone about it. In effect it is, of course, a response – the response of a Catholic to a Protestant, but also the response of a political thinker to an economist. If these lines of division are clear, the way in which they are connected is less so. On what level is Schmitt's opposition to Weber established in these texts? Or, further: what is the status of his discourse? Is he speaking as a Catholic theologian, or at least as a believer in the denomination of Catholicism, and does he claim for Catholicism the source of the structures of the modern world which Weber had attributed to Calvinist and Puritan Protestantism? Or is his point of view, rather, determined by a political perspective, which Weber neglected in favour of the economy?

Schmitt himself states that his intention, in this case, is to act as sociologist. 'The Sociology of the Concept of Sovereignty and Political Theology' was the title under which three chapters in the work dedicated to Max Weber were published. In the third chapter, Schmitt explains his views on the aims of this sociology and, in so doing, sets it up against Weberian sociology. The analogies he develops between juridical and theological concepts are meant to be a contribution to the sociology of concepts, specifically to the concept of sovereignty. Such a step is definitely alien to a Marxist point of view, which wants to see only 'reflections', 'appearances' and 'disguises' (*TP*, p. 52) in the categories of law. But nor is it a matter of a 'spiritualist' history, which would explain the political and social transformations through a history of ideas: it was there that the step taken by the theoreticians of counter-revolution was to be found; Schmitt separates himself from this move in characterizing the nature of his own discourse.

So it is neither materialist history nor spiritualist history. What of its relationship with Weberian sociology, which Schmitt knows – though without lingering on it for too long – is neither one nor the other? He characterizes this sociology quite precisely, saying that it is used to draw out the elective affinities between certain ideas and the social milieux whose conditions favour the inacceptance or production (*TP*, p. 53). On the sociology of law, for example, Weber brings the differentiation of juridical fields, as well as the development of certain modes of debate, back to the formation of a body of specialized jurists. Schmitt argues that such a step cannot count as the sociology of a juridical concept. In his eyes, Weberian sociology is ultimately psychology,[13] or psychosociology, of which certain kinds of literary criticism are also capable (Schmitt cites Sainte-Beuve).

What is it that makes up this sociology of concepts (so far from psychosociology) which, Schmitt states with wonderful confidence, 'is alone in being able to expect scientific results' (*TP*, p. 54)? Its aim, he tells us, is to bring about the ultimate structure of a system of juridical concepts, and to compare this conceptual structure with the general conceptual organization which dominates the intellectual sphere at a given time in a given society. It is evident that this step is conditioned by a fundamental presupposition: that all of society, at any point in its history, possesses a kind of spiritual homogeneity; that the mode of thinking ['*die gesamte Bewusstseinslage*'][14] is articulated according to certain dominant 'logical' schemes which determine what is evident in each particular realm of thinking. A sociology of juridical concepts which draws these concepts back to the general conceptual universe of the time at which they were developed brings us to matters of the theological and the metaphysical. For 'the metaphysical image of the world created by a certain period has the same structure as whatever it is that is seen as being evident in matters of political organization'.

The identity of a period is of a metaphysical nature: unbeknown to the thinkers and the actors in the social and political game, it regulates the division between what is accepted as obvious and what is unacceptable or incomprehensible. It is this hypothesis which governs the odd conception of history which Schmitt reveals in 'The Age of Neutralizations', in which the reader is invited to follow the shifting of the centre of gravity of the European spirit[15] over the last four centuries: from theology to metaphysics; from metaphysics to humanitarian morality and economics. Here metaphysics is the name used to refer to a given intellectual universe, that of the seventeenth century. It could also be said, however, that theology, metaphysics, humanitarian morality and economics are simply different 'metaphysical images' of the world, taking the term 'metaphysics' in the broader sense in which it is understood in *Political Theology*.

Looking back on the 1922 text, the later *Political Theology II* (1969) offers a rather different interpretation of it. It was simply a matter of locating the structural analogies between certain key concepts in 'the systematic thought of the two historically most developed and most structured organisms in "western rationalism", namely the Catholic *Church*, with all its juridical rationalism, and the state of the *Jus Publicum Europaeum* – still assumed to be Christian in Thomas Hobbes's system' (*TP*, p. 168); it also involved identifying a 'proximity between systematic structures, which, in terms of the theory and practice of law, is set between theological concepts and juridical ones.' (*TP*, p. 160, n.1). In the mind of the author, these structural similarities have nothing contingent about them: modern political thought would, without his knowledge, acknowledge the debt linking it to medieval theology. 'Secularization' is the term Schmitt uses to refer to this process of conceptual transfer from the theological to the political, and by way of example he willingly offers the concept of charismatic legitimacy which Weber borrows from the Protestant canonist Rudolf Sohm,[16] and which, in Schmitt's words, would be 'the most striking example, for theologians and non-theologians alike, of the most recent political theology' (*TP*, p. 126). In the charismatic legitimacy of Paul the Apostle – *triskaidekatos*, the thirteenth in relation to the Twelve – 'can be found the theological origin of everything which Max Weber, as a sociologist, could say on the subject of charisma' (*TP*, p. 118).

At first sight, this proposal seems more defined and more precise than that of the sociology of concepts drafted in the 1922 text. This modesty, however, is only apparent. For if, in this retrospective interpretation of the first *Political Theology*, it is no longer a question of reaching the 'metaphysical image a period makes of the world', it is not merely a question of restoring analogies and pointing out conceptual genealogies either. Reduced to these tasks, political theology would resemble the history of ideas, and would be of interest only to the curiosity of the erudite. Schmitt had different aims, as we shall see: in bringing to light the theological sources of modern political thought, even in the work of its least religious representatives (Weber), he intends to free juridical theory from the influence exerted upon it by 'naturalist' scientificity, which today is hegemonic. In his covert debate with Weber, the idea of science and the definition of the rational are stakes which are at least as fundamental as the opposition between Catholicism and Protestantism.

To Schmitt's eyes, Weber's work looks like an emblematic expression of the hegemony attained by 'economicist thought' and its most extreme form, technicist thought, in the nineteenth and twentieth centuries.[17] Schmitt attributes the pertinence of his diagnostic to Weber: the evolution of institutions in collective life after over a century moves towards an increasing subjection of human lives to objectivized orders (bureaucratic politics and economics) – that is, to what the German language of the time termed *Sachlichkeit*.[18] Weber, along with others (most notably

Ernst Troeltsch and Rathenau), recognized a process in the growing power of technique which led to 'the domination of the mind by that from which the mind is absent'[19] – that is, by the mechanistic logic of systems of action. Weber, a lucid analyst of the conditions of modern Western culture, was in a sense also a critic of this culture: like all the great sociologists of his time, he saw a threat to civilization itself in the direction of the course being taken by European civilization.[20] As a result, Schmitt uses everything in Weber which serves his own critique of the time: a time which enshrines the domination of mechanistic objective powers over human life, to the detriment of any political idea. 'The kind of economic and technical thought which is dominant today is incapable of conceiving of a political idea,' he observes in *Political Theology* (TP, p. 73), supporting this remark with a reference to Weber's definition of the state as a large firm. In other words, Weber grasped the reality of the state well in an age dominated by economic-technical thought, and this state is characterized precisely by its not being interpreted politically. Likewise, the supplanting of all true legitimacy in the definition of the legal state's specific mode of domination, and also the affirmation of the victory of a conception which is strictly instrumental of law, faithfully translate a tendency inherent in the civilization of our time.

The convergences between Schmitt and Weber, however, end with this diagnostic. Weber's attempt to reintroduce elements of charismatic legitimation into the functioning of modern institutions, through the 'plebiscite democracy of leaders', aimed at preventing, as far as possible, the progress of the functionalization of the political. But for him this 'possible' was extremely limited. Objectivization of structures in collective life, capitalist economics and the bureaucratization of the political seemed to him to be too narrowly bound to the specific rationality of the modern West for it to be possible to envisage a real alternative. This is a very different approach from Schmitt's, which, while recognizing the factual pertinence of Weber's analyses, none the less refuses to see an unavoidable destiny in the evolution they observe. This alleged destiny is, to Schmitt, no more than a sign of the inability of 'economic and technical thought' to grasp a political idea: an inability which is shared with 'American financiers, industrial technicians, Marxist socialists and anarchic-unionist revolutionaries', all united to 'eliminate the non-objective [*unsachlich*] domination of the political over the objectivity [*Sachlichkeit*] of economic life' (TP, p. 73). There is some complicity between American financiers and Russian Bolsheviks, he observes likewise in *Römischer Katholizismus*, 'in the struggle for economic thought, that is, in the struggle against the politicians and the jurists' (RK, p. 22).

It is in this context, where the conflict between faculties (politics and law against economic theory) symbolizes the dilemma with which Western civilization must now come to terms, that the praise of Catholicism expressed in the 1923 pamphlet begins to make sense. It is easy to be mistaken about the meaning of this praise. For today's French reader (and certainly for a German one) the significance and implications of Catholicism, as professed by Carl Schmitt, are extremely hard to grasp. Compared to the naturally secular nature of the work of most twentieth-century political theorists and jurists (a secularism independent of their own personal beliefs), Schmitt's juridical-political theology is rather odd, a mixture of genres which break the elementary rules governing scientific thought. As we shall see, this infraction is deliberate, and the anachronism which people are in such a hurry to criticize is there by the author's design, and indeed is presumed by him. Nevertheless, the idea that to show the existence of Catholic premises in Schmittian thought is sufficient to make this thought invalid is a simplistic one. *Römischer Katholizismus und politische Form*, perhaps the only work where Schmitt speaks absolutely frankly, is not a declaration of allegiance to a Catholic faith involving a generally accepted dogma. Rather the contrary is the case: Schmitt takes up a position against what he sees as the dominant tendencies of Catholicism at the time: he criticizes its bending towards a private and subjective belief (a process of evolution borne out by the complicity existing between Catholic and Romantic milieux since the nineteenth century); he maintains that Catholicism loses its way when it seeks only to bring another soul to a world condemned to the grip of economic and technical rationality, or to be (in his own words) 'an institute for cleanliness, aimed at tending the sufferings from the competitive struggle, a Sunday escape or a summer break for those living in the large towns' (*RK*, p. 20). Catholicism in general cannot be invoked as the reason behind Schmitt's political logic, in so far as his political theology is quite as much an intervention in theology as it is an intervention in juridical and political theory. In both these cases, his position goes directly against tendencies prevalent in his time. Schmitt seeks support for his political theory in a fundamentally heterodox conception of Catholicism. His theological thinking about politics is developed via a *political* interpretation of Catholicism, one that is quite alien to twentieth-century theologians.

Interpreted appropriately – that is, condensed to its political essence – Catholicism embodies a kind of rationality which our contemporaries are unable to understand, since it is obsessed by the objectivist rationalism which dominates modern thought to the exclusion of all else:

> The Church has its own particular rationalism. This rationalism is to be found in its institutional nature, and it is essentially juridical. (*RK*, p. 23)

Catholicism is political, in the most distinguished sense of the word, different from that absolute economic objectivity which monopolizes the attention of contemporary theorists. (*RK*, p. 27.)

Economic thought, however, is not the only issue here. If economicism benefits from such evidence, it is because it maintains close complicity with the concept of truth dominating scientific ventures since the establishment of the natural sciences in the seventeenth century. *Römischer Katholizismus* indicates the link between the mechanistic conception of nature imposed in the seventeenth century, and the 'objectivization' [*Versachlichung*], 'already frequently depicted', of all social relations (*RK*, p. 28). Ten years later, in 'The Age of Neutralizations', Schmitt was again to state his conviction that 'in European history the most striking and influential intellectual watershed was the shift in the seventeenth century from traditional Christian theology to a natural scientific system', in the way in which it would determine 'the rules which would govern the movement of European history over the coming centuries, and preside over its formation of a concept of truth' (*NP*, pp. 144–5).[21]

As a result, from his very earliest texts, Schmitt's questioning is aimed both at modern ideals of scientificity and at the way in which its proponents tend to conceive the forces which govern the collective being of humanity. In the strikingly anachronistic Catholicism which he sketches in *Römischer Katholizismus*, he seeks both a concept of scientificity and a model of social rationality which are able to match those in favour with our contemporaries: a model which makes it possible to affirm the primacy of the political over economics, of decision over impersonal structural constraints, of the Idea over matter.

This search for another rationality explains (albeit only in passing) some of the oddest and probably most debatable aspects of the exegesis of Hobbes which Schmitt offers, especially in the 1965 text 'Die vollendete Reformation'.[22] In opposition to the more classical interpretation – in opposition even to the letter of the texts themselves – Schmitt refuses to see Hobbes as the founder of a political science, in so far as we give the word 'science' those connotations which we attach to it today. Quite casually, he attributes the author's explicit methodological justifications to the simple matter of timeliness: the state of the theological controversies left him no choice (*VR*, p. 64). The flimsiness of the argument is obvious, and we ought to pause to consider it. What interest did Schmitt have in denying the methodological premises declared in the Hobbesian construction? Did Hobbes not want to be the Galileo of the political sciences, and does this ambition not justify considering him one of the initiators of the process of secularization – that is, of 'dechristianization and the removing of the divine from public life': whose final product is the current 'scientific-technical-industrial civilization' (*VR*, p. 61)?

This kind of reading does not, however, allow Schmitt to twist Hobbes's thinking to his own ends, to make it the link ensuring a continuity between medieval Catholicism and the theory of the modern state. The spiritual and temporal hegemony of the Roman Church, celebrated earlier in *Römischer Katholizismus*, is too distant and too manifestly outdated a historical figure to constitute a credible alternative to modern (theoretical and practical) rationality. Schmitt's position is indisputably stronger if one accepts that he succeeds in showing that the 'particular rationality' illustrated by the medieval Church did not disappear when its political power did; rather, it survived, in another form, just as the different elements of another kind of (now naturalist and technical) rationality were being established, providing rules for the contemporary world. This is why he had to rule out everything in Hobbes's work which links it to the concept of science whose precursors are in Galileo and Descartes. The theory of the *Jus Publicum Europaeum* – created by Hobbes, among others – draws on the same fundamental logic as Christian law. So it is inconceivable that Hobbes seriously meant to link his argument to the logic of 'naturalist scientificity'. What Hobbes achieves:

> is not of the order of natural sciences. He is neither a great mathematician, nor a physicist, nor a philosopher in the 'natural sciences' sense. His scientific achievements belong entirely to the realm of *practical philosophy* ... For Hobbes, philosophy still is not a simple theory of mathematical or physical natural science. It is located in the intellectual tradition developed in the Roman Church since the eleventh century, and which found its fulfilment partly in theological and metaphysical ideas, partly in canonical law. (*VR*, pp. 64–5.)

The detour via Hobbes clarifies the paradigmatic role assigned to Roman Catholicism in the 1923 text (*Römischer Katholizismus*). Schmitt clearly did not plan to accord the Roman Church the power she lost at the end of the wars of religion. In the seventeenth century the ecclesiastical institution was definitively replaced by the state. *Quis judicabit?*, the political question *par excellence*, was resolved in favour of the latter. However, the specific rationality which – in an exemplary way – characterized the medieval Church did not disappear at the same time. Hobbes really reveals the political essence of the Church at exactly the point where he passes to the secular state the ultimate power of judging what is proper to political power. But it is precisely for this reason that he 'is neither scientist nor technocrat' (*VR*, p. 67). By making the question of the sovereign being – that is, of authority for the ultimate decision – the key question of authentic political thought, he is theoretically assuming the heritage of Catholicism.[23] This is why, at its heart, his thought is 'inadequate to a period of scientific-technical civilization, even incommensurable with it' (VR, p. 67): infinitely closer to the Catholicism it was replacing than to the modernity which in some ways it was establishing.

The theme of continuity between the rationality of the medieval Church and that of the juridical-political thought of the *Jus Publicum Europaeum*, which from 1923 was implicit in the opposition between economicism and the political Idea, may be found in another form in *Political Theology II*. Setting himself in opposition to the views of Peterson, the Protestant theologian who maintained an apolitical vocation for theology, Schmitt maintains instead that theology and law are related sciences. The systematic science of law, as it was developed from the Christian Middle Ages first under the auspices of canonical law, is a 'sister-science to theology' (TP, p. 159). Hence the fact that the concepts used by these two disciplines are *structurally compatible* (TP, p. 158). In other words, theology and the science of law are sciences in the same way – that is, they speak the same language. If, today, theology seems on the whole to be denied the status of a science, this is because 'a concept entirely different from science' has imposed itself, precisely that of the objective or functionalist science[24] which has 'succeeded in holding religion and its theology back in the depths of its kind of secularism [*in die Untergründe seiner Art von Weltlichkeit*] and to write them off, after the fashion of psychoanalysis, as anachronisms and neuroses' (TP, p. 158; German text, p. 99). The rationalism arising from canonical law prepared for that of secular law. Here Schmitt quotes from Weber's *Sociology of Law*: 'For secular law, canonical law is a guide to the path of rationalization. The relatively decisive factor is the Catholic church's nature as a rational institution, which is not to be found elsewhere.' The lay law of the secular state prolongs a process begun before the state existed.[25]

The incommensurability of Hobbes's thought with the logic of the functionalist sciences of technical-scientific civilization is the counterpart to the compatibility of the concepts of theology and law. The political interpretation of Roman Catholicism, set up as a model of an alternative rationality to that of the modern world, effectively resulted in the science of law being accorded the status of an exception in the area of contemporary thought. If law inherits the rules of its discourse from theology, the discontinuity is not merely a historical one, but crosses the boundaries between scientific discourses of our time. The decisive questions of authentic juridical thought cannot be dealt with using the conceptual means common in modern sciences. *Quis judicabit?* The 'legal objective regularities' [*Sachgesetzlichkeiten*] provide no answer to this question; a science which aims exclusively at the knowledge of such natural laws is not even in a position to ask it.[26]

Without doubt, the kinship between theology and law does not prevent conflicts between theologians and jurists: the masters they serve are not the same. The secular state has been an important opponent of the institutional Church, in their dispute (won by the former, as we know) over the power to make ultimate decisions. But these conflicts are expressed in a language as comprehensible to the one as to the other: the language of concrete orders, of institutions confronting each other as warring parties (*TP*, pp. 164–5).[27] *Römischer Katholizismus* highlights the idea of representation, linked to that of a personal authority, as the heart of the Catholic kind of political thinking. What Schmitt finds in Hobbes is precisely a 'specifically juridical personalism', by which he distinguishes himself from all 'naturalist scientism, as from all mythical scientism' (*VR*, p. 65).

I would need more space than is available here to expound on the organization of this juridical-political thought and the reasons behind it, set out as it is around notions of authority (as opposed to substance), of concrete order, of form and of representation. There is indeed a readily discernible continuity, one which leads from the thematics of visibility of the Church,[28] – that is, the manifestation on earth of a transcendent God, already developed in a pamphlet published by Schmitt in 1917 – to that of representation or form, as we find it in *Römischer Katholizismus* or *Politische Romantik*,[29] and even later, in the 1950s, to the concept of *nomos*. This continuity fits in with Schmitt's conviction that public space – that is, the space for collective life – can be structured only through a purely authoritarian act of institution.

Our aim here, however, is limited to bringing out the underlying themes in the polemic Schmitt conducts against the economicism of the 1920s. This polemic sometimes seems only to reiterate certain *topoi* of the criticism of culture which flourished in Germany, as a reaction to the rushed development of industrialization and urbanization which that country experienced from the last decades of the nineteenth century: the denunciation of a system of production which was adaptable to the most contingent demands of consumption, the denunciation of the uprooting of the inhabitants of cities, and so on. *Römischer Katholizismus* does not even avoid crude schematizing – for example, opposing the affective bond between Catholics (predominantly rural, according to Schmitt) and the land of their birth, to which the Protestants are indifferent. If a Protestant can establish his industry anywhere, if any ground can be the site for his professional work and his 'terrestrial asceticism' (*RK*, p. 18: the allusion to Weber here is evident), then it is because for him nature is only matter to be subjugated, and the earth has no significance as the site of the motherland.

Naturally, the interest of the work resides not in recalling these common bonds, but in the fact that in counterpoint it asks of Catholicism not only different ways of conceiving the forms of human sociality, but also – and perhaps principally – a theoretical logic different from that ruling modernist scientificity.

According to Schmitt, the future of juridical science depended on the restoring of this apparently obsolete way of thinking. If the former yielded to the dominant tendencies of the period, bringing its concepts and arguments into conformity with the demands of 'naturalist' science, it would definitively break its links with *philosophia practica*. It seems important to emphasize this point, which is generally ignored by those who see Schmitt primarily as the author of *The Concept of the Political*. With admittedly unusual references (to Catholicism rather than to ancient philosophy), this unusual jurist fought in his own way to save practical philosophy, threatened with extinction by scientific ideology.

As we have seen, Schmitt's rather unorthodox interpretation of Hobbes aimed to link the latter with the field of *philosophia practica*. It was enough that Hobbes had asked the question of the authority who decides or interprets for Schmitt to state that his thought 'is entirely founded in moral, juridical practical philosophy' (*VR*, p. 65). In that way the authentically political nature of his theory of law was asserted, capable, after the fashion of the medieval Church, of giving 'a substantial configuration to historical and social reality' (*RK*, p. 14). Such a theory can provide humanity with something which technical-economic rationalism cannot: points of reference, a basis on which to judge and act – in other words, a 'guide' (*RK*, p. 24) or 'normative direction for human social existence' (*RK*, p. 21). In this the moral signification of politically comprehended Catholicism was to be found. The objection Schmitt raises to what he calls 'neutralization' – or, to use a more 'classical' term, 'secularization' – aims at the modern concept of scientific objectivity to the extent that the latter, in so far as it manages to impose itself on the science of law itself, would mark the end of *philosophia practica* – that is, of that thought which questions 'the only essential rationality, that of the aim' which eliminates the system of modern economics and technique (*RK*, p. 26).

In this context the strategic nature of the confrontation with Max Weber is easy to explain. In effect he was both the theoretician of 'sociality without norms',[30] describing the inescapable progress of economic and bureaucratic rationality, and at the same time the fiercest defender of the independence of science with respect to values. A science associated only with the knowledge of legal regularities is doubtless

perfectly suited to a world entirely enslaved to the constraints of impersonal systems. The intellectual asceticism to which Weber submits himself in working, without compromise, from the perspective of an
axiologically neutral science is the only coherent approach of an objectivized world. His scientific ethics are therefore entirely adequate to the
logic of the world from which he elaborates the theory.[31] Schmitt is just
as coherent in his refusal of both approaches.

On the theoretical plane, Schmitt fought against the tendency, accurately diagnosed by Weber, to consider law as a simple rational technical
tool. On an epistemological plane, he was against bringing juridical
science into line with the canon of the free science of values. For him,
these were two facets of a single and unique struggle. To yield on the
second point would be to revert to surrender, and to the acceptance of
the rule of the *Sachlichkeit* as inescapable destiny. Coupling juridical
science to theology seemed to him to be the only way of preventing its
subjugation to the norms of the dominant scientificity. What was at stake
in this definition of the place of the science of law in the arrangement of
disciplines was the existence of this science itself. It is in this light that
one should understand a comment in the *Glossarium*, dated 20 April
1948: 'Jurists, today we find ourselves in between theology and technique, in a tiresome alternative which might ultimately destroy us.'
Schmitt reiterates this assertion in the preface to *Der Nomos der Erde*
where, locating his work in the tradition of Savigny and Bachofen, he
observes that what is in question is 'the very existence of the science of
law, which today is crushed between theology and technique' (*NE*, p. 6).
Theology, a *rational* discourse rooted in transcendence, and technicist-
functionalist science, the final offshoot of the concepts of immanence for
which nineteenth-century German idealist philosophy had already
paved the way,[32] are for Schmitt the two poles defining the field in
which the science of law should be situated. This is as much as to say
that a jurist has no choice but to be a theologian if he wants to maintain
the science of law as a *practical* science – that is, as a science capable of
assigning its aims to the collective being, and so to direct action.

Schmitt's sympathy with canonists Theodor Andrès Marcos, Hans
Barion and, with some reservations, Rudolf Sohm,[33] can of course be
explained with recourse to the details of his intellectual biography.
Nevertheless, his one ambition was to convert the uncomfortable
position in which he found himself – between theologians and jurists of
terrestrial law – into a decision concerning the future of the science of
law. 'I am a theologian of jurisprudence,' he summarized in a passage in
the *Glossarium* (3 October 1947). He doubtless knew that in such a
capacity, at a time of 'mass secularism', he was doomed to marginalization, but he was equally convinced that he occupied the only position

from which it would be possible to rescue law from a technicization which would ultimately result in its loss.

Translated by Daniel Hahn

Notes

1. *Théologie politique II*, in Carl Schmitt, *Théologie politique* (hereafter *TP*), Paris: Gallimard, 1988, p. 170. The work which appeared under this title was the French translation, supervised by Jean-Louis Schlegel, of two of Schmitt's works, which were originally separated by some fifty years: *Théologie politique: quatre chapitres sur la théorie de la souveraineté* (1922) and *Théologie politique. Une légende: la liquidation de toute théologie politique* (1969).

2. At the end of his speech to the fifteenth colloquium on German sociology, in 1964. See Jürgen Habermas, *Zur Logik der Sozialwissenschaften*, Frankfurt: Suhrkamp, 1982, p. 85. Habermas accepted a colleague's suggestion: rather than seeing Schmitt as a legitimate disciple of Weber he could, rather, be considered his 'natural son'.

3. Carl Schmitt, *Legalität und Legitimität* (1932), in *Verfassungsrechtliche Aufsätze*, Berlin: Duncker & Humblot, 1985.

4. Cited by Carl Schmitt in *Legalität und Legitimität*, p. 269.

5. See the last two chapters (VII: 'Les qualités formelles du droit d'essence révolutionnaire' and VIII: 'Les qualités formelles du droit moderne') of Max Weber, *Sociologie du droit*, Paris: Presses Universitaires de France, 1986.

6. Carl Schmitt, *Glossarium*, Berlin: Duncker & Humblot, 1991; this is a journal kept by Schmitt between 1947 and 1951.

7. This work appeared in 1952 as *Legitimität und Legalität in Max Webers Herrschaftssoziologie*, Tübingen: J.C.B. Mohr (Paul Siebeck).

8. Translated from *Wirtschaft und Gesellschaft II*, Tübingen: J.C.B. Mohr (Paul Siebeck), 1952, p. 513.

9. This text began as Schmitt's speech following a conference on Ernst Forsthoff, under the title 'Tugend und Wert in der Staatslehre' [Virtue and valour in the theory of the state]. It was published in a volume of *Ebracher Studien* devoted to Forsthoff to mark his sixtieth birthday (*Sakularisation und Utopie*, 1965), republished in 1979 as *Die Tyrannei der Werte* (Hamburg: Lutherisches Verlaghaus).

10. *Römischer Katholizismus und politische Form* (hereafter *RK*), Stuttgart: Klett-Cotta, 1984.

11. G.L.Ulmen, 'Politische theologie und politische Ökonomie – Über Carl Schmitt und Max Weber', in H. Quaritsch (ed.), *Complexio Oppositorum, Über Carl Schmitt*, Berlin: Duncker & Humblot, 1988, p. 342.

12. See Catherine Colliot-Thélène, 'Rationalisation et désenchantement du monde: problèmes d'interprétation de la sociologie des religions de Max Weber', in *Archives de sociologie des religions 89, January–March 1995, pp. 61–81*.

13. 'Bringing a conceptual result back to its sociological bearer is a kind of psychology, and an ascribing of a certain kind of motivation to human action.' Translated from *TP*, p. 53–4.

14. *Politische Theologie*, Berlin: Duncker & Humblot, 1985, p. 59; the French translation renders the whole of this phrase, rather simply, as 'la mentalité' – 'mentality' (*TP*, p. 55).

15. See 'L'ère des neutralisations et des dépolitisations', in *La notion de politique – Théorie du partisan* (hereafter *NP*), Paris: Calmann-Lévy, 1972, pp. 131–53. The text specifies that it is concerned with the intellectual life 'of the active elite which makes up the avant-gardes' (*NP*, p. 135).

16. See *Wirtschaft und Gesellschaft I*, Tübingen: J.C.B. Mohr (Paul Siebeck), p. 124, para. 2, n. 1.

17. I will not linger here upon the differences Schmitt sometimes draws between

economy and techniques, as he himself uses the expression 'economic-technical thought' (for example, *RK*, pp. 46, 47).

18. Elsewhere I have emphasized the importance of this in Weber's thought, and I will allow myself to refer back to these analyses: *Le désenchantement de l'État. De Hegel à Max Weber*, Paris: Minuit, 1992, pp. 162 ff., 247. The objectivizing (*Versachlichung*) of the logics of collective action is, for Weber, linked to the issue of predictability (*Berechenbarkeit*). These same associations can be found in Schmitt, for whom the nature of the rationalism of economic thought is made from predictability and objectivization. See *RK*, p. 25: 'The rationalism of economic thought is used to counting on certain needs and to seeing only what it can "satisfy". In the large modern towns, this rationalism was a construction in which everything that took place was predictable. This system of unshakeable objectivity can be alarming to a pious Catholic, by its very rationality.'

19. 'L'ère des neutralisations', *NP*, p. 149.

20. See *NP*, p. 150; See also *Glossarium*, 5 October 1948, where Schmitt refers to Bernanos's work *La France contre les robots*: 'It is basically a critique of the technical age, which we in Germany have known since the beginning of the century through Max Weber and Walther Rathenau.'

21. See in the 1922 *Théologie politique* (*TP*, p. 57), a passage inspired by the same subject, where Schmitt directly calls into question the subjection of juridical and ethical thought to the logical norms of modern science.

22. 'Die vollendete Reformation' (hereafter *VR*), *Der Staat* 4, 1965, pp. 51–65.

23. Hobbes's 'personalism' had already been emphasized in *Théologie Politique* in 1922: *TP*, p. 56: 'In spite of his nominalism and his attachment to the natural sciences, . . . Hobbes none the less remains personalist and postulates the authority for a correct and final decision . . .'

24. See *VR*, p. 65: The question *Quis judicabitur?* is a formal one, and not a material one: 'It is not, however, scientific in the way that mathematics or geometry are, or in the sense of a functionalist, naturalist scientificity.'

25. I have used Jacques Grosclaude's translation, *Sociologie du droit*, p. 183. This passage is quoted by Schmitt at some length (*TP*, p. 160).

26. See *VR*, p. 67.

27. See also *TP*, p. 160.

28. 'Die Sichtbarkeit der Kirche. Eine scholastische Erwagung', *Summa I* (1917–18).

29. *Politische Romantik*, Berlin: Duncker & Humblot, 1982 (Ist edn 1919).

30. I have borrowed this expression from Jürgen Habermas.

31. A few phrases from the *Glossarium* confirm the link existing for Schmitt between Max Weber's scientific ideal and the political structures of the contemporary world. For example, he establishes a relationship between the bureaucrat who is respectful of legality to the point that he obeys an order which seems to him questionable, and the axiological abstention advocated by Weber in the realm of science. In both these cases it is a matter of asceticism, whose motivations are doubtless identical (25 November 1947). A passage appearing under the date 12 March 1948 is evidence of Schmitt's basic dislike of this ascetic practice of science. Having just immersed himself in works on Weber's sociology of religions, he affirmed ill-temperedly: 'How sad and ugly this seething rationality is, which seeks to cover itself in rational vine-leaves at the cost of continual cramps. The power of the wise man's ascetic honesty is an ethical *plus*, but it is not scientific.'

32. On the increasing diffusion, throughout the nineteenth century, of 'representations of immanence', see *TP*, pp. 58–60.

33. Schmitt states his sympathy with Theodor Andrès Marcos and Hans Barion in the *Glossarium*, in the entry for 3 October 1947. His relation to Rudolf Sohm is more complex: in effect Sohm is a Protestant theologian who, in his *Kirchenrecht*, denounces the juridical organization of the Catholic Church as a perversion of originary Christianity. Various passages from the *Glossarium* do, however, show the admiration Schmitt felt for Sohm, sometimes borrowing analyses and concepts from him.

9

Political Order and Democracy: Carl Schmitt and His Influence

Ulrich K. Preuss

Introduction

Undoubtedly, Carl Schmitt belongs among the most equivocal and notorious European intellectuals of the twentieth century – his scholarly work has fascinated several generations of academics and political essayists; his personal conduct shortly before and during the Nazi regime has aroused the most discrepant reactions, ranging from disgust, and even hatred, to rationalization, apology and justification. Although in West Germany's postwar political, academic and intellectual life we could find numerous people who were far more compromised by their collaboration with the Nazis, the academic community has reacted much more moderately with respect to them than to Schmitt. He was banned from postwar academic life because he was regarded as *the* political theorist of the collapse of the Weimar Republic and of the Nazi regime. To be sure, he could not have gained this paradigmatic significance if his work had lost all relevance after the eradication of the Nazi regime, or if it had slumped to a mere object of *Geistesgeschichte*. His rise to a 'case' appears understandable only if his work still has some significance for us, be it that it is a kind of paradigm for still menacing and perhaps even seductive theoretical fallacies; be it that there is an inherent and irritating affinity between his possibly still convincing analyses of politics on the one hand and his wholly unacceptable personal alliance with the Nazis on the other; be it, finally, that his work confronts us with insights into structural characteristics of constitutional democracy which incite our aversion because there might be some truth in them.

In my opinion, all three elements play a role in this intellectual drama, but I do not intend to demonstrate this here at full length. I restrict myself exclusively to the question: to which degree are some doctrinal elements of Schmitt's constitutional theory still current in the constitutional discourse of the Federal Republic? It is therefore not my ambition to develop a new and original interpretation of Schmitt's work as a whole, or of some of his ideas, but, rather, to give an Anglo-Saxon audience a necessarily somewhat schematic overview and an impression of the relevance – albeit declining – of some of the questions he raised and the answers he gave. From that it follows that I am not prepared to deal with the intellectual influence of those circles which, in a sometimes sectarian manner, behave like guardians of the Holy Grail of Schmitt's work, occasionally revealing the resentful attitude that a critique of his tenets is a kind of sacrilege which can be explained only by intellectual inferiority, envy, or political enmity (see Maschke 1987; Willms 1987, p. 577). This is a topic for the sociology of knowledge; hence it does not concern us here.

A rough outline of Schmitt's constitutional approach

As is now widely acknowledged, Schmitt was an 'occasionalist' thinker who did not elaborate a theoretical system (Quaritsch 1987, p. 21). Even his *Verfassungslehre*, a comprehensive treatise of a liberal-democratic constitution pertaining predominantly to the Weimar constitution, first published in 1928 and reprinted several times after World War II, is more a remodelling of the main topics of constitutional law than the invention of a new theoretical system for the understanding of constitutional democracy. But this restructuring has one dominant 'leitmotiv' which is deeply engraved in his interpretation of almost every constitutional institution: the essential relevance of 'the political' for the operation of all constitutional processes. To put it in a different manner, the threatening presence of pre- and non-constitutional political energies within the constitution is the dominant property of Schmitt's constitutional thought. Hence it is important to understand his notion of 'the political' because it is the key element of his constitutional reasoning. 'The political' delineates the character of a social conflict in that it refers to its potentially highest intensity and escalation to the existential antagonism of 'friend' and 'enemy'. The paradigmatic constellation is a group's contention of its 'sameness' and 'identity' against the 'otherness' of a different group; it is this assertive consciousness – or, more precisely, this assertive common feeling of 'sameness' based on race, ethnicity, common history, culture, or language, which for Schmitt forges the members of the group into the 'oneness' of a 'people' – that constitutes the political quality of a group. As a consequence, the notion of 'the political' antecedes the notion of the state, because the common feeling of a group's oneness is the determining state-building social energy; the state – the institutional order of the political quality of a people – rests on 'the political' as its preceding condition. The most succinct version of this argument appears in the first sentence of *The Concept of the Political*: 'The concept of the state presupposes the concept of the political' (Schmitt 1976 [1927/1932]). Parenthetically, I should direct attention to Schmitt's rather strange use of the term 'the political' – a nominalization of an adjective – which avoids the noun 'politics' or the adjective 'political'. This vagueness has been interpreted as a syntactic strategy which entails the dissolution and blurring of the connections between order, state and politics, with the consequence that every concrete order can be transformed into a political conflict, and hence reduced to its very basis (Altmann 1988, pp. 306 f.).

Be this as it may, it is Schmitt's ardent emphasis on the political element of constitutional democracy that has made him a conspicuous figure among constitutional and political theorists. To be sure, it has been a commonplace that constitutional law is 'political law' in that it deals with political institutions, procedures and decisions; Schmitt did not refer to this truism. His distinctive approach includes the message that – contrary to the essential rationale of any constitutional theory, and hence contrary to almost all constitutional authors – 'the political' cannot and must not be entirely domesticated and, by virtue of the rules of the constitution, depoliticized and transformed into institutions. What he states about the relation between 'the political' and the state applies even more to the interrelation between the political and the constitution: the political order is antecedent to the constitution. 'The political' is the pre-constitutional foundation of the constitution: the pre-institutional political oneness of the people is prior to the legal or constitutional order: 'prior' in a logical as well as a historical sense (Schmitt 1979 [1922/1933], pp. 16, 18 f.; 1965 [1928], pp. 237 ff.). This relation is not a transitory one; it applies not only to the 'disorder' of a revolution, when an old order is abolished by political forces which create the foundation of a new order; rather, it persists and slumbers as a latent potential in the constitution. Evidently this is a fundamental challenge to the basic tenet of constitutional democracy, according to which the political order is created by the constitution which, as it were, has 'consumed' and legally tamed the political energies which enabled its creation.

This has a far-reaching consequence – probably the one which, next to the notorious friend–enemy theory of the political, has instigated the most fervent resistance, at least among constitutional lawyers: the consequence that the integrity of the political order can – and sometimes even must – be sustained against the constitution, through the breach of the constitution, because the essence of the political order is not the constitution but the undamaged oneness of the people. In technical terms Schmitt made the distinction between the 'constitution' [*Verfassung*] and 'constitutional law' [*Verfassungsgesetz*], the first including the pre-constitutional political substance or, in other words, the political decisions of the constitutional order (Schmitt 1965, pp. 18 ff., 108 ff.), the latter consisting of nothing but provisions about more or less inferior issues which, as a result of compromises between pluralistic social groups, had been incorporated into the constitution in order to protect particularistic interests against social and political change through the barrier of the two-thirds majority required for constitutional amendments (Schmitt 1965 [1928], pp. 23 ff., 32; 1969 [1931], p. 48). Hence a military *coup d'état* which claims to save the political essence of the 'constitution' against the 'disorder' of the antagonistic struggles of pluralistic social groups and parties could well be justified as substantively constitutional, although it violates the formal constitutional law. This 'essentialist' constitutionalism is also the key to the understanding of Schmitt's fascination with the 'exception' and his preference for such topics as dictatorship, state of emergency, war, and so on. Incidentally, Schmitt himself bore out the correctness of this conclusion in that he – in the dramatic months before the final collapse of the Weimar Republic at the turn of the years 1932 to 1933, in autumn 1932 – was personally involved in the preparations of such a coup as a legal adviser to the Papen and Schleicher governments (Huber 1988).

The nineteenth-century tradition and the challenge of the Weimar constitution

In this context it seems appropriate to give a short account of the sociopolitical background of Schmitt's biography, the better to understand his preoccupation with the pre-constitutional elements of the constitution or, in other words, with the latency of dictatorship within the normalcy of the constitution (in the aforementioned sense of 'constitutional law' [*Verfassungsgesetz*]). Schmitt was thirty years old in 1918, when the Revolution overthrew the constitution of Imperial Germany, but already the prewar crises and the war itself had clearly confirmed that the nineteenth century had ended ten years earlier. The quest for security could no longer be satisfied in the institutional framework of the Bismarck Reich, which – more or less successfully – had excluded the dominant social conflict, the class struggle between the bourgeoisie and the working class, from the political realm. Although Schmitt was certainly an antibourgeois who had close connections to the exponents of modernism in art and literature (Kennedy 1988), he was none the less deeply connected with the nineteenth-century legal culture and its basic concepts. It should be mentioned that he was a student of Paul Laband, the eminent and most influential constitutional lawyer of legal positivism in the last third of the nineteenth century. Schmitt did not follow Laband's strict distinction between law and politics, and rejected his expulsion of politics from the sphere of constitutional law, but he clung to Laband's influential and widely accepted premiss that the state's unity is represented by the head of the executive branch of government. During Laband's lifetime this was the monarch, so that after the abolition of the monarchy there was a vacuum. The Weimar constitution embodied the democratic enterprise: to fill this vacuum by substituting the people as the exclusive source of legitimacy for the monarch and the monarchic–bureaucratic–military state apparatus which had been subordinated to his will.

In contrast, Schmitt tried to maintain the concept of the homogeneity and oneness of political power, and its undisputed superiority over the social divisions and cleavages of society. However, his approach was quite distinct and far more original than the constitutional reasoning of most of his colleagues – straightforward reactionaries who lamented the abolition of the monarchy and cultivated their hostile resentments against the democratic republic. Schmitt was less an ultraconservative of that kind than a bourgeois revolutionary who struggled for the preservation of bourgeois order under the conditions of the intensifying class struggles of the twentieth century; not entirely falsely, he has been called the 'Lenin of the bourgeoisie'. His concept consisted essentially in the use of the dynamics of mass democracy for the maintenance of the cardinal institutions of bourgeois social order: private property, the right of inheritance, the freedoms of trade, commerce, contract and investment. As is known, the Weimar constitution tried to reconcile – or at least, to diminish the discrepancy between – capitalism and political democracy through the creation of universal suffrage, a competitive party system on the basis of a purely proportional electoral system, and through institutions of collective bargaining and workers' co-determination in companies. All this entailed a 'democracy of organizations' which, in Schmitt's view, made the political acts of the government, particularly the laws, appear as mere products of the power relations and bartering skills of particularistic *pouvoirs de fait*. This state bore no similarity whatsoever to the Hegelian 'objective spirit' and its pretension to represent something like collective reason. In Schmitt's view the vacuum which the faded monarchy had abandoned could not be filled by its restoration, because this would have meant a solution in terms of the nineteenth century. But pluralist democracy, much less the struggle of antagonist classes and groups for political power, was no solution either. More or less random majorities were no warranty of political unity which, for him, glowed with the aura of reason and objective political truth. However, he accepted the democratic challenge of the Weimar constitution. His constitutional approach can be read as an attempt to reconcile his quest for security and stable order with his experience of the wavering and menacing dynamics of mass democracy. Both his notion of order and his doctrine of democracy are linked by his concept of the political, which is deeply ingrained in both.

The concept of order

Schmitt raised the question to which every constitution has to respond, in a fundamental crisis if not before: what is the essence of a social order which has to be safeguarded by the constitution, and who is responsible for its preservation? He rejected the idea that freedom could be the substance of a political order. In contrast to the liberals' optimism, he did not believe in the cunning of reason, the invisible hand, the transformation of private vices into public benefits and virtues, or similar constructions which envisaged a prestabilized harmony of individual freedom and social order. 'Freedom does not constitute anything,' he declared (Schmitt 1965, p. 200); on the contrary, freedom presupposes order which embodies the inherent quality and reason of collective life, and hence determines and restricts individual liberties. Schmitt's concern was less the inescapable tension between freedom and order than the endangerment of order by chaos which he presumed in the subjectivity of men, and which led him to suspect individual liberty. He does not yield to the current distinction of political theories according to which man's nature is supposed as either inherently 'good' or 'bad' but, rather, envisages man as a dynamic, and hence 'dangerous', being that is prone to threaten order (Schmitt 1979, p. 61).

Paradoxically, it is his very quest for the good that makes man incalculable and 'dangerous'. Alluding to the religious civil wars of the sixteenth and seventeenth centuries and referring to Hobbes, with whom he agrees, he considers the discovery and ongoing recognition of the individual's conscience as the source not only of subjective rights, but also of the objective law – which, in the continental European legal tradition, has long been conceived of as the expression of a homogeneous will, not as the solution of a problem but, rather, as the problem of a solution (Schmitt 1978, pp. 21 ff.). On the basis of the unequivocal voice of his or her conscience, everybody can claim to know the right content of a just law; and in a society split by intense religious and ideological conflict, this entails permanent struggle and, in the last instance, the Hobbesian 'war of every man against every man' (Hobbes 1991, Part I, ch. 13). The conviction that a person has to obey his or her conscience more than the law of the state threatens peace and order. And more: it jeopardizes the state's monopolistic right to issue binding laws for every citizen, and thus challenges its very political quality. The state's capacity to safeguard peace and order by mastering all particularistic social forces which may endanger social coherence and undermine its attempt to integrate the chaotic multitude of individuals and interests into the unity of one political body is the distinctive quality which makes up its political character. This requires the institutional superiority of a sovereign power over any other authority which claims to determine or co-determine the content of the law. Therefore the benefit of the law consists not in its inherent justness – this will always be disputable and, indeed, disputed – but in its ability to terminate the struggle about justice (Schmitt 1978, p. 22).

In the religious civil wars of the sixteenth and seventeenth centuries the struggle for the establishment of the political character of power took place in the battles between, on the one hand, feudal corporations, the Church and the new religious denominations and, on the other, the exponents of the concept of the territorial state. In modern mass democracy the challenge to the state's monopoly of the political has been secularized. Here, according to Schmitt, the state has to struggle against the political aspirations of such pluralist intermediate forces as the churches, the unions or economic associations, in order to relativize and neutralize them politically – that is, to push them back into the status of mere private associations of citizens. If the state has the monopoly of the political, the preservation of order within the state is essentially a problem not of politics, but of the police (Schmitt 1963, pp. 10 f., 30 f.; Böckenförde 1987, p. 285). Politics comes into play only if *any pouvoir de feit* – or, as Schmitt called them, 'indirect power' – tries to impose its very conceptions of justice and the common good on the state. To acknowledge and yield to this claim would be a threat to the state's quality as a political body.

The definitive criterion is whether the state has the 'last word' in a quarrel about the content of a law or any other governmental decision which cannot be resolved by compromise or other peaceful means. The situation which seriously raises this question, is, so to speak, the 'moment of truth' and the state of exception. This explains the succinct first sentence in Schmitt's *Political Theology*: 'The sovereign is the one who decides about the state of exception' (1979, p. 11; 1978, p. 24). In the context of modern constitutionalism this sentence applies not only to the relation 'state' versus *pouvoirs de fait*, but also to the relation between the legislature, the judiciary and the executive branch. Regarding the judiciary as essentially unpolitical and the legislature as having fallen prey to the pluralist cartel of economic and social organizations, Schmitt stated in 1929, at the beginning of the fatal crisis of the Weimar Republic, that in this situation of unstable party coalitions and volatile parliamentary majorities it was the *Reichspräsident* who was to be viewed as the representative of political unity and the genuinely political 'guardian of the constitution' (Schmitt 1969 [1931]).

The concept of democracy

As I have already mentioned, Carl Schmitt did not elude the challenge of the dynamics of mass democracy. But he fiercely rejected the Weimar constitution's notion of democracy – a combination of party competition and liberal corporatism – which, in his opinion, excluded democratic accountability for the whole of the political body. The sovereignty of the people, stipulated in Article 1 of the Weimar constitution, was to be understood almost literally as the 'rule of the people' as opposed to the 'rule of law'. For Schmitt, the political character of democratic order was characterized not by good rules but by good rulers, where 'good' means representing the pre-normative existential quality of 'the people'. In a purely empirical sense, 'the people' is only a multitude of individuals within a distinct territory, but in a political sense 'the people' consists in the ethnic and cultural oneness of this multitude, which entails its capacity to realize its otherness in relation both to other peoples and to the liberal-universalist category of mankind (Schmitt 1965, pp. 227 ff.). For him, the essence of the political in a democratic order is the will of the people to preserve its distinctive property and its oneness, and to impose this will on the economic, social, cultural and political cleavages of society.

This means, in the first instance, the exclusion of all 'non-homogeneous' members of society from their affiliation to 'the people' and, as a consequence, from the enjoyment of equal political rights (like the right to vote, to free speech, to freedom of assembly) (Schmitt 1965 [1928], pp. 228 ff., 234; 1988 [1923]). Moreover, from this it follows that 'the people', in this existential and quasi-naturalistic sense of a preconstitutional homogeneous entity, becomes the antipode of 'the people' in the sense of citizenry, who, although they are the holders of sovereignty, cannot exercise their sovereign power except according to the standards of the constitution, and whose political will is therefore channelled and mediated in manifold ways. It comes as no surprise that Schmitt regarded the constitutionally 'unalienated' people, its ethnic and national sameness, as the 'true' foundation of democracy. Democracy is the rule of 'the people's will', whose essence is collective authenticity; this quality cannot be achieved by mere aggregation of private individual wills, the attribute of elections in liberal democracies. Referring to Rousseau – and at the same time misunderstanding him – Schmitt contends that the best precondition for the inherent authenticity and existential oneness of the people's will is the unqualified immediacy of its expression.

The ideal model is the assembly of a small community, which, of course, is not available in the extended territory of the modern nation-state; but Schmitt's concept of genuine democracy is derived from this ideal hypothesis:

> Only an actually assembled people is a people and only an actually assembled people can do what distictively belongs to the actions of this people: it can acclaim, that is, express its consent or its rejection through simple shouts, cry Up or Down, hallow a leader or a proposal, venerate the king or anybody else, or reject acclamation through silence or grumbling. (Schmitt 1965 [1928], pp. 243 f.)

Within the institutional framework of mass democracy, the ultimate attainable degree of authenticity and congruity of the people's will with its very essence is to be achieved by representation. By representation Schmitt does not mean the complex process of constitutional aggregation of many divergent and antagonistic interests and opinions, channelled and processed through rights, procedures, institutions, associations, and so on, characteristic of constitutional democracy. Rather, he suggests a kind of symbolic reappearance of the essential qualities of the people, and their incarnation in a person who has the capacity to express the 'true' self of the people.

This concept of democratic representation clearly reveals the close connection between plebiscitarian democracy and authoritarian rule – an affinity which led Schmitt to the (at first glance paradoxical) contention that a true dictatorship can be founded only on a democratic basis (Schmitt 1965 [1928], p. 237; 1978 [1921], pp. XII ff.). According to this view, democracy and dictatorship are not essentially antagonistic; dictatorship is, rather, a kind of democracy. By the way, this contention is one of the reasons why the Left has always taken great interest in Carl Schmitt, who, after World War II, was allegedly astonished that the Russians did not try to gain his co-operation in favour of their political ideology.

Although Schmitt's concept of democracy seems to foreshadow and to justify Hitler's *Führerdiktatur*, it would hardly be correct to portray him as a Nazi partisan in the years before 1933. Clearly he was, like many academics of his generation, a nationalist, appalled by the Versailles peace treaty and taking offence at the Revolution of 1918, which was widely resented as the starting point of the debasement of the German people; along with many others, he deemed pluralist party democracy to be inappropriate to the political character of the Germans.

But at the same time he clung to the idea of constitutionalism, although his reading of the constitution was quite different from a liberal understanding and its references to Locke, Montesquieu, or the Federalists. His concern was to overcome what he called the 'empty functionalism' of parliamentarianism – that is, the compromises and bargaining processes which precede political decisions and which, in his opinion, were doomed to suffocate the political element. He looked for the persistence of the sovereign in the routine of everyday politics – 'the people' in the aforementioned sense of a homogeneous and authentic self. To put it in a different manner: he tried to keep the spirit of the people's will as 'one', to keep its sameness alive, and to oppose it to the inherent tendency of the people to 'regress' into a multitude of egoist individuals and particularistic social forces.

In this affection for sameness and identity one can detect a hidden negative sentiment towards the intrinsic proclivity of modern society to differentiate and to change ever more rapidly. Consequently Schmitt, quite in line with contemporary tendencies, resorts to non-universalistic 'existential' [seinsmäpige], even biological categories when he calls for homogeneity and identity of species (or co-specificity) [Artgleichheit, Gleichartigkeit] in order to mobilize unchangeable and hence unhistorical elements of order against the centrifugal and threatening tendencies of modern society. In a methodological view, this position raises the hermeneutic question of how to interpret the constitution, which we have to understand as the legal authentication of an act of foundation, and very frequently also as the final result of a revolution (in the broad sense of this term): is the constitution to be considered a law that contains normative rules and principles which, if and to the extent to which they are obeyed, create normalcy under changing circumstances? Or do we have to conceive of it as a coherent set of substantive political decisions that embody the revolutionary spirit of the founding generation and have to be kept viable in order to survive beyond the compromising routine of political everyday life, with the consequence that the political order exists in a state of permanent militant defence against the menace of degeneration of the political essence of the act of foundation? To put the alternatives more pointedly: does the constitution terminate revolution or, conversely, is it the institutionalization of the permanence of revolution? Not surprisingly, Schmitt opts for the second alternative. It includes the latency of the state of exception within the normalcy of the constitution, whose susceptibility to being permanently threatened through degeneration is clearly expressed in Schmitt's invention of the category 'guardian of the constitution', which plays a pivotal role in his constitutional reasoning (Schmitt 1958 [1929], pp. 63 ff.; 1965, pp. 133 ff.; 1969 [1931]). As we have seen, in the Weimar Republic he proclaimed the *Reichspräsident* as the 'guardian of the constitution', who – by virtue of his election by immediate vote of the people in a quasi-plebiscitarian manner, and due to his power to maintain the political order and security of the people (according to the famous Article 48 of the Weimar constitution) – was best qualified for a kind of 'democratic dictatorship', and hence for the reconciliation of the two concerns of Carl Schmitt: order and democracy. While this is now only of historical interest, the methodological approach can be applied to any constitution, and this explains the persistence of Schmitt's theoretical relevance for our own time.

Carl Schmitt's influence on the constitutional discourse of the Federal Republic of Germany

As I said in my introductory remarks, it is not possible to give a full account of the theoretical influence of Schmitt's doctrines on the constitutional reasoning in the Federal Republic here. In this rather selective overview I restrict myself to two examples, the first having a more conceptual, the second a more political impact. Finally, I want to give an assessment of the actual process of constitution-making in Eastern Europe in a perspective which, so to speak, tries to put the political viability of Schmitt's ideas to the test.

The nature of the constitution and its relation to the state

Presumably, the most accepted – albeit frequently unconscious – incorporation of Schmitt's doctrinal elements is his understanding of the constitution as a political decision. Although the German Federal Constitutional Court does not use the term 'political decision', it qualifies, quite in line with Schmitt, the declaration of the principles of rule of law, of democracy, of the social state or the guarantee of the bill of rights in the Basic Law as 'fundamental constitutional decisions' which reflect and continue the political will of the founders for succeeding generations. This does not mean that the Court clings to the empirical will of the people involved in order to expound the content of the constitution – the contrary is true. The methodological approach, rather, acknowledges the distinction between the wording of the text and the political essence of the constitution which, in the language of the Constitutional Court, forms a 'value order'. Hence the Basic Law consists of decisions for different values – like the dignity of the person, the rule of law, the democratic principle, and so on – which have to be contended, and require a guardian. Consequently, the Constitutional Court has widely been regarded as the 'guardian of the constitution'. This is understandable only if one realizes that the Basic Law confers on the Constitutional Court the power not only to perform the rather conventional task of settling – for instance – cases relating to the separation of powers, or the federal–state division; or to determine whether or not a given subject is placed beyond governmental control; but – presuming that the essential values of the constitution are prone to degeneration – also to authenticate the genuine content and the spirit of the so-called 'free democratic order'.

Bearing in mind the circumstances of the end of the Weimar constitution, the Parliamentary Council which devised the Basic Law alluded to the potentiality of democratic self-destruction, that is, the abolition of democracy through democratic means, intended to save the 'identity' of the constitution against a potentially destructive majority will. This includes the power of the Constitutional Court to pronounce the forfeiture of basic rights of citizens who abuse their democratic liberties 'to combat the free democratic basic order' (Article 18) and to declare the unconstitutionality of parties which seek to impair or abolish the free democratic basic order (Article 21 para. 2). These stipulations not only mirror the militant character of the constitution, but imply the aforementioned Schmittian distinction between constitutional law [*Verfassungsgesetz*] and constitution [*Verfassung*], the latter representing the very political essence and 'identity' of the constitution which cannot become subject to any amendment. The Basic Law has confirmed this concept in the so-called 'eternity clause' of Article 79 paragraph 3, according to which 'amendments of this Basic Law affecting the division of the Federation into Länder, the participation on principle of the Länder in legislation, or the basic principles laid down in Articles 1 and 20, shall be inadmissible'. Article 1 declares the inviolability of the dignity of man; Article 20 contains essentially the principles of democracy, of the rule of law and the constitutional state, and of the social state.

After the war, Schmitt praised himself – in the indirect manner of quoting another legal author affirmatively – for having developed the underlying idea of the 'eternity clause' of the Basic Law (Schmitt 1958, p. 345; see also 1965, p. vii). But it is worth mentioning that Article 79 paragraph 3 of the Basic Law eliminated the ambiguities of Schmitt's concept in that it defined the content of the 'spirit' of the constitution. In the *Verfassungslehre* published in 1928, Schmitt had sharply opposed the elements of the constitutional state [*Rechtsstaat*] to the genuinely political components which, as I have already stated, hold logical priority over the former, and are essentially identified with the democratic state as the embodiment of the people's will to oneness and political identity. The elements of the constitutional state [*Rechtsstaat*] are not ingredients of 'the state' in this emphatic sense but, rather, external restraints on its political actions. If the state is threatened by war, or internal turmoil and disorder, the components of the constitutional state, having no constitutive significance for the political existence of the people, can and even must be suspended because they thwart actions which are intended to safeguard the integrity of the order (Schmitt 1965 [1928], pp. 110, 125, 204).

In *Legality and Legitimacy*, which came out in 1932, Schmitt devises a different opposition. Here he identifies the 'functionalist majority system' of parliamentarianism – which, in his opinion, allows the formation of destructive majorities – and consequently any constitutional amendment which may annihilate even the substantive foundations of the constitution, as essentially subordinate to the 'substantive order' of the Second Main Part of the Weimar constitution, entitled *The Basic Rights and Duties of the Germans*. In the former opposition he finds the guarantee of political unity in the pre-constitutional oneness of the people; in the latter, which visibly mirrors the fundamental cleavages of German society shortly before the end of the Weimar Republic, he emphasizes the importance and integrative force of the basic values of the liberal-bourgeois order as expressed in individualist liberties, and attributes to them the dignity of a *super-légalité constitutionelle*, a super-legal quality on behalf of which the system of parliamentarian legality and the whole complex of pluralist democracy can – and, at that time, must – be suspended (Schmitt 1958 [1932], p. 311).

In this context it would not be appropriate to pursue the details of Schmitt's different versions and modifications of his main distinction between the political essence of the constitution – which confers the superior legality of certain values, and which he calls legitimacy – and those parts which embody the rights, institutions and procedures of an inferior notion of legality, which essentially apply to the practice of pluralist democracy. Instead, I want to direct attention to the continuance of this theoretical legacy in the constitutional discourse of the Federal Republic.

From a theoretical point of view, it is not so important *how* the boundary line between the two components of the constitution is drawn; the problem is that there is such a division at all. This approach implies the inescapable consequence that in the case of a serious conflict or a crisis, the substantive values claim priority to the formal and procedural provisions of the constitution which allow the process of democratic self-regulation for civil society. To put it in a less abstract manner: those social and political forces which are in a position to assert successfully that they are the exponents of the 'true', 'genuine', or 'authentic' spirit of the constitution have the power to define the 'enemies of the constitution', and hence to demarcate the realm of – in their view – 'legitimate' and loyal democratic dissent. In a slightly modified phrase of Carl Schmitt: they collect an extra-constitutional premium for the possession of the 'spirit of the constitution'. In view of this potentiality, the framers of the Basic Law instituted, as I have already said, the Constitutional Court as the 'guardian of the constitution'; but, as a careful observer of West German politics will confirm, the structural militancy of the Basic Law permeates many acts of government – legislative, administrative, or judicial – in which political questions play a role, and which are therefore susceptible to more or less subtle distinctions between a 'loyal' and a 'disloyal' use of civic rights and duties. The tacit justification is an obscure combination of civil religion and 'constitutional patriotism' which has been operating as a substitute for the traumatized national self-esteem of the West Germans, and which at times has entailed a reduced capacity of their society to endure dissent. The unexpected unification of the two German states will certainly raise the question whether this Schmittian legacy – the concern for political identity and substantive oneness, be it in ethnic, national, or ideological terms – can be disposed of.

I want to conclude this section, which deals with Schmitt's influence on the conceptual dimension of the Basic Law, with a brief reference to another, no less relevant instance of his influence on the theoretical understanding of the constitution. It entails a certain relation between state and constitution. The United States understands her constitution as the document of her foundation to the effect that without the constitution there would be no political body. The Lockeian social contract has not only served as a yardstick for the assessment of political rule but has also, to a certain degree, been understood as describing a political reality. As we know, the historical experience of continental Europe has been far more influenced by Hobbes than by Locke (Arendt 1963, pp. 139 ff.; 1972, pp. 51 ff.). While France drew radical-egalitarian consequences from the authoritarian Hobbesian concept, and developed an original version of democracy (Offe/Preuss 1991), the German practice of political rule continued until 1918 to rest on the dichotomy of the monarchic state including the bureaucracy, the military force and also the Protestant Church, and simultaneously monopolizing the political on the one hand, and the unpolitical spheres of commerce, trade and culture that constitute bourgeois society on the other.

The German constitutionalist movement essentially strived for the political representation of bourgeois society, aiming at co-determination in areas concerning freedom and property. It did not challenge the priority of the state but, rather, intended its legal domestication. If we, following Hannah Arendt, distinguish between two kinds of social

contract – '[o]ne was concluded between individual persons and supposedly gave birth to society; the other was concluded between a people
and its ruler and supposedly resulted in legitimate government' (Arendt
1963, p. 169) – then the German case implies a third notion: it was a
contract between a ruler who already possessed legitimacy independently of the people and the people in order to restrict the ruler's power
and to allow the people to voice its interests *vis-à-vis* him. The Revolution
of 1918 pushed Germany into the second kind of social contract by
which – again in the words of Hannah Arendt – the individual 'expresses
his "consent" to be ruled by the government, whose power consists of
the sum total of forces which all individual persons have channeled into
it and which are monopolized by the government for the alleged benefit
of all subjects' (Arendt 1963, p. 170). In this version it is the constitution
which establishes political rule.

While Schmitt – as I have already explained – does not deny the
state's quality as embodying the political unity of the people, he fer-
vently rejects the idea of the creative character of the constitution for this
unity. According to his concept, political unity is based on some pre-
political qualities, like ethnicity and nationality, which definitely require
its institutional representation in the state; but this state is defined by
only one condition – the monopoly of power in order to preserve peace
and security – whereas the content and the limits of this state's power
are the ensuing and, so to speak, secondary tasks of a constitution. The
persistence of the state does not depend on any normative rules and
individuals' compliance with them; rather, it is an existential fact of
collective life (Schmitt 1965, pp. 125, 200; Böckenförde 1987, p. 288).
Hence political unity and its incarnation in the state are perfectly
conceivable without a constitution. And if there is a constitution, it is
devised not as an instrument of self-regulation of civil society but as a
device to preserve political unity against its degeneration through 'dom-
estic pluralization . . . human rights universalism, and utopian discourse
ideals' (Isensee 1987, p. 592) – political eccentricities which acknowledge
the state and the integrity of its institutions not as an antecedent
condition of security, civil liberties and welfare, but as a never-attained
goal of a free discourse directed and inspired by the constitution.

The quotation I used comes not from Carl Schmitt but from a
contemporary author, and I selected it in order to demonstrate that
constitutional reasoning in the Federal Republic is largely dominated by
these two theoretical currents. One is the 'statist' tendency which, more
or less consciously, relies on the doctrine of the pre-constitutional political existence of the people and its incarnation in the state, being concerned in the first instance with the preservation of the unity,
homogeneity and integrity of its power. The other current is represented

by the 'pluralists' who regard political unity not as the pre-constitutional starting point of politics but, rather, as the uncertain result of a free political process in which the meaning of the constitution is permanently reinterpreted and reshaped according to the changing needs and interests within civil society. It is the old battle about the political priority of order or liberty, a dispute which can probably never be settled through theoretical devices. Presumably nobody has provided the contemporary 'statists' with more – and more brilliantly elaborated arguments for their position than Carl Schmitt. It is he who allows them to accept democracy without renouncing their unequivocal preference for order, though their concept of democracy, presupposing a prepolitical oneness of the people, is no less disputable and no less piercingly open to debate than Schmitt's was.

Democracy and homogeneity

In this section I want to give a – necessarily very rough – impression of the ongoing political impact of Schmitt's doctrine on contemporary West German debates which take place in an area where constitutional and political reasoning overlap. I refer to the dispute over whether immigrants who have been living and working in the Federal Republic for a minimum of five years (and do not have German citizenship) should qualify for the right to vote and to stand as candidates at municipal elections. Although this seems to be an issue of limited importance – the problem is not over the degree to which the government should restrain immigration, nor is the question, by now, whether immigrants should enjoy the right to vote during elections to the parliaments of the Länder or the Federation – it has nevertheless raised important considerations on the notion of democracy. In this case the argument is particularly concerned with the issue of 'homogeneity'. In German constitutional discourse, at least, it is a common assumption that the functioning of democracy requires some minimal homogeneity of the citizenry. The dispute centres around the meaning of 'homogeneity'. In the light of the divisive effects of economic and social deprivation, and the class struggle, 'homogeneity' has been defined predominantly in terms of economic and social equality. Too-large differences with respect to income, status, education and life chances in general have been regarded as threatening the formation of political consent, after the most disintegrative factor of the pre-constitutional era – namely, religion – had been tamed, albeit precariously, by the separation of state and Church and the guarantee of the freedoms of religion and of conscience.

Schmitt put forth a quite different meaning of 'homogeneity'. His conception completely evades socioeconomic notions or, more correctly,

he translates them into ontological ideas which then, for instance, lead
him to read 'appropriation' as 'taking' or 'seizing' [Nahme], distribution
as 'partitioning' [Teilen], and production as 'pasturing' [Weiden] (Schmitt
1958, pp. 489 ff.). In claiming to have thus identified the fundamental
categories of each and every economic order, he reveals that he is more
concerned with ahistorical entities than with historically changing structures. Hence 'homogeneity' means, not surprisingly, a quasi-natural
'existential' [seinsmäpige] equality of the members of a people as the
warranty of its capacity to become politically one (Schmitt 1965,
pp. 226 ff.). Whereas the development of democracy in the last two
hundred years has been characterized by an increasing inclusiveness (in
terms of economic barriers, gender, and age), his notion is extremely
restrictive, and potentially even violent. For him democracy requires the
exclusion and: 'if the need arises – the elimination or eradication of
heterogeneity' (Schmitt 1988 [1923], p. 14), and from this it follows that
political rights, such as the right to vote, can be assigned only to
nationals.

It goes without saying that this violent bias, which proved so susceptible to the racist ideology of the Nazis, has no support in contemporary
West German constitutional discourse. But the core of the argument –
namely, the claim that democracy requires homogeneity, and homogeneity has to be defined in terms of substantive equality prior to economic
and social equality – is readily made by numerous authors; the Constitutional Court is expected to assess this argument next time it has to
decide on the question of the constitutionality of a law of one of the
Länder.* The argument is essentially that the citizens' right to participate
in the political affairs of a state (including local communities) originates
not in their being subject to the actions of government – this applies to
non-nationals who enter the state's territory, too – but in the inescapable
commonness of their collective destiny which forces them to share the
weaknesses and dangers of the state as well as its benefits. This barrier
to the extension of political rights to aliens couid be surmounted by a
generous practice of naturalization, but here a much more severe obstacle
stands in the way – more severe in that it cannot be abolished by means
of economic, social, or immigration policy. It is the notion of substantive
equality which designates a pre-legal property of individuals in terms of
a common national history, language, and culture which define their
'sameness' or 'identity' as opposed to the characteristic of other people,
and even of individual citizens of other nations. Although it is not

---

* In the meantime the Court has decided that aliens do not have the right to vote (or to
stand as a candidate) at municipal elections. In order to allow the implementation of the
Treaty of Maastricht, the Basic Law has been amended to the effect that nationals of
Member States of the EC are now admitted to municipal elections.

disputed that national commonness and substantive equality can rest on a common political confession, this possibility is excluded for Germany. It is claimed that the German nation is based on 'ethnic-cultural' homogeneity, which allegedly precludes an integration of ethnic-cultural diversity in one state, as is the case in the USA (Böckenförde 1987, pp. 903, 918). The remarkable thing about this reasoning is less the particularistic concept of nation than the connection of this concept with the idea of democracy which, as we know, is inseparably linked to the universalistic tenets of the French Revolution. And this version of democratic rule, too, is a legacy of Carl Schmitt.

A test of the viability of Schmitt's constitutional approach

The overthrow of communist rule in all Eastern European countries has correctly been described as a political alteration of major historical significance with as yet unknown effects on European and world politics. But this development is no less astounding and consequential for the internal social and political structure of the respective societies. At first glance the revocation of the leading role of the working class and its political incarnations, the Communist Parties, from the constitutions has a purely institutional – albeit important – meaning, in that it entails an institutional separation of party and state power and, consequently, also the realization of the principle of separation of state powers and their democratic legitimation through free elections. It is therefore appropriate to speak of a political revolution. But at the same time, it is more than that. It is hardly mistaken to assume that the ongoing processes of constitution-making in Eastern Europe will entail different variations on three essential principles of their socioeconomic and sociopolitical orders: the institution of human and civil rights, including the right to private ownership of means of production; the establishment of market regulation instead of central economic and social planning; and the creation of a system of autonomous collective bargaining involving unions and business associations which will determine the price of labour for the majority of wage-workers and employees. Compared to the *ancien régime* of one-party rule and the monopolistic command of its leading cadres, who claimed to be the political embodiment of the thorough emancipation of the working class, and even the starting point for the universal liberation of mankind at large, this development seems to have taken on the quality of a social revolution. By social revolution I mean, roughly speaking, a fundamental change in the given distribution of societal wealth and the rules which regulate it. Do we have to understand the revolutions in Eastern Europe as political or as social, or do we have to consider a different theoretical framework? Can we expect Schmitt to give us an appropriate perception of the constitutional implications, since his approach is, so to speak, specialized in the interpretation of states of exception?

Since the end of the eighteenth century, almost all revolutions have been fought on behalf of popular rule. Today there is no principle of political legitimacy which can seriously challenge the democratic axiom. Hence the question is not who is the sovereign, but who can credibly identify himself with 'the people' and claim to be 'the people'. In Europe the response to this question has been given predominantly in terms of class categories: both the two 'Great Revolutions' of the last two hundred years – the French and the Russian – identified 'the people' with the impoverished and exploited classes as opposed to the ruling classes: in the former case it was the bourgeoisie that claimed to be 'the people'; in the latter it was the proletariat. As Hannah Arendt has convincingly shown, these revolutions connected the concept of popular rule with the idea of fundamental social change (Arendt 1963, pp. 14 ff.); this explains why a radical social change was broadly thought to imply a no less radical change in political institutions and, conversely, why the need for a fundamental change in political institutions was considered possible only if it was paralleled by similar social changes. This coupling is due to the underlying continental European concept that 'the people', as the holder of sovereignty, utilized its political will to empower the state with the authority to exercise a unitary control over society. Viewed from the perspective of constitutional theory, revolutions did not aim at the substitution of a new holder of sovereignty for the former, but, rather, at the identification of one social class with 'the people' as the undisputed holder of sovereignty. Hence the cruelty of revolutions in which all parties involved arrogate the omnipotence of the sovereign people for their respective cause. In this continental European frame of reference, revolutions have become more or less concealed class struggles – or, in other words, class struggle has been politicized, with the consequence that the economic and social conflict has escalated almost to the level of modern religious civil wars. This class struggle evidently lurks in the background of Schmitt's concept of the political, which could exercise its suggestive force, and even claim some plausibility, only because the struggle of the diverse social groups for identification with 'the people' implied the inherent tendency to exterminate those members of society who obstinately resisted that identification. And – as Schmitt readily admitted – since it would be inhumane and absolutely unjustifiable to kill people on the basis of socioeconomic interests, he was driven to qualify this struggle for identification with 'the people' as having an 'existential' character which implies the extermination of 'the others' for the sake of preserving 'sameness' beyond all normative justifications. Eccentric and grotesque as this concept is, we should not forget that, in the last instance, it is based on the fundamental axiom that democracy means the command of the unitary will of 'the people' over society, thus combining the concept of democracy with the 'social question'.

Coming back to the revolutions in the Eastern European countries, I want to give a brief assessment of whether they fit into this theoretical framework of understanding revolutions in Europe, which broadly conforms to Schmitt's approach in that it tries to reveal its inherent logic. I restrict myself to the specifically constitutional problems. The question is, then, first, who claims to be 'the people' – that is, who claims to incarnate its 'oneness'; and, second, what is the constitutional design which, after the termination of the revolutionary state of exception, would determine where the power to preserve this oneness is placed within the constitution? In the present pre-constitutional situation, it is easy to understand that the almost universal popular opposition to the dictatorial rule of the *ancien régime* forges the many citizens into 'one people' to the extent that it indeed appears justifiable to speak of the political oneness of the people. Following Schmitt's approach, this would require a clear-cut 'political' – as opposed to legal – reprisal against the exponents of the overturned rule: 'political' punishment of the leading lights of the old regime, through courts specially convened, or without any legal procedure. That means that the question of whether and to what degree they have to be punished depends not on the law (which law?) but on the principle of how best to protect the achievements of the revolution against their political dangerousness and enmity; this is the meaning of 'political justice'. 'Political justice' would involve, furthermore, the dissolution of all political organizations of the old regime, such as the leading party, the unions, and the associated mass organizations; the implicit or explicit revocation of the old constitution in favour of the re-establishment of the 'genuine' people's will as the only legitimate source of order; and last, but not least, the expropriation of their property without any compensation and irrespective of the original manner of acquiring this property, because all entitlements acquired by the beneficiaries of the old order have been wholly delegitimized.

In other words: the characteristic of this revolutionary situation would be the passing of the sovereign power of the people from those who had claimed to incarnate the people's political oneness to 'the people' themselves. But since 'the people' cannot act permanently in the form of immediate mass rallies in the streets, it has to install, by the constitution, new representative agencies which transform its revolutionary spirit into permanent structures, and now represent its political oneness. A framer of the new constitution, having Schmitt's approach in mind, would now

create procedures and powers designed to preserve this unifying political spirit for the times of normalcy to come. He or she would establish
an institution – a president, a powerful or even democratically omnipotent parliament, or a constitutional court – which, irrespective of the
institution of the separation of powers, could claim in times of crisis and
exception to incarnate the political oneness of the people, the spirit of
the founding political ideas, and hence the unitary power which has
now taken command over society. This institution would then be the
new 'guardian of the constitution' – that is, the latent dictator within
constitutional normalcy. And if we take into account the fact that
according to this model of explaining revolutions, the rational nucleus of
the aspiration for 'oneness' and for identification with 'the people' is
ultimately the 'social question', then the 'guardian of the constitution'
wouid have to protect unequivocally the interests of that social group
which had prevailed at the time of the revolution.

Would this pattern of untangling and analysing the present predica-
ments of constitution-making in East Europe provide a satisfying explanation? I have serious doubts. Certainly the situation is still fluid, and less
than clear. What is striking, however, is that apart from the somewhat
different constellation of Romania, the political movements which overturned the old communist regimes have completely resisted the temptation to push forward political purges in the aforementioned sense of
'political justice' on behalf of a constitutionally unbound political will of
the sovereign people. As we know, in the DDR several members of the
former ruling elite have been arrested, but they are supposed to be
charged and judged according to the ordinary penal code before ordinary
civil courts. This implies the grotesque consequence that Erich Honecker
is charged with the crime of high treason according to the still valid penal
code of the old order; of course he did not attack this order but, rather,
protected it with all available and – in the sense of the old order –
legitimate, if not necessarily legal, means, so that he certainly must be
acquitted. There are, of course, calls for the coercive dissolution of the
SED [Communist state party], but among the leading circles of the
political opposition no claim has been made for the exclusion of this party
from the elections to be held in mid March; the legitimacy of the extended
properties of the SED has been contested, but the 'expropriation' takes the
form of the party's search for old documents about the legal origin of its
entitlements, and its autonomous decision about the degree to which it
should give its properties to the state or to the SPD (which was coercively
united with the KPD in 1946, and then had to transfer its properties to the
new party dominated by the communists). Finally, the foundation of the
new order, although essentially driven and enforced by permanent mass
rallies of the citizens, is to be guaranteed by regular parliamentary

elections, whereas in the meantime – a period of about four months – the parliament as well as the government of the old order are still in power, though modified through a 'round table' which unites the political opposition and the representatives of the old regime. The Prime Minister, elected by the old parliament according to the still valid old constitution, couid accurately claim that he was not in office due to a *coup d'état*, but he avoided a positive definition of his legitimacy; indeed, he did not come into power as the representative of the rebellious people in the streets, either, but, rather, as a person entrusted with the task of managing a 'soft' transition from the old order to the new.

All these details and many others bear sufficient evidence to the fact that the political battle – which will presumably go on for several months – does not focus on the Schmittian problem of who is to be the new embodiment of the people's sovereignty, of its political oneness and its unitary will. They reveal, rather, the attempt of an oppressed society whose creative capacity for self-regulation had been suffocated for more than fifty years (counting the years of Nazi rule followed by occupation) to liberate and to constitute itself as a *civil society* that is mature enough to reject its submission to the rule of a unitary power, notwithstanding the fact that this homogeneous state authority has been identified with the sovereign will of 'the people' and justified quasi-eschatologically as the manifestation of historical progress. What has been happening in Eastern Europe is neither a political nor a social but an *institutional revolution* which indeed has far-reaching political and social implications and consequences. European – particularly German – political thought has been preoccupied not so much with civil but with 'bourgeois society' and the devastating consequences of individualism, egotism and the disregard of social solidarity. There have been different – in fact contrary – responses to this worry about societal self-alienation, the most famous and consequential being those of Hobbes, Rousseau, Hegel, Marx, Lenin and, to a certain extent, also of the German Social Democratic Party. Despite their fundamental differences they share the idea that the coherence of society has to be provided through the unitary power of the state. Since the split multitude of individuals and the 'disorder' of society cannot create collective reason, it is the homogeneity and unity of 'the state', and its sovereign power, which forges and represents the quasi-transcendental destiny of society. Schmitt is a conspicuous representative of this statist tradition in the twentieth century; he radicalizes the antinomy between the heterogeneity of society and its incapacity to generate collective reason on the one hand, and the unifying force of a sovereign power that embodies reason on the other. But while the Hegelian assumption of an inherent reasonableness of the state had become unconvincing in the twentieth century and the Marxist–Leninist identification of the proletariat's class interest with the universal interest and destiny of mankind was visibly doomed to degenerate into the rule of Communist Party elites, Schmitt looked for a different concept to reconcile collective reason and power on the basis of the tenets of democracy. Referring to and misunderstanding Rousseau, he found it in a pre-constitutional and even pre-statist concept of the political (Schmitt 1963) which essentially consists in the idea of the contentious will of the people to preserve its quasi-natural ethnic, national and cultural 'sameness' against 'others'. Hence he claims that the will of 'the people' is inherently reasonable (Schmitt 1965 [1928], p. 235), thus finding a vindication for the unification of reason and popular power, and their united command over the heterogeneity of society.

I leave open the question of whether the attempt to reconcile collective reason, power and democratic self-determination is fallacious in its very origin or whether, instead, it represents a viable and valuable utopia. What seems to be evident is the insight that state power, however legitimized, has become a more and more inappropriate medium of societal regulation, at least for modern societies approaching the twenty-first century. The concept of civil society, though it is not yet fully adapted to the needs of contemporary societies, is a response to this experience (Held 1987, pp. 283 ff.; Roedel et al. 1989). In the first instance it requires a constitutional political economy which has to involve some kind of economic democracy (Dahl 1985) and will have to be based on predominantly voluntary associations and communities, respecting social, ethnic, cultural and political diversity, encouraging communicative forms of creating consensus and learning to cope with dissent without trying to forge conformity and unity by the force of an irresistible sovereign will. I have the impression that this is the – more or less unconsciously developed – model of civil society which inspires the revolutions in East Europe. If this is so, they mark a radical breach with the concept of the European revolutions of the last two hundred years, separating the 'social question' of the nineteenth century and the first half of the twentieth from the 'democratic question' (Roedel et al. 1989), and reversing their historic relation: the energies of socioeconomic conflict will not invade and threaten the integrity of the sphere of political institutions, whereas a reasonable institutional mechanism can contribute to the rationalization and civilization of socioeconomic conflicts. Of course, that does not mean that they have already found the adequate answers to the 'democratic question'. In fact, there will never be a definite answer, because the adequate manner in which we can cope with this question will probably consist in the persistent search for responsive institutions in a perpetual learning process.

If this assessment is fairly correct, the social and political preconditions of Schmitt's thought have been fading away. His thought belongs to the age of European revolutions which released the dynamics of capitalist society, and his intellectual originality consisted in the uncompromising and unrivalled radicalism with which he tried to preserve the values of nineteenth-century bourgeois order under conditions of mass democracy and its social and political struggles during the first half of the twentieth century. The fact that, despite his personal moral failure during Nazi rule, his reasoning has been equally attractive to right and left intellectuals since World War II, is certainly due to the promise, in his approach, of the reconciliation of reason and power: a promise which proved wholly illusory and dangerous.

Carl Schmitt is neither a political theorist without significance nor a author of such eternal relevance as Hobbes, Locke or Machiavelli. Rather, his significance is clearly bound to a particular historical epoch which is about to vanish.

References

Altmann, R. (1988) 'Intervention.' In *Complexio Oppositorum. Über Carl Schmitt*, ed. H. Quaritsch. Berlin: Duncker & Humblot, pp. 306–7.

Arendt, H. (1963) *On Revolution*. New York: Viking Press.

Arendt, H. (1972) *Crises of the Republic*. New York: Harcourt Brace Jovanovich.

Böckenförde, E. (1987) 'Demokratie als Verfassungsprinzip'. In *Handbuch des Staatsrechts*, ed. J. Isensee and P. Kirchhof, vol. 1. Heidelberg: C.F. Müller, pp. 887–952.

Böckenförde, E. (1988) 'Der Begriff des Politischen als Schlüssel zum staatsrechtlichen Werk Carl Schmitts'. In *Complexio Oppositorum. Über Carl Schmitt*, ed. H. Quaritsch. Berlin: Duncker & Humblot, pp. 283–99.

Dahl, R.A. (1985) *A Preface to Economic Democracy*. Berkeley and Los Angeles: University of California Press.

Held, D. (1987) *Models of Democracy*. Stanford, CA: Stanford University Press.

Hobbes, T. (1991 [1651]) *Leviathan, or the Matter, Forme, & Power of a common-Wealth Ecclesiastical and Civil*. Cambridge: Cambridge University Press.

Huber, E.R. (1988) 'Carl Schmitt in der Reichskrise der Weimarer Endzeit'. In *Complexio Oppositorum. Über Carl Schmitt*, ed. H. Quaritsch. Berlin: Duncker & Humblot, pp. 33–50.

Isensee, J. (1987) 'Staat und Verfassung'. In *Handbuch des Staatsrechts*, ed. J. Isensee and P. Kirchhoff, vol. 1. Heidelberg: C.F. Müller, pp. 591–661.

Kennedy, E. (1988) 'Politischer Expressionismus: Die kulturkritischen und metaphysischen Ursprünge des Begriffs des Politischen von Carl Schmitt'. In *Complexio Oppositorum. Über Carl Schmitt*, ed. H. Quaritsch. Berlin: Duncker & Humblot, pp. 233–51.

Maschke, G. (1987) *Der Tod des Carl Schmitt. Apologie und Polemik.* Vienna: Karolinger.

Offe, C. and Preuss, U.K. (1991) 'Democratic Institutions and Moral Resources'. In *Political Theory Today*, ed. D. Held. Cambridge: Polity Press, pp. 143–71.

Quaritsch, H. (1987) 'Einleitung: Über den Umgang mit Person und Werk Carl Schmitts'. In *Complexio Oppositorum. Über Carl Schmitt*, ed. H. Quaritsch. Berlin: Duncker & Humblot, pp. 13–21.

Roedel, U., Frankenberg, G. and Dubiel, H. (1989) *Die demokratische Frage. Ein Essay.* Frankfurt: Suhrkamp.

Schmitt, C. (1958 [1929]) 'Das Reichsgericht als Hüter der Verfassung'. In Carl Schmitt, *Verfassungsrechtliche Aufsätze aus den Jahren 1924–1954. Materialien zu einer Verfassungslehre.* Berlin: Duncker & Humblot, pp. 63–109.

Schmitt, C. (1958 [1932]) 'Legalität und Legitimität'. In Carl Schmitt *Verfassungsrechtliche Aufsätze aus den Jahren 1924–1954. Materialien zu einer Verfassungslehre.* Berlin: Duncker & Humblot, pp. 263–350.

Schmitt, C. (1958 [1953]) 'Nehmen/Teilen/Weiden'. In Carl Schmitt *Verfassungsrechtliche Aufsätze aus den Jahren 1924–1954. Materialien zu einer Verfassungslehre.* Berlin: Duncker & Humblot, pp. 489–504.

Schmitt, C. (1963 [1927/1932]) *Der Begriff des Politischen. Text von 1932 mit einem Vorwort und drei Corollarien.* Berlin: Duncker & Humblot.

Schmitt, C. (1965 [1928]) *Verfassungslehre* (4th edn) Berlin: Duncker & Humblot.

Schmitt, C. (1969 [1931]) *Der Höter der Verfassung* (2nd edn). Berlin: Duncker & Humblot.

Schmitt, C. (1976 [1927/1932]) *The Concept of the Political.* New Brunswick/NJ: Rutgers University Press.

Schmitt, C. (1978 [1921]) *Die Diktatur. Von den Anfängen des modernen Souveränitätsgedankens bis zum proletarischen Klassenkampf* (4th edn). Berlin: Duncker & Humblot.

Schmitt, C. (1979 [1922/1933]) *Politische Theologie. Vier Kapitel zur Lehre von der Souveränität.* (3rd edn). Berlin: Duncker & Humblot.

Schmitt, C. (1988 [1923]) *The Crisis of Parliamentary Democracy.* (trans. Ellen Kennedy). Cambridge, MA, London: MIT Press.

Willms, B. (1987) 'Carl Schmitt – Jüngster Klassiker des politischen Denkens?' In *Complexio Oppositorum. Über Carl Schmitt*, ed. H. Quaritsch. Berlin: Duncker & Humblot, pp. 577–97.

Carl Schmitt and European
Juridical Science

Agostino Carrino

> Peace cannot be based purely on human reason. It will not last if
> it remains merely a treaty agreed by men, and therefore, cannot
> constitute, at the same time, a sacred agreement.
>
> (Ernst Jünger, *Peace* [1945])

'Die Lage der europäischen Rechtswissenschaft',[1] written during the
worst period of the Second World War, is one of the most important
essays to consult for an insight into Carl Schmitt's complex and painstak-
ing thought. This can be seen from two points of view. The first refers to
the Schmittian doctrine of state and law; the second refers to the
relationship between Schmitt and the national Socialist regime.

Where Schmitt's political philosophy is concerned, the above-mentioned
essay shows the full importance of the juridical structure of Schmittian
thought – that is, the central role of *jus* in the structure of Schmitt's
works, which are based not on juridical doctrine but, rather, on concrete
reality (this is why he has been accused of 'occasionalism').[2]

For many years, the study of Schmitt has been left to political
scientists, political philosophers and historians of political doctrine.[3] In
'Die Lage . . .' Schmitt seems to assert that in essence he is a jurist, a
claim he was to make many years later when he declared, with pride: 'I
am a jurist!'[4] Therefore, this essay on European juridical science should
be read *en juriste*, in the awareness of the fact that he was a *great* jurist,
and that he was not (merely) interested in the mechanics of law; on the
contrary, he was open to the broader perspectives of juridical culture
and legal civilization. Another element that characterized Schmitt during
the period of the Weimar Republic should be taken into account: his
ambiguity, which led Erich Schwinge, in his essay on methodological

controversy in public law, to define Schmitt as 'the sphinx' of modern German legal experts.[5]

The first point which must be emphasized is the role of juridical science in Schmitt's historical perspective, and the connection between juridical science and law. In the early 1950s, Enrico Allorio believed that the correct interpretation of Schmitt's essay could be summed up in the theory that the production of law comes directly from juridical science, at least on the 'optative' level, and from his point of view – based on a formalistic and dogmatic-systematic conception – he rejected this.[6] However, does Schmitt really argue that 'juridical science' produces law? Furthermore, does he really believe that law can be produced? In this context, the Schmittian idea of 'acceptance' is extremely illuminating because it is not limited to the best-known phenomenon of the acceptance of Roman Law within modern legal systems but, rather, relates to the entire history of the peoples of Europe, and is interpreted as profoundly deep-rooted:

> It can even be argued, without exaggeration, that the entire story and development of the peoples of Europe has been, for thousands of years, the story of mutual acceptance, where 'acceptance' does not mean a passive process devoid of creativity, but an alternate process of incorporation, adaptation and perfection of laws, often linked to strong resistance, capable of affecting these laws, which must be evaluated case by case.[7]

To this, I would add the observation that in his essay, Schmitt suggests the idea (even if it is not fully developed) that law and juridical science (almost) overlap, until one cannot (logically) be the *product* of the other. The acceptance of Roman Law seems to be an eminently cultural phenomenon whereby the different peoples of Europe recognize that they share common roots, and that they inhabit the same land mass:

> From the work of the jurists of all the peoples of Europe, Roman Law became a common vocabulary, the language of the juridical science community, recognized as the model for juridical conceptualizing and, therefore, a conceptual and spiritual Common European Law, without which it would not even have been theoretically possible to achieve a common understanding between the jurists of different nations. This cultural edifice, based on the European spirit, is supported by this common base, produced by a common European legal science.[8]

In this essay, this common acknowledgement by the peoples of Europe as regards law assumes a peculiar characteristic: if, in fact, Schmitt believes that the state is a historically determined phenomenon that is destined to be superseded,[9] law remains the same – specific to European culture – so that a European consciousness alienated during the progressive and eventual disappearance of the state (which actually represented Europe's response to both the crisis of medieval Christian unity and the [civil] religious wars which followed) can attempt to rediscover the origins of the possibility of a new beginning. Therefore, this essay (which I would read in parallel with the essay – more or less contemporary – by Ernst Jünger in *Der Friede*, even if it could not be considered as good as his next work, *Nomos der Erde*) has, however, the undoubted merit of revealing a Schmitt who avoids the dangers of pessimism and attempts to look beyond the ruins of contemporary Europe.[10]

In effect, this work has a 'Catholic' dimension, in the sense that Schmitt both opens and is open to an optimism nourished by the strength of law, seen neither as commensurate with the state nor even identified (in a Kelsenian way) with the state. It is beyond the scope of this chapter to discuss the problem of the relationship between Schmitt and both natural law and juridical positivism; he criticized the latter, above all, as juridical legalism – in fact, in the last analysis, as 'statalism'. One of the most serious errors that still bedevils interpretations of Schmitt is the idea that he was a passionate supporter of the state as an institution; in fact, the opposite is true: for him, the state is a 'good evil' – good, because this product of European culture was magnificent during the process of overcoming civil war, because it knew how to develop as a 'mortal god', and therefore founded its own theological structure; but also bad, because the modern state, because it is modern, is necessarily subjected to the modern world; it therefore follows destiny, adjusting itself to a purely instrumental 'rationality'. Also, above all, because the state is the product of a theory which is itself the result of a division, an unresolved dualism: the dualism between thought and being, subject and object. For Schmitt, the state is both a response to civil war, and at the same time – with Bacon and Descartes, the relativist and anti-theological philosophy – the basis of the modern revolution.[11]

A rigorous analysis of the philosophical foundations of Schmittian thought is needed if we are to understand its opposition to the central problem of modernity, represented by Cartesian methodology. While it is impossible to carry out such an analysis here, the subject is reminiscent of an essay on Schmitt by Hugo Ball, where he wrote that the 'dismantling of the old ontological thought' started with Descartes;[12] however, Schmitt believed that ontological thought is vital if we are to understand the world. He is a realist, a man for whom things have their own lasting reality. This lasting reality, however, has been dismantled; the atom, indivisible by definition, has been divided. This is the contradiction that characterizes the world; therefore, it is also the contradiction within

Schmitt's thought: he is a great intellectual because he re-creates, within his own field of study, the aforementioned contradiction of both external reality and history. Schmittian decisionism (which never fails in this sense) is its own realism because it is reality that decides for or against the subject, sometimes shattering or superseding it; in so doing it brings about the tragedy (alienation) of both modern consciousness and philosophical thought from Kant onwards.

Therefore, reality is mortal for the modern man who has created a totalizing consciousness; at the same time, reality is also – as Heidegger would have put it – 'that which saves'. The law is part of this reality – or rather, it is identified with reality, which Schmitt himself defined as 'the concrete (juridical) order', or *jus* (later known as nomos), which is, in turn, law separated from positivistic law. Schmitt conceives law not as an obligation, pure *Sollen*, but as a way of being, *Sein* – indeed, being, in Schmitt's thought, is not contrasted with obligation [*Sollen*], as is the case in Kelsen's thought; it is, however, contrasted with *Nicht-Sein*.[13] Schmitt believes that being is not empirical or contingent; rather, he sees being in a historical sense, which is almost as Vico would conceive it, to the extent that in this essay Schmitt refers to Roman Law as it exists historically in the development of juridical science; law is not 'produced' by such a science but, rather, conceived consciously.

In this context, the underlining of the value and significance of the works of Savigny – founder of the school of history – is very important: the work of the German historian, as Schmitt puts it, 'is an existentialist reflection made by law itself'; it represents an appeal to legal science as the custodian of both ratified and non-ratified law'.[14] We can understand why law, given this element, has a new dimension which is similar to art: Europe is not only the sum of its cathedrals, churches, palaces, art galleries and music, it is also characterized by its juridical knowledge.

Europe, however, is also characterized by its *positive law*. In 'Die Lage...', the fact is that Schmitt is not a 'member of the school of natural law'; he does not contrast natural law with 'positive' law: in the positive nature of law, which is also its historical nature, lies positive law, which is ratified, and to a certain extent also written. This takes into account the theories of both Savigny and Hegel. Therefore, without doubt, the existential nature of law informs its 'positive nature', which implies that law is something which is 'given':

Schmitt argues that a particular Savignyan doctrine about the sources of law had an absolutely existentialist meaning. Through this theory, Savigny gives both the doctrine and the sources of law a new and profound meaning. Savigny and his unique notions of 'historical' and 'positive' can be understood only if one reflects on the fact that his doctrine and the image he gives of the sources of law are closely linked to the fight for survival by legal science. Law, as a concrete system, cannot be separated from its historical context. Real law is not set in stone; rather, it develops involuntarily. Real law can be defined as the concrete historical form of existence of a class of jurists who acknowledge this evolution. According to Savigny, the concept of the positive, as legal science understands it, is linked to a particular source of law, protected by jurists; in this source, law finds its origins in a specific way, as something which is given but not ratified.[15]

Therefore, nothing is more positive than this law of which the jurists are also the custodians and, therefore, somewhat distant from acritical positivism, or even from the criticism which, first, reduces law to a product derived from an arbitrary will; and, second, believes in the possibility of a purely scientific vision that is capable of producing the required unity and coherence of law made by the legislator. However, Schmitt perceives something more profound in both this juridical positivism and 'positive law' – their desire for power, and the fact that they are symbols of the age of reason: juridical positivism 'knows only fundamental causes and norms which are based on hypothesis. It does not seek law which is devoid of an objective; therefore, its ultimate objective is achievement of power and reason.'[16] To foresee an event in order to manage it is the motto of positivism, while an existentialist conception of both law and the world sees law like the fruit of a tree, the result of an object which has no other objective than to exist for itself. From this, the paradigmatic value is contrasted with the positive nature of law, and also the emblematic character of the debate between Savigny and Hegel, and its importance for Schmitt in this context:

> However fruitless the debate may have been due to its polemical nature, for him it testifies to the importance of such a debate, once more, before juridical science becomes all-powerful, and before the crisis that the state experiences, which is symbolized by the aforementioned debate. The breakdown of this dialogue is, among other historical factors, one of the reasons for the lack of juridical consciousness that characterizes the 'motorized legislator' of the twentieth century, for whom decrees, ordinances and administrative regulation have replaced the norm of the general law. However, such a legislator has not been able to deal with the juridical and political consequences.[17]

If all this is true, however, (my comments so far are totally provisional, and purely for the purposes of a working hypothesis), how can one explain not only the fact that Schmitt was linked with the Nazi regime for many years, but that he even regarded himself as its 'official' interpreter? It is true that many consider the Nazi phenomenon a kind of antimodern response to the modern world; however, if, as I believe, this interpretation is mistaken, and Nazism can be considered as a revolt (albeit completely contradictory) caused by Titanic forces, and therefore essentially modern, how can one reconcile all this with a Schmittian juridical philosophy which is itself a critique of modernity?

Above all, in order to support the thesis of both the 'Titanic nature' and the technical apparatus of nazism, I would like to mention a little-known author, the Nazi economic theorist Fritz Nonnenbruch: for Nonnenbruch, there is no separation between Nazism and its technical apparatus; rather, the contrary: the new system set up by Hitler is nothing but 'an infinite desire for a technical state'.[18]

If 'big capital' seems, for him, both stateless and branded as 'Hebrew', contemporary capitalism can be considered the enemy of technical progress, of which Nazism has made itself the champion.[19] If this is the argument made by the apologists for the other great 'decisionist' of the age, Martin Heidegger – that is, to develop an equal relationship between Nazism and technical progress – it confirms, for those who wish to believe it, that Heidegger (however indirectly) is also a critic of Nazism.[20] In other words, the exaltation of Titanism can be contrasted with those who have, instead, criticized modernity for its desire for technical supremacy and, therefore, absolute power.

So, by keeping to both the letter and the spirit of his thought, it is possible to see that there was an incompatibility between Schmitt and Nazism (which appears to be most evident in the essay on European juridical science), in that *Nazism was absolutely opposed to Roman Law*. Furthermore, within the constitution of the National Socialist Party, the battle against the corrupting spirit of Roman Law was even included within the dogma of the Nazi programme: 'The aim is to replace Roman Law, which is a law proper to a materialistic conception of the world, a common German law'. In particular, this was demonstrated over the issue of ownership; in reality, however, Roman Law was always subject to criticism by German conservatives.[21]

It is also evident that even a superficial reading of 'Die Lage . . .' demonstrates that Schmitt was not opposed to either Roman Law or roman juridical science. It is true that he generalizes the phenomenon of legal acceptance; nowhere in this essay, however, does he reject the notion of common law. Thus, this acknowledgement is more relevant because it is impossible to hide the fact that the relationship between Schmitt and juridical science was rather different between 1933 and 1936. I quote from 'Aufgabe und Notwendigket des deutschen Rechtsstandes' in order to clarify the gap between these two positions:[22] with the overcoming of the 'rule of Roman Law', writes Schmitt, 'the caste organization of the German guardianship of law' will also have to disappear:

> One is unthinkable without the other. When the robes fall, so also does the King. If we battle against the Roman Law already accepted, this is not solely a battle against the content of particular juridical propositions; one can perhaps argue against its compatibility; however, it is principally a battle for the creation of a totally German guardianship of law, which satisfies all the necessary conditions for organization and structure, in order to create and safeguard a common German law.[23]

It is impossible not to see the abyss that separates the Schmitt of 1936 from the Schmitt of 1943. It is beyond the scope of this chapter to explain why Schmitt made such an 'unnatural' conversion in order to support National Socialism, a conversion which 'is not noticeable in other intellectuals of the period';[24] one thing, however, is certain: during this period he was both an outstanding exponent and an authentic representative of Nazism – or, at least, this is both what he tried to be and what he is understood to be by many foreign jurists, for example, those in France and Italy.[25]

Is the Carl Schmitt of the Nazi time the necessary consequence of the Carl Schmitt of the Twenties? Personally, I do not believe so. Also, I do not believe that it is possible to question the break between the Nazi Schmitt and the Schmitt who was to follow.[26] Naturally, there has to be both a certain connection between the 'three Schmitts' and an explanation for students' attitudes to all his work. Furthermore, if one wanted to assert that Schmitt's connection was with the 'leader' rather than with the party – was with both the 'person' and the 'responsibilities' of the Führer, rather than with Nazi ideology, leading to a desire to accentuate the unity of Schmitt's thought – this would lead one to regard Schmitt's defence of Hitler after the Night of the Long Knives (the massacre of Röhm and the SA) as a consequence of regarding the leader as the protector of the law, the representative of a truly neutral state.[27]

In effect, the Nazi Schmitt – following a certain kind of Hegelian rebirth during this period[28] – emphasizes elements of a Hegelian interpretation of Prussia, or a Prussian interpretation of Hegel, neither of which has anything to do with his Catholicism: it is enough to recall the passage on Hegel in Schmitt's essay on the three types of juridical thought: in Hegel, writes Schmitt:

> once again, concrete institutional thought comes back to life – with an immediate impact that nobody could have expected, given the development of the theories of law and state during the seventeenth and eighteenth centuries – before the collapse of the following generations.

Hegel's state, which seems to Schmitt to resemble an imperial state rather than a purely modern state:

> is not a guarantee of tranquillity for the bourgeoisie, an institution which secures the functioning of the legal order. Neither is it sovereign body, the 'norm of all norms'. . . . It is the order above all other orders, the institution above all other institutions.[29]

During the period of the National Socialist regime, and after the 'decision' to adhere to the new order, Schmitt's thought undergoes a dramatic change where the elements of a break seem to prevail.

There is also, however, an implicit continuity within Schmittian thought on law, a continuity which is not usually considered relevant. I would mention the permanent status within Schmitt's thought of the notion of the superiority of the spiritual world, on the one hand, and of the spiritual nature of law, on the other:[30] for Schmitt, law is not and never has been a 'fact'. It is incorrect to think that the 'concrete' dimension of law is some kind of materialist empiricism; here, concreteness is always related to the history of a people and its law, and is not the result of some kind of materialist or voluntarist determinism ('blood').

When he wrote, in his early essay on the state, that law is an abstract idea, independent of facts and without relevance for them,[31] Schmitt wanted to say what can also be read – albeit permeated with pathos and a certain rhetoric which can indeed be justified by new and tragic experiences – in his essay on European juridical science:

> also, even within the terror of the instruments of destruction which the modern science of nature puts into the hands of those in power, a juridical science which is completely restored to itself will know how to find the mysterious in which the essence of its spirit is protected against every enemy.[32]

Therefore, law is not positive, and juridical science cannot be identified with the frenetic activity of the 'motorized legislator'; rather, both find their roots in a positive but invisible reality, divorced from modern humanity's desire for power.

Therefore, the essay on European juridical science represents Schmitt's 'return' to his pre-Nazi phase, and was perhaps even the prelude to a re-evaluation of his early ideas, which were to re-emerge as new experiences in the postwar period (the 'experience of the cell'). This also certainly represents a disowning but not, if we understand it correctly, a repudiation of his past. However, he was not only disowning his Nazi past, but at the same time accepting responsibility for what he had done.

Only fools or the weak can (pretend to) repudiate the past (which, in a Heideggerian sense, would mean repudiating oneself): through his mistakes, Schmitt was able to re-evaluate both the modern world and the possibility of man's salvation.

Thus, once again, he rediscovers his status as a jurist rather than as a 'political theorist'; within this rediscovery, he naturally also rediscovers the philosophy of juridical theory which forms part of the German cultural consciousness. I do not know if this is the best place to discuss the impact of a Christian and Augustinian vision, a Hegelian vision, or a particular kind of Existentialist vision[33] on the specific 'philosophical' dimensions of Schmittian thought. For now, therefore, I will reserve judgement. However, Hugo Ball, who knew Schmitt well, picks out a particular aspect of his personality which, to some extent, could help us to understand many aspects of the man which still remain shrouded in mystery: his 'commitment to the absolute', a commitment which, however,

> does not lend itself in any way to notions of the abstract ... but, rather, is directed to the concrete.... Like any Kantian, Schmitt starts with a priori concepts, starting precisely with his ideology of law. However, he is not content to define such concepts solely in relation to each other.
>
> Rather, he seeks to characterize each of his juridical concepts by reference to both existing forms of states and by reference to tradition, in a progressive manner, following both their most recent relations and their form of secularization, compared to other superior categories (philosophy, art, theology).[34]

This passage is of interest to anybody who is familiar with the philosophical epistemology of the first two decades of this century: on the one hand, Schmitt starts as a Kantian, or perhaps even a 'neo-Kantian', according to a perspective (already created by the neo-Kantism of Baden and, more specifically, that of Emil Lask) developed in an ontological sense.[35] Therefore, anybody who wishes to study Schmitt seriously must investigate this. In other words, he deals with a neo-Platonic perspective – which, obviously, he interpreted through Catholic eyes – which becomes Augustinian (this is Beaud's recent interpretation) but which, in my opinion, should remain the same (neo-Platonic) even when the Catholic element disappears (as during the Nazi years). However, I would hope to return to this subject in a future work in order to develop these ideas. The fact is that with this perspective, if it is correct, one must characterize the twofold nature of all phenomena, within their particular transient or perennial historical context. It is not by chance that Schmitt tries to stretch the definition of the concept (essence) of the political in order to include the historicity of the state, a fact which requires some analysis.[36]

In fact, at the same time, Schmitt emphasizes the historicity of the state and its decisive role in the modern era of the Western world. If it is true that he is not a 'statalist' – which is the opposite view to the one usually attributed both to him and to other authors close to him, such as the Italian Costamagna[37] – it must also be true that for Schmitt the state represents a vital phenomenon, even if he could not avoid deprecating all those phenomena which actually ended up destroying state sovereignty.[38] Nevertheless, Schmitt is, above all, a lucid and clinical analyst of historical processes; he characterizes, in effect, two connected phenomena within the gradual erosion of sovereignty: first, the socialization of the state; second, the statalization (juridicalization) of society (these ideas were subsequently analysed by one of Schmitt's most important students, Ernst Forsthoff[39]). The result of this certainly not only ensures the adoption of a position, but also – more importantly – pinpoints the real problem. As Nigro has noted:

Schmitt is credited with having anticipated, with real genius, the process of the fusion of state and society, in the twofold form of the organizing of society, and the socializing of the state. He also recognizes the existence of diffuse phenomena of confusion and impotence that the present state exhibits, particularly with the ever-growing acceptance of pluralism, especially as the latter is seen not as the antithesis, and the element which corrupts the administrative state, but rather as providing its dialectical solution.[40]

In other words, Schmittian discourse appears liable to exploitation, despite the unambiguous position Schmitt adopts; he demonstrates that only a clinical analysis allows one to develop a worthwhile discourse based on a conception of the world [Weltanschauung]. Such a conception does not depend on scientific analysis, but a historically justified conception of the world may never leave out of consideration a disenchanted diagnosis of the state of the world.

From this point of view, Schmitt reveals his debt to another important figure within contemporary thought, Max Weber. Schmitt cannot be understood without reference to Weber's political and juridical sociology; the former is the most important student of the latter.[41] I would like to suggest that the main link between Schmitt and Weber lies in the rejection of the notion that one dimension of life is sovereign over all others. It could be argued that this is going too far, as Schmitt could easily rank alongside those who believe that 'everything is political', so that politics, from the Maurrassian point of view, comes before everything else [politique d'abord]; anyway, it is not difficult to find in Schmitt elements which support this interpretation, but it is also possible to draw the opposite interpretation, as suggested in the essay on European juridical science.

In conclusion, the reading of Schmitt's essay is vital if we are to achieve a correct understanding of his thought, since it acts as a link between two different periods. Furthermore, it confirms Schmitt's appeal, as Cantimori found in the 1930s. In fact, this is the attraction of an era full of events and high-profile protagonists. Schmitt's works are both important and meaningful because they compete with rival works and ideas. Schmitt is interesting because it is possible to study him as part of an era which fascinates us because of its richness of intellectual and cultural activity, compared to the poverty of the present. When Schmitt is studied outside his cultural-historical context, it is sometimes difficult to read and comprehend his work, and it can also be reduced to a fruitless exercise. I seem to recall reading somewhere that when he was in Spain, Schmitt apologized to his host, because he wanted to return to Germany as soon as possible, by saying (more or less): 'I need my enemies'. Furthermore, Schmitt's works in isolation from other works – from Savigny to Laband, Kelsen, Radbruch, Heller, Smend, Triepel, Kirchheimer, and others – are pointless.

Within this perspective, the period during which Schmitt supported the Nazi regime can be considered a necessary failure. Destiny decreed that he should play this role; the question of whether it was congenial to him remains open, and goes beyond the scope of this chapter. In fact, I believe that the notion that there was a congenial relationship between Schmitt and the Nazis should be called into question.

The 'Carl Schmitt question' remains open, and this German jurist, who could be considered one of the metaphors of the twentieth century (another being Hans Kelsen), is still in need of exhaustive study.[42] However, this will not be possible unless it is conceived as one chapter in the history of political doctrine; in such a perspective Schmitt is – and will always be – the 'villain'. On the contrary, what is required is to relocate him in his own world – that is, the world of law – because there, and only there, he is intelligible. Schmitt's vocation was law, and throughout his life he was a great constitutionalist and theorist of the state, in line with the German tradition. Within law, politics can be found; within juridical theology, political theology can be found. It is the task of academics to discover the real and profound relationship between law, politics and theology (but also art and literature). *Sine ira et studio.*

Translated by Jorge del Rio Fernandez

Notes

1. C. Schmitt, 'Die Lage der europäischen Rechtswissenschaft' (1950), in *Verfassungs-rechtliche Aufsätze aus den Jahren 1924–1954. Materialen zu einer Verfassungslehre*, Berlin: Duncker & Humblot, 1958, pp. 386–429. First published in Hungarian in *Gazdasági Jog*, 1944, 5, pp. 257–70, with the title 'Az Europai Jogtudomány Mai Helyzete' (translated by Professor Kuncz Ödön). This chapter is a slightly abridged version of my article 'Europa und das Recht. Kritische Anmerkungen zu Carl Schmitts "Die Lage der europäischen Rechtswissenschaft', in *Staat und Recht. Festschrift für Günther Winkler*, Vienna – New York, 1997, pp. 161–77.

2. See K. Löwith, 'Il decisionismo occasionale di Carl Schmitt' (1935), in *Marx, Weber, Schmitt*, Roma-Bari: Laterza, 1994, pp. 124–66. 'Nothing meaningful can be said about culture and history without being aware of one's own historical and cultural situation': C. Schmitt, 'Das Zeitalter der Neutralisierungen und Entpolitisierungen' (1929), in *Positionen und Begriffe im Kampf mit Weimar-Genf-Versailles 1923–1939*, Berlin: Duncker & Humblot, 1988 (1940), p. 121: Schmitt shares this attitude, *mutatis mutandis*, with Weber and Hegel, and cannot therefore be easily interpreted as 'occasionalistic'.

3. See G. Maschke, 'Carl Schmitt in die Händen der Nicht-Juristen. Zur Neueren Literatur', *Der Statat* 34, 1 (1995), pp. 104–29.

4. 'I feel a hundred per cent a jurist and nothing else. Furthermore, I do not want to be anything else. I will be a jurist until I die, and endure all the misfortune of being a jurist that is involved': in F. Lanchester (ed.), 'Un giurista davanti a se stesso. Intervista a Carl Schmitt', *Quaderni costituzionali* III, 1 (1983), p. 34.

5. 'Carl Schmitt is the sphinx of the modern doctrine of public law, because from the first moment, he avoids precise classification': E. Schwinge, *Der Methodenstreit in der heutigen Rechtswissenschaft*, Bonn: Ludwig Rohrscheid Verlag, 1930, p. 19.

6. E. Allorio, 'Scienza giuridica europea', *Jus*, 1952; reprinted in Allorio, *La vita e la scienza del diritto in Italia e in Europa e altri studi*, Milan: Giuffrè, 1957, p. 65: 'I believe that this discussion also relates to the science of law. This does not either "create" law, or form its basis, therefore, one should not hope it is or that it will become so, as Carl Schmitt seems to do.'

7. Schmitt, 'Die Lage der europäischen Rechtswissenschaft', p. 391.

8. Ibid, p. 396.

9. See C. Schmitt, 'Staat als ein konkreter, an eine geschichtliche Epoche gebundener Begriff' (1941), in *Verfassungsrechtliche Aufsätze aus den Jahren 1924–1954. Materialen zu einer Verfassungslehre*, Berlin: Duncker & Humblot, 1958, pp. 375–85.

10. E. Jünger, *Der Friede* (1945), in *Sämtliche Werke*, vol. 7, Stuttgart: Klett-Cotta, 1980, pp. 193 f. As for Jünger and his influence on Schmitt, we see it in Schmitt's essay in, among other things, the last lines on pain. 'Let us recall the history of our tortuous labour, given that our strength is based upon our knowledge of pain' (p. 88) reminds us of Jünger's wonderful essay on pain (1934), and the contemporary relationship with the pain of the worker, that is, the figure who represents being thrown into Titanic modernity, and assumes the responsibility of bearing all pain: see A. Carrino, 'L'Operaio di Jünger tra tecnica e dolore', *Democrazia e diritto* XXXIII, 1 (1993), pp. 169–82.

11. See A. Carrino, 'Stato e rivoluzione nell'età del nichilismo' (1987), in Carrino (ed.), *Il diritto nella società moderna*, Naples: Edizioni Scientifiche Italiane, 1995, pp. 241–66.

12. H. Ball, 'Carl Schmitts Politische Theologie', *Hochland* 21 (April–September), S. 261–284; now published in J. Taubes (ed.), *Der Furst dieser Welt. Carl Schmitt und die Folgen*, Munich/Vienna/Zurich: Ferdinand Schoningh-Wilhelm Fink Verlag, 1983, p. 103.

13. See H. Hofmann, *Legitimität gegen Legalität* (1964; Berlin: Duncker & Humblot, 1992), p. 21. (This is one of the few high-profile books on Schmittian thought.)

14. Schmitt, 'Die Lage . . .' p. 411.

15. Ibid.

16. Ibid.

.

17. See J.-F. Kervégan, *Carl Schmitt, Hegel. Le politique entre spéculation et positivité*, Paris: Presses Universitaires de France, 1992, p. 142.

18. F. Nonnenbruch, *Die dynamische Wirtschaft*, Munich: Zentralverlag der NSDAP, 1936, 2. Aufl., p. 154. see also Nonnenbruch, *Politik, Technik und Geist*, Munich: Hoheneichen Verlag, 1939.

19. On Nonnenbruch, see E. Waibl, *Ökonomie und Ethik, Der Kapitalismusdebatte in der Philosophie der Neuzeit*, Stuttgart-Bad Cannstatt: Frommann-Holzboog, 1988–89, vol. 2, pp. 156–71.

20. See, for example, S. Vietta, *Heideggers Kritik am Nationalsozialismus und an der Technik*, Tübingen: Max Niemeyer Verlag, 1989, where not only should Heidegger not be regarded as a supporter of National Socialism (or as having an anti-Semitic and racist ideology) but, indeed, the opposite is the case; therefore he should be considered one of its critics: Heidegger, writes Vietta, 'leaves no room for doubt about the fact that he considers National Socialism an extreme form of contemporary Nihilism where man "forgets his *raison d'être*"' (p. 101). In this sense, Nazism itself becomes the subject of a radical critique by Heidegger of the notion of technical supremacy, in order to develop his 'radical distancing from the subjectivity of the modern', a distancing influenced specifically by his study of Nietzsche; however, there is a letter where, rather than seeing Nietzsche as negating Nihilism, Heidegger perceives him as having radicalized it (p. 67). For Heideggerian interpretation of Nietzsche Vietta goes back to the second half of the 1930s. Not only does he criticize the 'Nazi' interpretation, he sees Heidegger's university lectures, which were published after the war, as a first-class 'political act' against the Nazi totalitarian system (p. 51): 'Both Nietzsche and Heidegger recognize the Nihilism within real National Socialism' (p. 50) which, behind the 'ideas' and the 'values', was merely the ultimate expression of the desire for power (pp. 48–9). On the basis of a selection of some Heideggerian texts, Vietta considers 1938 the turning point: from this moment on, critiques of both technical supremacy and Nazism converge into a 'revelation' of the alienation of man within modernity, and of the project of the 'technical' subjection and exploitation of the world, of which Nazism is the highest expression.

21. If we stay within the sphere of the movement known as the 'Conservative revolution', of which Oswald Spengler was considered part, it is enough to limit ourselves to the works of Spengler in order to understand that Roman Law is the real phenomenon which represents the corruption of true 'Germanic liberty'. Spengler writes: 'Roman Law has corrupted us. It promotes, in a dangerous way, the tendency of the ordinary German to dream, to swallow whole everything that exists' ('Neubau des Reiches' [1924], in *Politische Schriften*, Munich: Beck, 1933, pp. 241 f).

22. C. Schmitt, 'Aufgabe und Notwendigkeit des deutschen Rechtsstandes', *Deutsches Recht* 6 (1936), pp. 181–85.

23. See ibid., pp. 181–2. Both Schmitt and prominent students of his work, such as Ernst Forsthoff – who wrote an essay on the 'Total State' in 1933 – were in complete agreement with the directives of the new regime.

24. See F. Lanchester, 'Carl Schmitt: un giurista scomodo', in: *Momenti e figure nel diritto costituzionale in Italia e Germania*, Milan: Giuffrè, 1994, p. 234. In explaining this conversion, Lanchester suggests on the one hand 'voluptas potestatis'; on the other, fear.

25. See, for example, F. Perroux, *Des mythes hitlériens à l'Europe allemande*, Paris: Librairie Générale de Droit et de Jurisprudence, 1940; A. Volpicelli, Preface to C. Schmitt, *Principii politici del nazionalsocialismo, Scritti scelti e tradotti da D. Cantimori*, Florence: Sansoni, 1935, p. v: 'Carl Schmitt, one of the official intellectuals of National Socialism'.

26. It has already been demonstrated that there is a real break in the 'development' of Schmittian thought. The fact is that in the second edition of *Der Begriff des Politischen* (1935), the Bibliography does not list any texts by the 'young' Schmitt, not even the 1924 essay on Roman Catholicism (a kind of self-censorship *à la* Lukács?).

27. One is reminded that in Schmitt, absolute sovereignty is never above the law but, rather, embodies it:

> The absolute sovereign is, at all times, above the relativity of the moment; he is not important as an individual; he does not experience changes of mood or enjoy

entertainment; he has become in everything 'the law'; he is no more above the law than he is above grammar. (C. Schmitt, *Der Wert des Staates und die Bedeutung des Einzelnen*, Helleray Hegner, 1917, p. 95)

This is followed immediately by:

The dignity that he demands and which he is attributed is solely related to his functions, and is not for the mere mortal. Thanks to his similarity to God, the absolute monarch embodies 'living law'; he is subject to the law, like the theological God whose omnipotent will cannot desire anything bad or irrational. (p. 96)

The functional nature of absolute sovereignty over law is what was to allow Schmitt his 'Prussian change'; thus, from this point of view, it would even be possible to interpret Schmitt's article on Hitler as protector of the law, written as a comment on the 'Night of the Long Knives' in a less negative way than usual. The essay ('Der Führer schätz das Recht, 1934) is in *Positonen und Begriffe im Kampf mit Weimar-Genf-Versailles, 1923–1939*, pp. 199–203.

28. See, on this point, the R. Treves's important essay *La filosofia di Hegel e le nuove concezioni del diritto e dello Stato*, Messina: Principato, 1935.

29. C. Schmitt, *Über die drei Arten des rechtswissenschaftlichen Denkens, Zweite Auflage* (1934), Berlin: Duncker & Humblot, 1993, pp. 38–9.

30. This idea has been one of the reasons for this 'understanding' of Schmitt and Nazism: the core of Schmitt's attitude to Nazism – writes P. Noack in *Carl Schmitt, Eine Biographie*, Berlin-Frankfurt: Propläen, 1993, pp. 211–12 –

lies, for me, in the fact that the representative of a spiritual world regarded himself, to a large extent, as superior to those who aspired to such a position. His assertion 'I feel completely and spiritually superior to Hitler' has already been cited. This goes back to his Hegelian origins. This man thought the worst of human beings, and longed for the day when the spiritual world would reveal itself as superior to all other worlds.

31. Schmitt, *Der Wert des Staates*, pp. 37–8.

32. Schmitt, 'Die Lage . . .' p. 426. This part does not exist in the 1944 Hungarian version, the only original version published at that time. No doubt the Jüngerian tone of these lines tries to help the reader to understand what he himself understands: that behind the 'persecutor' is Hitler. This would mean making Schmitt an open enemy of National Socialism, which he deserves only in part. In fact, while B. Rüthers (*Carl Schmitt im Dritten Reich*, Munich: Beck, 1990, pp. 99 ff.) – who, like me, has based the German text of 1950 on the earlier Hungarian one – is inclined to emphasize the failures of the 1944 text, I think that Schmitt's arguments are, at their core, unchanged: in the paper presented at several European Universities there are references to the old 'Aryan' law, which disappeared in 1950 (in fact, there are some references to Leist's scientific work *Altarisches Recht*, 1888); while the new and slightly enlarged text is filled instead with shifts of emphasis, hints and underscored passages which are not present in the Hungarian text of 1944, and try to say more than is necessary to understand it. Notwithstanding, the new essence of Schmitt's thought is easy to grasp: the vindication of the Roman Law and of the science of Roman Law is unchanged both in the 1944 text and in that of 1950.

Here I would like to thank my colleague from Budapest University, Professor Dr Gábor Hamza, who, with his perfect knowledge of both Italian and German, had the patience to confront page after page of the Hungarian and German texts.

33. O. Beaud opens his introduction to the French translation of Schmittian *Verfassungslehre*, on Schmitt's Augustinianism, in 'Carl Schmitt ou le juriste engagé', Preface to C. Schmitt, *Théorie de la Constitution*, Paris: PUF, 1993, pp. 5–113.

34. Ball, 'Carl Schmitts Politische theologie', p. 98.

35. On this, see A. Carrino, 'Law and Social Theory in Emil Lask', in *Festschrift für Werner Krawietz*, Berlin: Duncker & Humblot, 1993, pp. 209–31. Schmitt mentions Lask in the 1922 essay on political theology, in relation to the notion of a correspondence with

Kelsen's doctrine of the state – without giving an opinion, but in terms which, however subjective, denote an understanding of Lask's role within the theory of consciousness.

36. 'Schmitt uses, in an original way, the historicist method (given as a sign of the dominance of juridical formalism) in order to analyse, at different times (also relativizing them), existing institutions. In this sense, Schmitt is undoubtedly a participant in the complex development of German history; however, he distances himself in a peculiar way'. (F. Lanchester, 'Carl Schmitt e la storia costituzionale', in *Momenti e figure*, p. 245.

37. However, Carlo Costamagna was effectively a 'statalist', in the sense that for him the state represents: *'par excellence*, the concrete fact of life' (*Dottrina del fascismo*, 1940, 3 vols, Padua: Edizioni di Ar, 1990, vol. 1, p. 36); so the doctrine of the state comes to assume a 'supreme position' in the sphere of moral science, in that it is the science of the common good of a *particular* political society – not, therefore, as it was in Schmitt, 'a total political society', and therefore the total state; but, rather, the notion of constitutionality – that is, the notion of a concrete, unified and living people.

38. See T. Vesting, 'Erosionen staatlicher Herrschaft, Zum Begriff des Polititschen bei Carl Schmitt', *Archiv des öffentlichen Rechts*, 1, (1992), p. 29.

39. See Forsthoff for the most recent analysis of Schmitt, particularly during the years of the German Federal Republic: D. van Laak, *Gespräche in der Sicherheit des Schweigens. Carl Schmitt in der politischen Geistesgeschichte der frühen Bundesrepublik*, Berlin: Akademie Verlag, 1993, pp. 240–46.

40. M. Nigro, *Carl Schmitt e lo stato amministrativo*, in the 'Rivista trimestrale di diritto e procedura civile', 1986, p. 793.

41. On the relationship between Weber and Schmitt, see G. L. Ulmen, *Politische Mehrwert, Eine Studie über Max Weber und Carl Schmitt*, Weinheim, 1991; and C. Colliot-Thélène, 'Carl Schmitt contre Max Weber: rationalité juridique et rationalité économique', in C. M. Herrera, *Le droit, la politique. Autour de Max Weber, Hans Kelsen, Carl Schmitt*, Paris, 1995 (translated in this volume, Chapter 8 above).

42. Notwithstanding Andreas Koenen's rather detailed (all of 979 pages!) book *Der Fall Carl Schmitt, Sein Aufstieg zum 'Kronjuristen' des Dritten Reiches*, Darmstadt: Wissenschaftliche Buchgesellschaft, 1995.

Ethic of State and Pluralistic State[1]

Carl Schmitt

I

The most widespread and dominant evaluation of the state today is best indicated in the title of Ernest Barker's much-cited essay of 1915 – 'The Discredited State'. Even in very strong states such as the United States of America and England, states whose external political power and internal political order are not threatened, the traditional understandings of the state have, since the war, been subject to lively criticism, and the ancient demand of the state to be the sovereign unity and totality has been shaken up. As early as 1907 the syndicalist theorists in France had proclaimed: 'The state is dead'. Here, for over twenty years, a sociological and juristic literature has existed which disputes every aspect of the supremacy of the state and law, and subordinates both to society. One might cite here, as the most interesting and significant figures among contemporary jurists, Léon Duguit and Maxime Leroy. In Germany the crisis opened with the collapse of the Bismarckian empire, as the understandings of state and government which had until then been thought unshakeable fell away. Since 1919, a massive crisis in literature has come into existence. Suffice it to recall here the title of Alfred Weber's book – *The Crisis of European Thought*. Accompanying this was an extensive body of theoretical work on the state and international law which sought to destroy the concept of sovereignty and, with it, the customary understanding of the state as a unity transcending all other groups.

To shake up the state is always simultaneously to shake up the ethic of state. For all traditional understandings of the ethic of state share the fate of the concrete state – an entity they always presuppose – and fall with it into discredit. When the 'earthly god' falls from his throne, and the kingdom of objective reason and ethics turns into a 'magnum latrocinium',[2] then political parties slaughter the mighty Leviathan, and each cuts from its corpse a piece of flesh for itself. What can 'ethic of state' mean then? This blow does not reach only Hegel's ethic of state, which makes the state the bearer and creator of its own ethic; nor only the idea of the *stato etico* in the sense of fascist doctrine. It also hits the ethic of state of Kant, and of liberal individualism.

These last do not regard the state as bearer and subject of an autonomous ethic. Rather, their ethic of state consists above all in binding the state to ethical norms. As a result – with the exception of some radical anarchists – all presuppose that the state is the highest authority, the judge who prescribes over 'mine and thine', through whom the merely normative, and therefore judgeless, state of nature – a *status justitia* (more accurately *judice*) *vacuus*,[3] one in which each is judge in his own cause, is overcome. Without an understanding of the state as a transcendent unity and power, all the practical results of the Kantian ethic of state are contradictory and weakened. This is particularly clear in the theory of the right of resistance. Despite all his rationalistic relativization of the state, Kant rejected the right of resistance outright because it contradicted the idea of the unity of the state.

II

More recent Anglo-Saxon theories of the state (here G.D.H. Cole and Harold I. Laski[4] are the most interesting) call themselves 'pluralistic'. They want thereby to negate not only the state as the supreme comprehensive unity but also, first and foremost, its ethical demand to create a different and higher kind of obligation than any of the other associations in which men live. The state then becomes a social group or association which at most stands next to, but never above, the other associations. The ethical consequence is that the individual lives in a multiplicity of unordered, equally valid social obligations and loyalty relationships: in a religious community; in economic associations like unions, combines, and other organizations; in a political party or club; in cultural or social societies; in the family; and in a multitude of other social groups. He finds obligations of loyalty and fidelity everywhere. Everywhere an ethic springs up: church ethic, estate ethic, union ethic, family ethic, association ethic, office ethic, commercial ethic, and so on. In all this complex of duties, in the 'plurality of loyalties', there is no 'hierarchy of duties', no unconditional prescriptive principle of super- and subordination. In particular, the ethical bond to the state, the duty of fidelity and loyalty, appears as only one instance alongside other bonds – alongside loyalty to the church, the economy, or the family; loyalty to the state has no precedence, and the ethic of state is a special ethic among many other special ethics. Neither Cole nor Laski is clear about whether there is still a total social ethic; the former speaks vaguely of an apparently all-encompassing 'society'; the latter of 'humanity'.

III

There are sound reasons for the great impression these theories perforce make today, and these reasons are also philosophically interesting. When pluralistic social theorists like Cole and Laski are primarily preoccupied with the empirical realm, this is because they are pragmatists, and they remain consistent with the philosophy of pragmatism on which Laski explicitly relies. Laski is especially interesting, since he takes over for the state both the perspective, and also apparently the results, of William James's pluralistic philosophical picture of the world. He extracts an argument about the dissolution of the monistic unity of the universe into a multiverse in order to dissolve the political unity of the state into a plurality. Because of this, his interpretation of the state belongs to that intellectual and historical array of phenomena which I have called 'political theology'. The correspondence of theological and metaphysical world-pictures with the picture of the state is best grasped within the history of human thought. Its simplest examples are in the structural relationships of ideas between monarchy and monotheism, constitution-alism and deism. The structural relationship can be explained neither materialistically as a mere 'ideological superstructure', a reflex or 'reflec-tion', nor, conversely, idealistically or spiritually as a 'material foundation'.

One finds, as a further instance of intellectual historical interest, the fact that the pluralistic arguments are in no way absolutely new; rather, they are bound to old theories of the philosophy of state, and to that extent belong to a great tradition. Cole's social ethic justifies above all a very modern union or guild-socialist state; and Laski's pluralistic theory is likewise entwined with the aim and ideal of the union movement. The French critics of state sovereignty also have a syndicalist federalism in view. Thus one might seem at first glance to encounter an altogether new, very modern theory. From the intellectual historical perspective, however, the real surprise in the theoretical situation is that the argu-ments and viewpoints which served the social philosophers of the Roman Catholic Church, or of other churches or religious sects, in their quest to relativize the state against the church work from now on in the interest of a union or syndicalist socialism. One of Laski's favourite arguments refers to Bismarck's cultural struggle, in which the hitherto so powerful German empire could not overcome the Roman Church.

One of the most important books in the foundation of Anglo-Saxon pluralistic theory is (with Gierke and Maitland) John Neville Figgis's *Churches in the Modern State* (1913); and Laski relies on a name which, through the well-known work by Görre,[5] became a symbol of the universal Church's struggle against the state – that of Saint Athanasius, the most militant of the Fathers of the Church, whose shadow Laski resurrects for his socialism of the Second International.

Above all, the pluralistic interpretation corresponds with the actual empirical situation which one can observe today in most industrial states. In this way, pluralistic theory is very modern and topical. The state, in fact, does appear to be largely dependent on social groups, sometimes as sacrifice to, sometimes as a result of, their negotiations – an object of compromise among the powerful social and economic groups, an agglomeration of heterogeneous factors, political parties, combines, unions, churches, and so on, which come to understandings with each other. The state is weakened and relativized in the compromise of social forces – even rendered problematic, because it is difficult to see what independent significance it might have. It appears, if not altogether the servant or instrument of a dominant class or party, to have become the mere product of an equilibrium between several conflicting groups, at most a *pouvoir neutre*[6] and intermediary, a neutral mediator, a moment of equilibrium between the conflicting groups, a kind of clearing office,[7] a peacemaker. As such, it refrains from authoritative decision-making, renouncing completely the control of social, economic and religious antitheses, which it indeed ignores and cannot officially recognize. It becomes an 'agnostic' state, the *stato agnostico* which fascistic criticism disparages. In the face of such a figure, the ethical question of fidelity and loyalty must get a different answer from the one it gets in the case of a univocal, transcendent and comprehensive unity. As a result, in many states today the single individual feels that he is in a plurality of ethical bonds and is bound by religious communities, economic asocia-tions, cultural groups and parties, without the possibility of a determi-nate decision in the case of conflict between the series of these many bonds.

Philosophy should not neglect to interpret the empirical reality of such a situation. For any reference to empirical reality in the case of a subject like the state involves, fundamentally, a philosophical and moral argument. The value of the state lies equally for all state philosophers, whether individualist or collectivist, in its concrete reality, and a state which is not real cannot be the bearer or addressee of the concrete demands, duties, and feelings of an ethic of state. Ethical relationships like fidelity and loyalty are possible only in the reality of concrete life, only with concretely existing people or institutions, not with constructions and fictions. Thus from the perspective of a philosophy of the state or an ethic of the state it is not a matter of indifference whether the earlier demand of the state to be superior to all other groups has fallen away. Even for an individualistic interpretation, the achievement of the state is that it determines the concrete situation in which moral and legal norms can be at all valid. That is, every norm presupposes a normal situation. No norm is valid in a vacuum, nor in an abnormal (with respect to the normal) situation. If the state 'puts in place the external conditions for ethical life', that entails that it creates the normal situation. Just for that very reason it is (in Locke as in Kant) the highest judge. Once one or other social group, and not the state, determines the concrete normality of the situation in which individuals live, so the ethical demand of the state to fidelity and loyalty falls away.

IV

Despite its agreement with empirical considerations and its considerable philosophical noteworthiness, a pluralism of this sort cannot be the last word on contemporary problems of state ethics. From the intellectual historical perspective, all those pluralistic arguments against the unitary state are not in any respect as extraordinarily new and modern as they might at first appear. Even when one is strongly impressed by the rapid reshufflings in contemporary social life, one need only recall that for thousands of years all philosophers of state, from Plato to Hegel, understood the unity of the state as the highest value. To be sure, one finds in all these philosophers at many levels the strongest critique of exaggerated monistic tendencies, and many reservations favourable to independent social groups of very different kinds.

Aristotle's objections against Plato's exaggeration of political monism are well known. The *polis*,[8] in his opinion, must be a unity, *mian einai*,[9] as well as the *oikia*[10], *all' ou pantos*,[11] but not altogether (*Politics* II2, 19 and many other places in the second book). Thomas Aquinas's monism is at the front and the centre because of his monotheism. He discovers its value in the unity of the state, and equates unity with peace [*et ideo id ad quod tendit intentio multitudinem gubernantis est unitas sive pax: Summa Theologicae*, Ia. Q. 103 Art. 3].[12] Nevertheless, he joins Aristotle in saying that unity driven to the limit will destroy the state [*maxima unitas destruit civitatem*]. Besides, for him, as for all Catholic philosophers, the church is an independent *societas perfecta*[13] alongside the state, which is likewise a *societas perfecta*. This amounts to a dualism which, as in any surrender of simple unity, invites many arguments which broaden out towards pluralism.

One can clarify from this particular stance towards the state the – at first glance somewhat strange – intellectual historical alliance between the Roman Catholic Church and unionist federalism which one finds today in Laski. At the same time, one can demonstrate that Laski's state theoretic pluralism requires a deeper philosophical grounding if he is not to be caught by the obvious objection that the arguments he exploits of a Catholic philosophy of state stem from a particularly decisive universalism. The Roman Catholic Church is no pluralistic construction, and pluralism in its struggle against the state has – at least since the sixteenth century – been on the side of national states. A pluralistic social theory contradicts itself when it secularizes the monism and universalism of the Roman Catholic Church into the universalism of the Second or Third International, and plays them off against the state while always still desiring to remain pluralistic.

The ambiguities of such an intellectual historical coalition suffice to show that the pluralism of modern social theory is vague and in itself problematic. It is polemically directed against, and seeks to relativize, the established unity of the state. At the same time, the pluralistic theorists, for the most part, speak a highly individualistic language when it comes to the most decisive points of their arguments. In particular, their answer to the obvious and decisive question of how to decide the inevitable conflict of many different relationships of fidelity and loyalty is that the single individual must decide for himself. This brings about a double contradiction.

First, at issue is a social situation, one which the individual comprehends, but cannot change at will; at issue, that is, is a matter of social ethics, not of the inner autonomy of the individual. It is of course appropriate to an Anglo-Saxon sensibility to answer such a problem individualistically, and to let the ultimate decision reside with the individual, but a pluralistic social ethic immediately throws away its interesting and worthwhile features: the appreciation of the concrete empirical power of social groups, and of the empirical situation as it is determined by the ways in which individuals belong to several of such social groups. Besides, it is an empirical mistake to suppose that an individual, not a social group, decides. Perhaps there exists a nimble and agile individual who can succeed in the feat of maintaining his freedom between social groups, as one might hop from ice-floe to ice-floe. But this kind of freedom-as-balance could not be put forward as the normal ethical duty for the mass of ordinary citizens. In addition, it is the converse of a decisive resolution of social conflicts. When the unity of the state falls away, different social groups as such will probably make the decision of their own accord – that is, on the basis of their group interests. But in the case of the single individual, experience tells us that there is no space for his freedom other than what a strong state guarantees. When social pluralism is opposed to state unity, it means nothing other than abandoning the conflict of social duties to the decision of social groups. And that means the sovereignty of social groups, but not the freedom and autonomy of the single individual.

The second contradiction resides in the fact that ethical individualism has its correlate in the concept of humanity. The empirical individual is not sufficient unto himself, and his individuality cannot decide the ethical conflicts of social life. For an ethic of individuality, the individual has value only as a human being; the prescriptive concept is, correspondingly, humanity. In fact, for Laski humanity appears to be the highest factor, even humanity taken as a whole. And by the word 'society', Cole means – though not unambiguously – something similar to humanity. But just that is quintessential universalism and monism, and completely different from a pluralistic theory.

Just as ambiguous as pluralism itself is any position which can be grouped with pluralism because it opposes all theories of the state as a unity. From the above philosophical and historical remarks we can see that political unity cannot be, and never is, conceived as so absolutely monistic, so destructive of all other social groups, as the 'pluralists', for polemical reasons, often present it, and as it is often depicted in the simplifying formulae of jurists. When jurists speak of the 'omnipotence' of the sovereign, king or parliament, one must understand their baroque exaggerated formulae in the context of the state's quest to prevail against the pluralistic chaos of churches and estates between the sixteenth and eighteenth centuries. One makes the task too easy when one sticks to such modes of expression. Even the absolute prince of the seventeenth and eighteenth centuries was forced to respect divine and natural law – that is, to speak sociologically, church and family – and to take into account the manifold aspects of traditional institutions and established rights.

The unity of the state has always been a unity of social multiplicity. In different times and in different states, it was always complex and, in a special sense, internally pluralist. One can perhaps oppose an exaggerated monism on the basis of this self-evident complexity, but one does not thereby resolve the problem of political unity. Besides, even abstracting from any complexity, there are many possible ways of building political unity. There is unity from above (through command and power) and unity from below (from the substantive homogeneity of the people); unity through enduring association and compromise between social groups or through an equilibrium achieved somehow by some other means between such groups; unity which comes from within, and one which rests only on external pressure; a more static and a permanently dynamic, functionally integrated unity; finally, there is unity by force and unity by consensus. This last simple opposition dominates pluralism's ethic of state, whose ethical meaning evidently resides in the fact that it considers only consensual unity to be ethically valid. And rightly so. But that is where the real problem begins. For every consensus, even a 'free' one, is somehow motivated and brought into existence. Power produces consensus and often, to be sure, a rational and ethically justified consensus. Conversely, consensus produces power, and then often an irrational and – despite the consensus – ethically repugnant power. From a pragmatic and empirical perspective, the question arises of who controls the means of bringing about the 'free' consensus of the masses: the economic, educational, psychotechnical means of very different kinds with whose help, as we know from experience, one can achieve a consensus. If these means are in the hands of social groups or of single individuals, and removed from state control, then everything which officially still gets called 'state' is at an end, and political power has become invisible and unaccountable; but the social ethical problem is not solved with this observation.

The last and most profound cause of all such ambiguities and thus contradictions, stems from the obscurity of the pluralist state theorists' depiction of the state. For the most part they have in mind, for purely polemical reasons, the residues of the old 'absolutist' states of the seventeenth and eighteenth centuries. State then comes to mean apparatus of government, administrative machinery – in short, things which self-evidently can be assessed only for their instrumental value, but cannot attract fidelity or loyalty, and which the different social groups rightly control, since they share out the residues. But in addition the state is, even in pluralist eyes, the political unity which always integrates itself anew, even if this results from the compromises of social groups which, as such, can make certain ethical demands, albeit only the demand that the negotiations and compromises take place. That amounts to an ethic – albeit a very problematic one – of *'pacta sunt servanda'*.[14] It is, of course, possible to confine the word 'state' historically to the absolute state of the seventeenth and eighteenth centuries. That then makes it easy to contest the state on ethical grounds. But the issue has nothing to do with a word whose history has – and can – become unmodern; rather, it has to do with the problem of the political unity of a people.

An error which mostly goes unnoticed, and thus uncriticized, dominates thinking here and almost everywhere else, including among pluralist social theorists. It is that the political means a particular substance alongside other substances of 'social asociations', that it can be given a particular content alongside religion, economy, language, culture, and law, and that consequently the political groups can be set up alongside the other groups in a co-ordinated fashion – alongside the churches, combines, national, cultural and legal communities of the most disparate kinds. If this were the case, political unity would become a particular new substantive unity in step with other unities. All interpretation and discussion about the nature of the state and of the political must run into error as long as the widespread conception dominates which has it that there could be a political sphere with its own substance alongside the other spheres. It is then also easy to lead the state as political unity *ad absurdum*, and to oppose it root and branch. For what remains of the state as the political unity when all other contents – the religious, the economic, the cultural, and so forth – are removed? Were the political merely the result of such a subtraction, it would in fact amount to absolutely nothing. But there we have the cause of the misunderstanding, for the political, correctly understood, is only the degree of intensity of a unity. Political unity can contain and comprehend different contents. But it always designates the most intensive degree of a unity, from which, consequently, the most intensive distinction – the grouping of friend and enemy – is determined.

Political unity is the highest unity – not because it is an omnipotent dictator, or because it levels out all other unities, but because it decides, and has the potential to prevent all other opposing groups from dissociating into a state of extreme enmity – that is, into civil war. Where a political unity exists, the social conflicts among individuals and social groups can be decided, so that an order – that is, a normal situation – is maintained. The most intensive unity either exists or does not exist. It can dissolve itself, in which case normal order falls away. But it is always inescapably a unity, for there is no plurality of normal situations, and the decision inevitably emanates from the unity as long as it in fact exists. Every social group, of whatever kind and with whatever content, is equally political to the extent that it participates in the decision, or that the decision is concentrated in it. Because the political has no substance of its own, the point of the political can be reached from any terrain, and any social group, church, union, combine, nation, becomes political, and thereby of the state, as it approaches the point of highest intensity. It infuses with its content and values the political unity which lives off the different areas of human life and thought, and draws its energies from science, culture, religion, law and language. All human life, even the highest spiritual spheres, has in its historical realization at least the potential to become a state, which waxes strong and powerful from such contents and substances, as did the mythical eagle of Zeus, which nourished itself from Prometheus' entrails.

V

The ambiguities and contradictions which are revealed in pluralistic social theory have their cause not in pluralism but in the inappropriate application of an appropriate pluralism, a pluralism which is inescapable in all problems of objective spirit. For the world of objective spirit is a pluralistic world; pluralism of races and peoples, of religions and cultures, of languages and of legal systems. The issue has nothing to do with the denial of the fact of this pluralism, and with violating it in concert with universalism and monism, but much more with the correct placing of pluralism.

Even the political world is in its nature pluralistic. And the bearers of this pluralism are the political unities as such – that is, the states. In particular, the modern European states in the sixteenth and seventeenth centuries developed from the dissolution of a universalism, and their concept of sovereignty was directed polemically as much against the universal demand for a world monarchy of the empires as against the likewise universal political demands of the papacy. It is an intellectual historical misunderstanding of an astonishing kind to want to dissolve these plural political unities in response to the call of universal and monistic representations, and to designate that as pluralist – even more so if, as in Laski's case, the call is William James's. In the system of 'Political Theology', the pluralism of James's picture of the world corresponds with the era of contemporary democratic national states, with their pluralism of peoples, whose statehood is imbued by national factors. In accordance with the tendency of its ideas and logic, the monarchy is the more universalistic because it must derive from God when it does not justify itself democratically through the will of the people. In contrast, democracy leads to the recognition of each of the many peoples as a political unity. Hence, as a philosopher of pluralism rightly said:

> Just as in social life now and forever the demos[15] has stepped to the fore, and therefore there can no longer be kings in the civilized world who are not servants of the people, so in the terrain of philosophy, Being itself in its totality and manifoldness, that is, the bathos[16] of experience, has stepped forward as prescriptive, and the time of different schematic arrangements and oblatenesses is irrevocably over.' (Boris Jakowenko, On the Nature of Pluralism, Bonn 1928).

The plurality of states – that is, of the political unities of the different peoples – is thus the genuine expression of a rightly understood pluralism. Universal monistic concepts like God, world, and humanity are the highest concepts, and are enthroned above – very high above – any plurality in concrete reality. They maintain their dignity as highest concepts only as long as they remain in their most high position. They change their nature, and mistake their meaning and task, when they become mixed up in the scuffles of political life, and are recipients of a false power and a false proximity. I prefer not to go so far as to analogize them to Max Scheler's conception of spirit, and to say of them that they are as impotent over the concrete life of peoples and social groups as Scheler's metaphysics of spirit is over life and the instincts. Yet they are only regulative ideas without direct or indirect power, and in that lies their value and their indispensability. Certainly, there is no human and no political life without the idea of humanity, but this idea constitutes nothing, certainly no distinguishable community. All peoples, all classes, all adherents of all religions, Christians and Saracens, capitalists and proletarians, good and evil, just and unjust, delinquent and judge, are people, and with the help of such a universal concept every distinction may be negated and every concrete community ruptured.

Such elevated ideas can and should temper and modify. However, as soon as particular peoples and social groups, or even individuals, make use of them in order to identify themselves with the others, the regulative idea is transformed into an awful instrument of human domination. Even within the narrow boundaries of the state – boundaries which have, at least for some time, been visible among the community of nations – it is a dangerous deception when one single group pursues its special interests in the name of the whole, and unjustifiably identifies itself with the state. For then the name of the state serves only political suppression and deprivation of rights. And when, for the first time, a supreme and universal concept like humanity is used politically so as to identify a single people or a particular social organization with it, then the potential arises for a most awful expansion and a murderous imperialism. In this regard, the name of humanity is no less abused than the name of God, and it could be that a feeling spreads very widely among many peoples whose authentic expression is to be found in the variations on Proudhon's elegant dictum: 'Who speaks of humanity desires to deceive'.

After the political erosion of such expansive totalities, it is less pretentious to take into account and to recognize peoples unified into states. It is modest in comparison with any world- and humanity-encompassing universalism, and it justifies itself through the immanent mass of the social whole. Each of the many political unities is, of course, only a piece of order, a fragment, in the context of the whole of the world and of humanity. Yet it is human work, and a piece that conduces to community. Deception and lies are just as possible within the state as in any human endeavour, but the fantastic dimensions of a universal deception comprehending world and humanity are not possible here. In a spiritual world ruled by the law of pluralism, a piece of concrete order is more valuable than any empty generalizations of a false totality. For it is an actual order, not a constructed and imaginary abstraction, a total situation of normal life, in which concrete people and social groups can have a concrete existence. It would be a false pluralism which played world-comprehending totalities off against the concrete actuality of such plural orders; it is rational and sensible to permit to remain valid the succession and proximity of peoples and states which have been put in place by the content of human history.

States and peoples come and go, and there are stronger and weaker peoples, healthy and sick, majestic and wretched states. One does not oppose the strong and the forceful by referring to the weak, sick, and the pitiful. In this regard, the sentence by Aristotle which Rousseau put right at the head of his *Discourse on Human Inequality* gets it right: *Non in depravitis sed in his quae bene secundum naturam se habent considerandum est quid sit naturale.*[17] In this way it becomes clear to what degree political unity is a human work and task, for it is a unity which, within the boundaries of general pluralism, becomes effective and prescriptive, a piece of concrete order, the normal situation. A greater effort and spiritual achievement are required to this end than for other associations and social unities. In particular, it is easier to bring into being an economic 'association' than a political unity, and it is evident – even self-evident – that people lose interest in such efforts in times of weariness and exhaustion. The higher and more intensive the community, the higher the consciousness and deed required to bring them about. And so much the greater is the risk of failure. The successful and complete state is, therefore, as grand as the failed state is morally and aesthetically repugnant and miserable. It is easy to think of today's examples of many failed attempts, and of the pitiful caricatures of states. But that is obviously not a theoretical, ethical, or empirical argument, and no solution to our set task.

*

This lecture was confined to a short overview of an intellectual and historical problem. I want to close with a short summary which brings my theses together.

One finds an ethic of state in many different, even contradictory, senses. It can mean the subjection of the state to ethical norms, in which case it grounds, above all, duties of state. That, as one sees especially in Kant's arguments about state ethics, presupposes an existing state – 'the already existing legislator', as Kant puts it – a state whose existence is unproblematically taken to be self-evident. In social reality, the subjection of the state to ethical norms means, of course, only control and domination by those men and social groups who, in the name of the ethical norms, come forward within the context of concrete reality against a concrete state, and bring those norms to realization. Furthermore, ethic of state can mean an ethic which the state as an autonomous ethical subject posits, through which are grounded specific duties to do with non-resistance against the state. But that presupposes an already existing state. If the state then becomes a pluralistic party state, the unity of the state can be maintained only as long as two or more parties agree to recognize common premisses. That unity then rests in particular on the constitution recognized by all parties, which must be respected without qualification as the common foundation. The ethic of state then amounts to a constitutional ethic. Depending on the substantivity, unequivocality and authority of the constitution, a very effective unity can be found there. But it can also be the case that the constitution dwindles into mere rules of the game, its ethic into a mere ethic of fair play;[18] and that it finally, in a pluralistic dissolution of the unity of the political whole, reaches the point where the unity is only an agglomeration of changing alliances between heterogeneous groups. The constitutional ethic then dwindles even further, to the point of the ethic of state being reduced in the proposition *pacta sunt servanda*.

In all the cases of ethic of state already mentioned, the state remains a unity – whether, as in the first two cases, the state is subjected to an ethic or represented as a supreme ethical subject. It is presupposed as a concrete, existing unity, whether it consists of the commonly recognized constitutional foundation or of the rules of the game, but in either case it is presupposed as a unity. Only the proposition *pacta sunt servanda* can found no ethic of state, since the individual social groups, in their role as contracting subjects, are then as such the prescriptive forces, who use the contract to cater to themselves, and are bound only by a contractual association. They stand in relation to each other as independent forces, and what unity there is is only the result of terminable agreements (as all agreements and contracts are terminable). The contract then has the meaning only of a conclusion of peace between the contracting groups, and a conclusion of peace always has – whether the parties like it or not – an eye on the possibility, albeit remote, of war. In the background of this kind of contractual ethic, an ethic of civil war always lurks. In the foreground stands the obvious inadequacy of the proposition *pacta sunt servanda*, which, in concrete terms, can mean nothing more than the legitimation of the contingent status quo, just as in private life it is capable of taking the role of a splendid ethic of usury. Once the reality of social life renders the unity of state problematic, an unbearable situation is created for each citizen of the state, for at the same time the normal situation falls away, together with the presupposition of every ethical and every legal norm. Then the concept of ethic of state acquires a new content, and a new task arises. It is the work involved in consciously bringing about that unity, the duty to participate to create a bit of concrete and actual order and to make the situation normal once again. Then there comes into being, alongside the duty of state which resides in its subjection to ethical norms, and alongside the duties against the state, a duty of ethic of state of a completely different kind – the duty towards statehood.

Translated by David Dyzenhaus
Reproduced by kind permission of the Schmitt Estate and George Schwab,
Schmitt's English-language executor

Translator's notes

1. I thank John P. McCormick for looking over my translation from the German, and David Scourfield for help with the Latin and the Greek. I also thank George Schwab, Schmitt's English-language executor, for kindly agreeing to publication of this translation. All errors are, of course, mine. Translations from languages other than German when these seem required, and Schmitt's use of English, are given in the notes in inverted commas.
2. 'a large band of robbers'.
3. 'a state void of justice, more accurately of judges'.
4. More accurately, Harold J. Laski.
5. Schmitt must be referring to Charles Gore, the English theologian and Anglican bishop.
6. 'a neutral power'.
7. 'clearing office' in English in the original.
8. 'state' or 'city-state'.
9. 'be one'.
10. 'the household'.
11. Here Schmitt supplies the translation – that is, 'but not altogether'.
12. 'and therefore the one who guides the multitude strives towards a goal which is unity or peace'.
13. 'a complete association'.
14. 'contracts must be honoured'.
15. 'the people'.
16. 'depth'.
17. 'One should determine what is natural by considering not the depraved but those who act appropriately in accordance with their nature.'
18. 'fair play' in English in the original.

Carl Schmitt in English Translation

Books

The Necessity of Politics: An Essay on the Representative Idea in the Church and Modern Europe, trans. E. M. Codd, with an Introduction by Christopher Dawson, Essays in Order no. 5, Catholic Book-a-Month Club, London: Sheed & Ward, 1931.

The Concept of the Political, trans. George Schwab. New Brunswick: Rutgers University Press, 1976.

The Crisis of Parliamentary Democracy, trans. Ellen Kennedy. Cambridge, MA: MIT Press, 1985.

Political Theology: Four Chapters on the Concept of Sovereignty, trans. George Schwab. Cambridge, MA: MIT Press, 1985.

Political Romanticism, trans. Guy Oakes. Cambridge, MA: MIT Press, 1986.

The Leviathan in the State Theory of Thomas Hobbes: Meaning and Failure of a Political Symbol, trans. George Schwab and Erna Hilfstein. Westport, CT: Greenwood Press, 1996.

Roman Catholicism and Political Form, trans. G. L. Ulmen. Westport, CT: Greenwood Press, 1996.

Articles (trans. G. L. Ulmen unless otherwise stated)

'The Legal World Revolution'. *Telos* 72 (Summer 1987).

'The Plight of European Jurisprudence'. *Telos* 83 (Spring 1990).

'The Constitutional Theory of Federation'. *Telos* 91 (Spring 1992).

'Appropriation/Distribution/Production: Toward a Proper Formulation of the Basic Questions of Any Social and Economic Order'. *Telos* 95 (Spring 1993).

'The Age of Neutralizations and Depoliticizations', trans. M. Konzett and J. P. McCormick. *Telos* 96 (Summer 1993).

Notes on the Contributors

Grigoris Ananiadis teaches political philosophy and social theory at the University of the Aegean (Lesbos), and is a member of the editorial board of the political and cultural journal *Synchrona Themata*. He is currently working on Hans Kelsen's contribution to social and democratic theory.

Agostino Carrino is Professor of Public Law and Theory of the State at Federico II University, Naples, and co-editor of the journal *Diritto e Cultura*. His most recent publications include 'Ideologica e coscienza', *Critical Legal Studies* (1995); *Il diritto nella società moderna* (1995); *Die Normenordnung* (1998); and *Costituzione e sovranità. Il dibattito giuspubblicistico in Italia prima e dopo Maastricht* (1998).

Catherine Colliot-Thélène is Maître de Conférences en Philosophie at L'École Nationale Supérieure de Fontenay-St-Cloud. Her publications include *Max Weber et l'histoire* (1990); *Le désenchantement de l'État* (1992); and numerous articles in journals such as *Actes de la Recherche en Sciences sociales*, *Philosophie*, *Lignes*, *Archives de Sciences sociales des Religions*, and *Critique*.

Jorge E. Dotti is Professor of Political Philosophy at the University of Buenos Aires, and Researcher at Argentina's National Research Council CONICET. His publications include *Dialéctica y derecho. El proyecto ético-politico hegeliano* (1983); *Las vetas del texto* (1990); *El mundo de J.-J. Rousseau* (1991); and *La letra gótica. Recepción de Kant en Argentina* (1992).

David Dyzenhaus is Professor of Law and Philosophy at the University of Toronto. His most recent publications are *Legality and Legitimacy: Carl Schmitt, Hans Kelsen and Hermann Heller in Weimar* (1997); and *Judging the Judges and Ourselves: Truth, Reconciliation and the Apartheid Legal Order* (1998).

Paul Hirst is Professor of Social Theory at Birkbeck College, University of London. He is a member of the *Political Quarterly* editorial board, the *Renewal* advisory board, and the Charter 88 Executive. His publications include *Associative Democracy* (1994); *Globalisation in Question* (1996); and *From Statism to Pluralism* (1997).

Jean-François Kervégan is Professor of Philosophy at the University of Cergy-Pontoise and Director of Research Group 456 (German juridical and political philosophy) at the Centre National de Recherche Scientifique. He is the author of *Hegel, Carl Schmitt. Le politique entre spéculation et positivité* (1992); a co-author of *Introduction à la logique de Hegel* (1982–87); and translator of *Hegel: Philosophy of Law* (1998); and has written several papers on Hegel, Schmitt and political philosophy.

Chantal Mouffe is a Senior Research Fellow at the Centre for Study of Democracy at the University of Westminster. She is author of, among other works, *The Return of the Political* (1993), *Hegemony and Socialist Strategy* (with Ernesto Laclau, 1995); *Dimensions of Radical Democracy* (1992); *Gramsci and Marxist Theory* (1979); and *Deconstruction and Pragmatism* (1996).

Ulrich K. Preuss is Professor of Law and Politics at the Free University, Berlin. He is the editor of *Zum Begriff der Verfassung. Die Ordnung des Politischen* (1994); his recent publications as author include *Constitutional Revolution: The Link between Constitutionalism and Progress* (1995); and (as co-author with Jon Elster and Claus Offe) *Institutional Design in Post-Communist Societies: Rebuilding the Ship at Sea* (1998).

Slavoj Žižek is Senior Researcher at the Institute for Social Studies, Ljubljana, Slovenia. His most recent publications include *The Indivisible Remainder: An Essay on Schelling and Related Matters* (1996); *The Plague of Fantasies* (1997); and *The Ticklish Subject: The Absent Centre of Political Ontology* (1999).

PHRONESIS TITLES FROM VERSO

ALREADY PUBLISHED

Islams and Modernities, Aziz Al-Azmeh

Ethics–Politics–Subjectivity: Essays on Derrida, Levinas and Contemporary French Thought, Simon Critchley

Politics of Friendship, Jacques Derrida

The Circular Structure of Power, Torben Dyrberg

Hegemony and Socialist Strategy, Ernesto Laclau and Chantal Mouffe

Emancipation(s), Ernesto Laclau

New Reflections on the Revolution of Our Time, Enesto Laclau

The Making of Political Identities, Ernesto Laclau (ed.)

The Challenge of Carl Schmitt, Chantal Mouffe (ed.)

Dimensions of Radical Democracy, Chantal Mouffe (ed.)

The Return of the Political, Chantal Mouffe

Deconstructing Apartheid Discourse, Aletta J. Norval

On the Shores of Politics, Jacques Rancière

Michel Foucault: Genealogy as Critique, Rudi Visker

For they know not what they do: Enjoyment as a political factor, Slavoj Žižek

The Sublime Object of Ideology, Slavoj Žižek

FORTHCOMING

(Dis)figurations, Ian Angus

Contingent Universalities: Dialogues on the Left in Late Modernity, Judith Butler, Ernesto Laclau and Slavoj Žižek

Between Cultures: Tensions in the Struggle for Recognition, Alexander García Düttmann

The Populist Reason, Ernesto Laclau and Francisco Panizza